www.wadsworth.com

www.wadsworth.com is the World Wide Web site for
Thomson Wadsworth and is your direct source to
dozens of online resources.

At *www.wadsworth.com* you can find out about
supplements, demonstration software, and student
resources. You can also send email to many of our
authors and preview new publications and exciting
new technologies.

www.wadsworth.com
Changing the way the world learns®

D1528720

Current Perspectives
Readings from InfoTrac® College Edition

Terrorism and Homeland Security

DIPAK K. GUPTA
San Diego State University

THOMSON
™
WADSWORTH

Australia • Canada • Mexico • Singapore • Spain
United Kingdom • United States

THOMSON
WADSWORTH

Current Perspectives: Readings from InfoTrac® College Edition:
Terrorism and Homeland Security
Dipak K. Gupta

Editor in Chief: *Eve Howard*
Assistant Editor: *Jana Davis*
Editorial Assistants: *Elise Smith and Rebecca Johnson*
Technology Project Manager: *Susan DeVanna*
Marketing Manager: *Terra Schultz*
Marketing Assistant: *Annabelle Yang*
Advertising Project Manager: *Stacey Purviance*
Project Manager, Editorial Production: *Brenda Ginty*

Creative Director: *Robert Hugel*
Print Buyer: *Karen Hunt*
Production Service: *Rozi Harris, Interactive Composition Corporation*
Permissions Editor: *Sarah Harkrader*
Cover Designer: *Larry Didona*
Cover Image: *Photolibrary.com/Photonica*
Cover and Text Printer: *Thomson West*
Compositor: *Interactive Composition Corporation*

For more information about our products, contact us at:
Thomson Learning Academic Resource Center
1-800-423-0563

For permission to use material from this text or product, submit a request online at http://www.thomsonrights.com.
Any additional questions about permissions can be submitted by email to thomsonrights@thomson.com.

Library of Congress Control Number:
2004116845

ISBN 0-495-00723-4

Thomson Higher Education
10 Davis Drive
Belmont, CA 94002-3098
USA

Asia (including India)
Thomson Learning
5 Shenton Way
#01-01 UIC Building
Singapore 068808

Australia/New Zealand
Thomson Learning Australia
102 Dodds Street
Southbank, Victoria 3006
Australia

Canada
Thomson Nelson
1120 Birchmount Road
Toronto, Ontario M1K 5G4
Canada

UK/Europe/Middle East/Africa
Thomson Learning
High Holborn House
50–51 Bedford Row
London WC1R 4LR
United Kingdom

Latin America
Thomson Learning
Seneca, 53
Colonia Polanco
11560 Mexico
D.F. Mexico

Spain (including Portugal)
Thomson Paraninfo
Calle Magallanes, 25
28015 Madrid, Spain

Contents

Preface

Terrorism's Trap

The two worlds were coming apart for some time. Most of us in the West did not realize the depth of this tectonic shift until the hijacked planes made a direct hit on September 11, 2001. Although a miniscule minority in the Muslim world carried out these extreme acts, there is no denying of the weight of history that has precipitated this rupture. Recently, Pakistani President Parvez Musharraf, by borrowing a phrase from Winston Churchill, warned that an iron curtain has descended between the West and the Islamic nations. The danger of this separation to the stability of the global community cannot be overestimated.

Our collection of essays starts with quotations from Osama bin Laden, the leader of al-Qaeda, responsible for the attacks of 9/11. In these passages, culled from various Internet sources, bin Laden explains the historical and religious contexts within which these actions must be understood. These passages were translated by individuals without the best command of English. I have made only minimal editorial changes in the fear of distorting the words of bin Laden. If we are to understand the rage and frustration felt widely in the Arab/Muslim world, which bin Laden has been able to exploit successfully, we must take a brief look at the long history of animosity and mistrust that has shaped the conflicting worldviews.

It was inevitable for two great civilizations living side by side to come in conflict. Soon after the death of Prophet Mohammad in the seventh century C.E., the newfound religion of Islam spread with lightning speed to conquer nearly two-thirds of the "known world," spanning from Spain to Indonesia. The spread of Islam brought it directly into confrontation with the Christian world. Feeling threatened by the growing Islamic power, the European princes responded to the call of the Pope Urban II and, between 1096 and 1270, launched eight Crusades to capture the Holy Land. Although these attempts failed to keep Jerusalem in Christian hands, the bitterness from such a protracted conflict left its permanent legacy in the minds of many in the Muslim community. Thus, while in the Christian West the term "crusade" implies drive for righteous cause, in the Islamic world, it signifies invasion of nonbelievers for rape and pillage.

The global dominance of Islam lasted over a thousand years. However, Islam's loss of global supremacy began with the expulsion of the Moors from Spain in the last decade of the 1400s. Since then, the rise of the Western power, aided by the discoveries of the New World, discovery of ocean routes to the Orient, and advancements in science and technology, saw a steady stream of subsequent Western victories over the Islamic Empires. One by one, the vast territory started falling into the hands of the European colonial powers. India fell to the British, Indonesia to the Dutch, and the Middle East and North Africa were carved out by France, Germany, and Italy, with the lion's share going to Great Britain. The destruction of the Ottoman Empire after World War I made the final demise of Islamic dominance manifestly clear. The long colonial rule added to the bitter legacy. When the former colonies gained independence after World War II, the Islamic world found itself fragmented, mired in poverty, and being ruled by corrupt authoritarian regimes.

The world kept on changing, but this change did not favor the Islamic world. While the economic gap between the two worlds widened, the forces of modernization burst open the door of these traditional societies and directly challenged the existing social, economic, and political power structures. Ideas inimical to orthodox Islam started to permeate the society. The process of modernization causes deep conflicts in every society, spanning history, culture, and geography. The Islamic world is no exception. If we are to understand the complex historical process that gave birth to the 9/11 attacks, we must do so within the broader historical, cultural, and religious context.

On the other side of the coin, we must also understand the impact of the 9/11 attacks in particular and the fight against terrorism in general on U.S. foreign policies. The enormity of these attacks on the psyche of a nation can be understood by the fact that these attacks not only took aim directly at the heart of the country, they claimed the lives of nearly 3,000 innocent civilians. Before these attacks, the highest number of casualties from a single attack stood at 329, when the Sikh militants brought down an Air India flight in 1985 off the coast of Ireland. The number of victims in the 9/11 attacks is nearly ten times the previous record of infamy. The scars created by the spectacular attacks are unlikely to heal anytime soon and will continue to claim their victims many times the original number for years, if not decades to come.

The problems of terrorism are age-old. No government can survive without taking a strong and immediate action in the aftermath of a catastrophic attack on its unarmed civilian population. Unfortunately, terrorist groups do not possess standing armies and, in fact, they often do not even have a strict hierarchy of command and control. It is not easy for an organized government with a strong military force to confront such an amorphous enemy. In absence of "hard targets" the use of brute force, which punishes an entire community, satisfies the domestic constituency of the political leaders, but such actions only help the perpetrators by enlarging their support base. This is the policy trap of terrorism.

Against this backdrop, the articles of this volume, written by some of the best-known researchers in the field, are selected to allow students to have an overview of the policy trap of terrorism facing the world. We begin our discussion by putting current terrorism in its proper historical context. In the aftermath of the 9/11 attacks, many in the United States came to two quick yet unsubstantiated conclusions. The first one was rarely publicly uttered by responsible leaders. The second one was extensively debated during the presidential campaign of 2004.

The first set of conclusions was that Islam as a religion was responsible for the terrorist attacks on the United States, and that the Muslims have been at the center of violence throughout history. These sweeping generalizations were on many minds, whether they had the temerity to articulate them or not. Suddenly, these deeply held suspicions, fears, and prejudices transformed the comfortable and often complacent suburban "soccer moms" into paranoid "security moms." No measure, however extreme in its assault on the core values of individual freedom, was unacceptable in the name of national security.

In the aftermath of the 9/11 attacks, President Bush declared war on terrorism and promised a rapid and decisive victory against this "evil." The U.S. forces gained quick military victories in Afghanistan. The president basked in the glory of a fabulous victory against Saddam Hussein's Iraq under the banner "Mission Accomplished" onboard an aircraft carrier. Yet threats of terrorism did not subside. Daily news reports flooded the media with shocking pictures of victims from Chechnya to Iraq, Israel to Spain. Confronting the unprecedented situation, many in a nation accustomed to instant results, including the two presidential contenders, tentatively reached the conclusion that the war against terrorism is unwinnable and may take generations to resolve. During the long and arduous presidential campaign, when either candidate wanted to appear thoughtful, he would quietly assert that we could not beat terrorism, which immediately drew scorn from the other. The ferocity of these back and forth bravados and accusations reflected our deep-down fear that we might not be able to quell the fire of terrorism in our lifetime. David C. Rapoport's careful historical analysis provides answers to both of these two national conundrums. He argues that, viewed from a global perspective, acts of terrorism tend to come in clusters. He identifies four waves of terrorism. The first wave was the "anarchist" movement that targeted the political leadership beginning in 1880s and culminated with the assassination of Austrian Archduke Franz Ferdinand and his wife by the Serbian nationalist Gavrilo Princip in 1914. These extremely high-profile assassinations triggered the spark that engulfed the entire world into a fighting frenzy. The second wave of terrorism was inspired by anticolonial movements and started in the early 1940s; it lasted nearly 30 years, when the European colonial rule came to an end in Asia and Africa. The third wave of terrorism was spawned by the leftist ideologies of the 1970s. For the last two decades, the world has been experiencing religion-inspired terrorism, much of which has been carried out by the Muslims. Rapoport's analysis helps us understand that the current wave of attacks by people of Islamic faith is but the latest in the 125-year history of terrorism. Therefore, the supposition that terrorism in inextricably linked with Islam is groundless. Second, his analysis assures us that if history is any guide, like other previous ideologies, this one will also run its own course. Although history does not tell us the exact point in time when it will run out of steam, it does show that, while acts of terrorism by disgruntled dissident groups are going to be with us as long we have organized society, any particular ideology has its own lifecycle.

If the world is to confront the threats of terrorism, it must first define the term and must provide accurate and measurable information. The unfortunate reality about terrorism research is our inability to define the term to everyone's satisfaction. The term "terrorism" traces its origin to the French Revolution. In stark contrast to its contemporary connotation, during the trying times of the post revolutionary chaos, terrorism was seen as a way of maintaining law and order by injecting fear in the minds of the potential miscreants. However, if there is a link between the term's original meaning and its current usage, it is that terrorism has always been "propaganda by deed": deliberate acts that effectively combine violence with public spectacle. During the reign of terror of 1793–1794, violence was systematically directed at the possible counter-revolutionaries. Their public beheading by the use of the guillotine was designed to serve notice to those who might be tempted to threaten the fledgling democracy of the republican France. Similarly, by carrying out spectacular attacks, today's terrorists mix violence with the theatrics of a macabre play produced on the global stage.

However, our ambivalence toward terrorism is amply reflected by our inability to formally define it. The common adage "one man's terrorist is another man's freedom fighter" is literally true. Those we call "suicide bombers" are known as "shaeed" or "martyrs" in the Middle East. The meaning of the two words is as wide as the views of the two opposing worlds. As a result, we recognize that "terrorism" is a political term and contains a large degree of subjective assessment. However, every term we use in social sciences is similarly ill-defined and is subject to interpretation and political manipulation. Responding to the threats of terrorism, the U.S. State Department started to compile data of global terrorism. However, just before the presidential election in 2004, the Bush Administration encountered a firestorm of criticism when it released the previous year's figures on global terrorism showing a discernable downward trend. In the face of mounting evidence, the State Department had to admit to the lack of veracity of the information. Since any policy analysis must start with adequate measurement, in their article Krueger and Laitin argue for a concerted effort at developing accurate databases for terrorism by stating that if the United States is serious about fighting terrorism, it must get its facts straight.

The following two articles examine some of the important causes of terrorism: religion and poverty. Although neither of the two are either necessary or sufficient causes for terrorism, the former supplies the essential base on which justifications of killings are made and the latter provides the fertile breeding ground of discontent from which young men and women are often recruited. Bernard Lewis examines the religious basis of terrorism. By delving into various interpretations of the Qur'an, he directs us toward understanding of the fires of religious zeal that can promote extremist behavior in the Islamic world.

We can be generous in prosperity. During times of economic hardship we tend to look at assistance to foreign countries as luxury and cut out economic assistance. Since poverty and social injustice breed desperate behavior, Strobe Talbott warns that the United States will make a grave mistake if it ignores global poverty due to the growing budget deficit and other domestic economic woes.

Witnessing the devastating impacts of terrorism, particularly those wrought by acts of suicide attacks, it is not too difficult to understand our penchant for considering terrorists as mentally unbalanced, or simply irrational religious fanatics. Ehud Sprinzak dispels this notion by carefully arguing that behind their acts, even suicide attacks, which assault the very concept of human rationality, are in fact strategic actions taken by the dissident groups to achieve certain political goals.

Because suicide bombings are on the rise all over the world, we must pay special attention to this phenomenon. In his article, Robert A. Pape, by studying incidents of suicide attacks, demonstrates that the terrorist groups have learned to use these human bombs (the smartest of all weapons) because they offer the most effective delivery system. Both physical and psychological impacts of these attacks are so devastating that the terrorist organizations, which can boast of ready supplies of human sacrifices for their causes, have seen that these weapons are the most effective in reaching their political goals.

While fighting terrorism, it is easy to lose sight of the fact that not all groups are the same. In the world of political communication, where simple answers are preferred over more thoughtful and nuanced observations, it is imperative that the policy makers do not fall into the dangerous temptation of covering every Islamic radicalism and political groups under one sweeping generalization. Groups that engage in violence are not formed on the basis of a single motivation. Some are formed with ideological goals of transforming the entire world in their own image of religious absolutism. In contrast, there are groups that are fighting over local or regional issues, and there are others yet who are interested more in the spoils of war. Journalist Steven Rogers points out the dangers of a one-size-fits-all approach to global terrorism. By grouping together every political movement conducted by Muslims into one single *jihadi* movement, we risk serious misunderstanding of a complex problem. Rogers points out that the Abu Syaaf group in the Philippines are basically a criminal gang, fighting over regional issues.

Having explained the strategies of terror attacks, we now turn to the question, why do some groups succeed? Jessica Stern explains that to a large extent, al-Qaeda's success in delivering the most lethal message of hate to the most powerful nation on earth rests with the group's ability to change its ideology over time.

As we differentiate between ideologies and their malleable nature in dealing with the threats emanating from *jihadi* groups like al-Qaeda, we should know that it is not Islam that confronts us. It is the collective frustration and anger resulting from myriad agendas and issues, which use Islam as a vehicle and vocabulary in the Muslim world. Graham E. Fuller takes a close look and concludes, "The West is not at war with the religion itself, but it is indeed challenged by the radicalism that some groups have embraced. Muslims may too readily blame the West for their own problems, but their frustrations and current grievances are real." He warns that to ignore some of the most pressing injustices, perceived or real, would take us deeper into the problem of terrorism.

During the height of the Cold War, when the smaller countries were often torn between the two warring superpowers, Julius Nyerere, the president of Tanzania, joked that when two elephants fight, it is the grass that suffers. When asked during the period of détente, when the United States and the Soviet Union were reveling in their newfound friendship, Nyerere quipped that when two elephants make love, it the grass that suffers. In today's world, where the United States is the only standing superpower, with its military, economic, and cultural dominance over the rest of the world unparalleled in history, it is important for us to realize the size of our footprint. Whatever the United States does—good or bad—gets hugely magnified in the global arena. When George W. Bush went to the White House, he took with him a group of scholars and experts who believed that it was about time the United States recognized that it was an imperial power and start behaving accordingly. In the following two articles, G. John Ikenberry and Eliot A. Cohen explain America's foreign policy dilemma. In the mono polar world of today, there are little restraints on the victorious superpower. Russia or the countries of the European Union do not provide a counterbalance to the military, economic, and cultural prowess of the United States. However, even in the face of overwhelming superiority, the choice for the United States is limited. In the Greek mythology, Hercules, the most powerful being on earth, was sent to fight a deadly serpent called Hydra. This disgusting being had several heads that grew back as soon as they were cut off. In this expedition, Hercules was accompanied by his nephew, Iolaus, who watched his uncle fight the dreaded beast from a distance. However, Hercules was getting tired. No sooner than he would cut off one of the heads, another head would grow. So Iolaus lit a torch and started sealing off each neck with fire to prevent it from growing back. Hydra was killed. The story illustrates that even the most powerful Hercules, the son of Zeus, the king of gods, could not defeat the serpent without the help of his much weaker ally, Iolaus. Similarly, in our global fight against terrorism, the mighty United States is unable to slay the monster without help from other countries. The United States can act like an imperialist, but in so doing it risks getting overextended, both militarily and economically. Therefore, the leaders of the United States, present and future, must learn to lead by being part of an international system based on the rule of law.

If the United States cannot defeat terrorism on its own, the rest of world must also recognize their responsibilities. Feinstein and Slaughter argue that the other nations of the world have a duty to work with the United States in their common goal of a peaceful and orderly world.

In his article, David Carr points out that in our effort to fight terrorism, we cannot transform the United States into a fortress; we cannot promote democracy and the rule of law in the world by becoming a police state ourselves. The vastness of the country and the multiplicity of potential targets make it impossible for us to develop a foolproof policy for preventing future acts of terrorism. There is no doubt that the horrors of 9/11 forever will be seared into our memories. And, in the foreseeable future it will be one of the most dominant events in shaping U.S. foreign and domestic policies. How we conduct ourselves in these trying times will determine our destiny. My essay concludes the volume by reminding that, while it is important to know what we are fighting against, it is perhaps even more important to recognize what we are fighting for.

When Jana Davis of Thomson Wadsworth approached me to put together this reader, I was in the middle of a project, funded by the United States Institute of Peace. The research for this reader is the outcome of this timely grant.

To the memory of Gouri Sankar Gupta and Karabi Sen.

Dipak K. Gupta
San Diego State University

1

In His Own Words: Excerpts from Osama bin Laden's Messages

Excerpts of Osama bin Laden's Broadcasts on the al-Jazeera Network

REASONS FOR 9/11 ATTACKS

I direct my speech to the American people to the best way to avoid another conflict.

You American people, my speech to you is the best way to avoid another conflict about the war and its reasons and results. I am telling you security is an important pillar of human life. And free people don't let go of their security contrary to [George W.] Bush's claims that we hate freedom. He should tell us why we didn't hit Sweden for instance. It's known that those who hate freedom don't have dignified souls like the 19 who were blessed. But we fought you because we are free people, we don't sleep on our oppression. We want to regain the freedom of our Muslim nation; as you spill our security, we spill your security.

"In His Own Words: Excerpts from Osama bin Laden's Messages" as printed at http://news.bbc.co.uk/2/hi/middle_east/2751019.stm.

I am so surprised by you. Although we are in the fourth year after the events of September 11, Bush is still practicing distortion and (is) misleading you, and obscuring the main reasons. Therefore the reasons are still existing to repeat what happened before. I will tell you the reasons behind theses incidents.

I will be honest with you on the moment when the decision was taken to understand. We never thought of hitting the (World Trade Center) towers. But after we were so fed up, and we saw the oppression of the American Israeli coalition on our people in Palestine and Lebanon, it came to my mind and the incidents that really touched me directly goes back to 1982 and the following incidents. When the US permitted the Israelis to invade Lebanon with the assistance of the 6th fleet. In these hard moments, it occurred to me so many meanings I can't explain but it resulted in a general feeling of rejecting oppression and gave me a hard determination to punish the oppressors. While I was looking at the destroyed towers in Lebanon, it came to my mind to punish the oppressor the same way and destroy towers in the US to get a taste of what they tasted, and quit killing our children and women.

We didn't find difficulty dealing with Bush and his administration due to the similarity of his regime and the regimes in our countries. Which half of them are ruled by military and the other half by sons of kings and presidents and our experience with them is long. Both parties are arrogant and stubborn and the greediness and taking money without right and that similarity appeared during the visits of Bush to the region while people from our side were impressed by the US and hoped that these visits would influence our countries. Here he is being influenced by these regimes, royal and military. And was feeling jealous they were staying for decades in power stealing the nations' finances without anybody overseeing them. So he transferred the oppression of freedom and tyranny to his son and they call it the Patriot Law to fight terrorism. He was bright in putting his sons as governors in states and he didn't forget to transfer his experience from the rulers of our region to Florida to falsify elections to benefit from it in critical times.

ON GEORGE W. BUSH'S RESPONSE
TO THE 9/11 ATTACKS

We agreed with Mohamed Atta (the leader of the al-Qaeda suicide squad), God bless him, to execute the whole operation in 20 minutes. Before Bush and his administration would pay attention and we never thought that the high commander of the US armies would leave 50 thousand of his citizens in both towers to face the horrors by themselves when they most needed him because it seemed to distract his attention from listening to the girl telling him about her goat butting was more important than paying attention to airplanes butting the towers which gave us three times the time to execute the operation thank god.

Your security is not in the hands of (Sen. John) Kerry or (George W.) Bush or al-Qaeda. Your security is in your hands. Each state that doesn't mess with our security has automatically secured their security.

RATIONALE FOR KILLING
INNOCENT CIVILIANS

Female Presenter (voice on the tape): In Bin Laden's message he approached other points. He pointed to the contradiction, which considers oppression and killing of innocents a legal act. They formed an international law as Bush the father did with the children of Iraq according to bin Laden. Bin Laden pointed to the millions of pounds of explosives dropped on Iraqi children as Bush his son had done, as he said to remove an old agent and install a new agent to help in stealing the oil of Iraq. And bin Laden said the events of 9/11 came as an answer to this oppression and said that if the answer to this oppression is considered bad terror, then we need to do it. And he stressed that he wants to deliver this message to the Americans in words and in deeds since the 9/11 events. He reminded Americans of a few warning messages through various news media like *Time* magazine and CNN and other Arab and correspondents since 1996. He warned them of the consequences of their countries policies. He talked about the damage Sept 11 caused the US economy and that it cost close to a trillion dollars. He talked about President Bush and that the emergency law requires more money.

11 FEBRUARY. 2003

In the name of God, the merciful, the compassionate.

A message to our Muslim brothers in Iraq, may God's peace, mercy, and blessings be upon you.

O you who believe fear Allah, by doing all that He has ordered and by abstaining from all that He has forbidden as He should be feared.

Obey Him, be thankful to Him, and remember Him always, and die not except in a state of Islam [as Muslims] with complete submission to Allah.

We are following up with great interest and extreme concern the crusaders preparations for war to occupy a former capital of Islam, loot Muslims wealth, and install an agent government, which would be a satellite for its masters in Washington and Tel Aviv, just like all the other treasonous and agent Arab governments.

This would be in preparation for establishing the Greater Israel.

Allah is sufficient for us and He is the best disposer of affairs.

"UNJUST WAR"

Amid this unjust war, the war of infidels and debauchees led by America along with its allies and agents, we would like to stress a number of important values:

First, showing good intentions. This means fighting should be for the sake of the one God.

It should not be for championing ethnic groups, or for championing the non-Islamic regimes in all Arab countries, including Iraq.

God Almighty says: "Those who believe fight in the cause of Allah, and those who reject faith fight in the cause of evil."

So fight ye against the friends of Satan: feeble indeed is the cunning of Satan.

Second, we remind that victory comes only from God and all we have to do is prepare and motivate for jihad.

God Almighty says: "Oh ye who believe! If ye will help the cause of Allah, He will help you and plant your feet firmly."

We must rush to seek God Almighty's forgiveness from sins, particularly the grave sins.

Prophet Muhammad, God's peace be upon him, said: "Avoid the seven grave sins; polytheism, sorcery, killing, unless permitted by God, usury, taking the money of orphans, fleeing from combat, and slandering innocent faithful women."

Also, all grave sins, such as consuming alcohol, committing adultery, disobeying parents, and committing perjury. We must obey God in general, and should in particular mention the name of God more before combat.

"MEDIA MACHINE"

Abu-al-Darda, may God be pleased with him, said: "Perform a good deed before an attack, because you are fighting with your deeds."

Third, we realized from our defense and fighting against the American enemy that, in combat, they mainly depend on psychological warfare.

This is in light of the huge media machine they have.

They also depend on massive air strikes so as to conceal their most prominent point of weakness, which is the fear, cowardliness, and the absence of combat spirit among US soldiers.

Those soldiers are completely convinced of the injustice and lying of their government.

They also lack a fair cause to defend. They only fight for capitalists, usury takers, and the merchants of arms and oil, including the gang of crime at the White House.

This is in addition to crusader and personal grudges by Bush the father.

TRENCH WARFARE

We also realized that one of the most effective and available methods of rendering the air force of the crusader enemy ineffective is by setting up roofed and disguised trenches in large numbers.

I had referred to that in a previous statement during the Tora Bora battle last year.

In that great battle, faith triumphed over all the materialistic forces of the people of evil, for principles were adhered to, thanks to God Almighty.

I will narrate to you part of that great battle, to show how cowardly they are on the one hand, and how effective trenches are in exhausting them on the other.

We were about 300 mujahideen [Islamic militants]. We dug 100 trenches that were spread in an area that does not exceed one square mile, one trench for every three brothers, so as to avoid the huge human losses resulting from the bombardment.

Since the first hour of the US campaign on 20 Rajab 1422, corresponding to 7 October 2001, our centres were exposed to a concentrated bombardment.

And this bombardment continued until mid-Ramadan.

On 17 Ramadan, a very fierce bombardment began, particularly after the US command was certain that some of al-Qaeda leaders were still in Tora Bora, including the humble servant to God [referring to himself] and the brother mujahid Dr Ayman al-Zawahiri.

The bombardment was round-the-clock and the warplanes continued to fly over us day and night.

WAR IN AFGHANISTAN

The US Pentagon, together with its allies, worked full time on blowing up and destroying this small spot, as well as on removing it entirely.

Planes poured their lava on us, particularly after accomplishing their main missions in Afghanistan.

The US forces attacked us with smart bombs, bombs that weigh thousands of pounds, cluster bombs, and bunker busters.

Bombers, like the B-52, used to fly overhead for more than two hours and drop between 20 to 30 bombs at a time.

The modified C-130 aircraft kept carpet-bombing us at night, using modern types of bombs.

The US forces dared not break into our positions, despite the unprecedented massive bombing and terrible propaganda targeting this completely besieged small area.

This is in addition to the forces of hypocrites, whom they prodded to fight us for 15 days non-stop.

Every time the latter attacked us, we forced them out of our area carrying their dead and wounded.

"ALLIANCE OF EVIL"

Is there any clearer evidence of their cowardice, fear, and lies regarding their legends about their alleged power.

To sum it up, the battle resulted in the complete failure of the international alliance of evil, with all its forces, [to overcome] a small number of mujahideen—300 mujahideen hunkered down in trenches spread over an area of one square mile under a temperature of −10 degrees Celsius.

The battle resulted in the injury of six percent of personnel—we hope God will accept them as martyrs—and the damage of two percent of the trenches, praise be to God.

If all the world forces of evil could not achieve their goals on a one square mile of area against a small number of mujahideen with very limited capabilities, how can these evil forces triumph over the Muslim world?

This is impossible, God willing, if people adhere to their religion and insist on jihad for its sake.

IRAQI "BROTHERS"

O mujahideen brothers in Iraq, do not be afraid of what the United States is propagating in terms of their lies about their power and their smart, laser-guided missiles.

The smart bombs will have no effect worth mentioning in the hills and in the trenches, on plains, and in forests.

They must have apparent targets. The well-camouflaged trenches and targets will not be reached by either the smart or the stupid missiles.

There will only be haphazard strikes that dissipate the enemy ammunition and waste its money. Dig many trenches.

The [early Muslim caliph] Umar, may God be pleased with him, stated: "Take the ground as a shield because this will ensure the exhaustion of all the stored enemy missiles within months."

Their daily production is too little and can be dealt with, God willing.

We also recommend luring the enemy forces into a protracted, close, and exhausting fight, using the camouflaged defensive positions in plains, farms, mountains, and cities.

The enemy fears city and street wars most, a war in which the enemy expects grave human losses.

MARTYRDOM OPERATIONS

We stress the importance of the martyrdom operations against the enemy—operations that inflicted harm on the United States and Israel that have been unprecedented in their history, thanks to Almighty God.

We also point out that whoever supported the United States, including the hypocrites of Iraq or the rulers of Arab countries, those who approved their actions and followed them in this crusade war by fighting with them or providing bases and administrative support, or any form of support, even by words, to kill the Muslims in Iraq, should know that they are apostates and outside the community of Muslims.

It is permissible to spill their blood and take their property.

God says: "O ye who believe! Take not the Jews and the Christians for your friends and protectors: they are but friends and protectors to each other."

And he amongst you that turns to them [for friendship] is of them.

Verily, Allah guideth not a people unjust.

MOBILIZING THE "ISLAMIC NATION"

We also stress to honest Muslims that they should move, incite, and mobilize the [Islamic] nation, amid such grave events and hot atmosphere so as to liberate themselves from those unjust and renegade ruling regimes, which are enslaved by the United States.

They should also do so to establish the rule of God on earth.

The most qualified regions for liberation are Jordan, Morocco, Nigeria, Pakistan, the land of the two holy mosques [Saudi Arabia], and Yemen.

Needless to say, this crusade war is primarily targeted against the people of Islam.

Regardless of the removal or the survival of the socialist party or Saddam, Muslims in general and the Iraqis in particular must brace themselves for jihad against this unjust campaign and acquire ammunition and weapons.

This is a prescribed duty. God says: "[And let them pray with thee] taking all precautions and bearing arms: the unbelievers wish if ye were negligent of your arms and your baggage, to assault you in a single rush."

Fighting in support of the non–Islamic banners is forbidden.

Muslims' doctrine and banner should be clear in fighting for the sake of God. He who fights to raise the word of God will fight for God's sake.

Under these circumstances, there will be no harm if the interests of Muslims converge with the interests of the socialists in the fight against the crusaders, despite our belief in the infidelity of socialists.

The jurisdiction of the socialists and those rulers has fallen a long time ago.

Socialists are infidels wherever they are, whether they are in Baghdad or Aden.

"HIGH MORALE"

The fighting, which is waging and which will be waged these days, is very much like the fighting of Muslims against the Byzantine in the past.

And the convergence of interests is not detrimental. The Muslims' fighting against the Byzantine converged with the interests of the Persians.

And this was not detrimental to the companions of the prophet.

Before concluding, we reiterate the importance of high morale and caution against false rumours, defeatism, uncertainty, and discouragement.

The prophet said: "Bring good omens and do not discourage people."

He also said: "The voice of Abu-Talhah [one of the prophet's companions] in the army is better than 100 men."

During the Al-Yarmuk Battle, a man told Khalid bin-al-Walid [an Islamic commander]: "The Byzantine soldiers are too many and the Muslims are few."

So, Khalid told him: "Shame on you. Armies do not triumph with large numbers but are defeated if the spirit of defeatism prevails."

Keep this saying before your eyes: "It is not fitting for a Prophet that he should have prisoners of war until he hath thoroughly subdued the land."

"Therefore, when ye meet the unbelievers (in fight), smite at their necks."

Your wish to the crusaders should be as came in this verse of poetry: "The only language between you and us is the sword that will strike your necks."

In the end, I advise myself and you to fear God covertly and openly and to be patient in the jihad.

Victory will be achieved with patience. I also advise myself and you to say more prayers.

O ye who believe! When ye meet a force, be firm, and call Allah in remembrance much (and often); That ye may prosper.

God, who sent the book unto the prophet, who drives the clouds, and who defeated the enemy parties, defeat them and make us victorious over them.

Our Lord! Give us good in this world and good in the Hereafter and save us from the torment of the Fire! [Koranic verse].

May God's peace and blessings be upon Prophet Muhammad and his household.

2

The Four Waves of Modern Terrorism

David C. Rapoport

September 11, 2001, is the most destructive day in the long, bloody history of terrorism. The casualties, economic damage, and outrage were unprecedented. It could turn out to be the most important day too, because it led President Bush to declare a "war (that) would not end until every terrorist group of global reach has been found, stopped, and defeated."[1]

However unprecedented September 11 was, President Bush's declaration was not altogether unique. Exactly 100 years ago, when an anarchist assassinated President William McKinley in September 1901, his successor Theodore Roosevelt called for a crusade to exterminate terrorism everywhere.[2]

No one knows if the current campaign will be more successful than its predecessors, but we can more fully appreciate the difficulties ahead by examining features of the history of rebel (nonstate) terror. That history shows how deeply implanted terrorism is in our culture, provides parallels worth pondering, and offers a perspective for understanding the uniqueness of September 11 and its aftermath.[3] To this end, in this chapter I examine the course of modern terror from its initial appearance 125 years ago; I emphasize continuities and change, particularly with respect to international ingredients.[4]

David Rapoport, "The Four Waves of Rebel Terror and September 11," from *Attacking Terrorism,* Audrey Cronin and James Ludes, eds., Georgetown University Press, 2004. Reprinted by permission of the author.

THE WAVE PHENOMENA

Modern terror began in Russia in the 1880s and within a decade appeared in Western Europe, the Balkans, and Asia. A generation later the wave was completed. Anarchists initiated the wave, and their primary strategy—assassination campaigns against prominent officials—was adopted by virtually all the other groups of the time, even those with nationalist aims in the Balkans and India.

Significant examples of secular rebel terror existed earlier, but they were specific to a particular time and country. The Ku Klux Klan (KKK), for example, made a striking contribution to the decision of the federal government to end Reconstruction, but the KKK had no contemporary parallels or emulators.[5]

The "Anarchist wave" was the first global or truly international terrorist experience in history;[6] three similar, consecutive, and overlapping expressions followed. The "anticolonial wave" began in the 1920s and lasted about forty years. Then came the "New Left wave," which diminished greatly as the twentieth century closed, leaving only a few groups still active today in Nepal, Spain, the United Kingdom, Peru, and Colombia. In 1979 a "religious wave" emerged; if the pattern of its three predecessors is relevant it could disappear by 2025, at which time a new wave might emerge.[7] The uniqueness and persistence of the wave experience indicates that terror is deeply rooted in modern culture.

The wave concept—an unfamiliar notion—is worth more attention. Academics focus on organizations, and there are good reasons for this orientation. Organizations launch terror campaigns, and governments are always primarily concerned to disable those organizations.[8] Students of terrorism also focus unduly on contemporary events, which makes us less sensitive to waves because the life cycle of a wave lasts at least a generation.[9]

What is a wave? It is a cycle of activity in a given time period—a cycle characterized by expansion and contraction phases. A crucial feature is its international character; similar activities occur in several countries, driven by a common predominant energy that shapes the participating groups' characteristics and mutual relationships. As their name—"Anarchist," "anticolonial," "New Left," and "Religious"—suggest, a different energy drives each.

Each wave's name reflects its dominant but not its only feature. Nationalist organizations in various numbers appear in all waves, for example, and each wave shaped its national elements differently. The Anarchists gave them tactics and often training. Third-wave nationalist groups displayed profoundly left-wing aspirations, and nationalism serves or reacts to religious purposes in the fourth wave. All groups in the second wave had nationalist aspirations, but the wave is termed anticolonial because the resisting states were powers that had become ambivalent about retaining their colonial status. That ambivalence explains why the wave produced the first terrorist successes. In other waves, that ambivalence is absent or very weak, and no nationalist struggle has succeeded.

A wave is composed of organizations, but waves and organizations have very different life rhythms. Normally, organizations disappear before the initial wave associated with them does. New Left organizations were particularly striking in this respect—typically lasting two years. Nonetheless, the wave retained sufficient energy to create a generation of successor or new groups. When a wave's energy cannot inspire new organizations, the wave disappears. Resistance, political concessions, and changes in the perceptions of generations are critical factors in explaining the disappearance.

Occasionally an organization survives its original wave. The Irish Republican Army (IRA), for example, is the oldest modern terrorist organization—emerging first in 1916, though not as a terror organization.[10] It then fought five campaigns in two successive waves (the fourth struggle, in the 1950s, used guerrilla tactics).[11] At least two offshoots—the Real IRA and Continuity IRA—are still active. The Palestine Liberation Organization (PLO), founded in 1964, became active in 1967. When the Viet Cong faded into history, the international connections and activity of the PLO made it the preeminent body of the New Left wave, although the PLO pursued largely nationalist ends. More recently, elements of the PLO (e.g., Fatah) have become active in the fourth wave, even though the organization initially was wholly secular. When an organization transcends a wave, it reflects the new wave's influence—a change that may pose special problems for the group and its constituencies, as we shall see.

The first three waves lasted about a generation each—a suggestive time frame closest in duration to that of a human life cycle, in which dreams inspiring parents lose their attractiveness for children.[12] Although the resistance of those attacked is crucial in explaining why terror organizations rarely succeed, the time span of the wave also suggests that the wave has its own momentum. Over time there are fewer organizations because the enterprise's problematic nature becomes more visible. The pattern is familiar to students of revolutionary states such as France, the Soviet Union, and Iran. The inheritors of the revolution do not value it in the same way its creators did. In the anticolonial wave, the process also seems relevant to the colonial powers. A new generation found it much easier to discard the colonial idea. The wave pattern calls one's attention to crucial political themes in the general culture—themes that distinguish the ethos of one generation from another.

There are many reasons the first wave occurred when it did, but two critical factors are conspicuous and facilitated successive waves. The first was the transformation in communication and transportation patterns. The telegraph, daily mass newspapers, and railroads flourished during the last quarter of the nineteenth century. Events in one country were known elsewhere in a day or so. Prominent Russian anarchists traveled extensively, helping to inspire sympathies and groups elsewhere; sometimes, as the journeys of Peter Prodhoun indicate, they had more influence abroad than at home. Mass transportation made large-scale emigrations possible and created diaspora communities, which then became significant in the politics of both their "new" and "old" countries. Subsequent innovations continued to shrink time and space.

A second factor contributing to the emergence of the first wave was doctrine or culture. Russian writers created a strategy for terror, which became an inheritance for successors to use, improve, and transmit. Sergei Nechaev was the leading figure in this effort; Nicholas Mozorov, Peter Kropotkin, Serge Stepniak, and others also made contributions.[13] Their efforts perpetuated the wave. The KKK had no emulators partly because it made no effort to explain its tactics. The Russian achievement becomes even more striking when we compare it to the practices of the ancient religious terrorists who always stayed within their own religious tradition—the source of their justifications and binding precedents. Each religious tradition produced its own kind of terrorist, and sometimes the tactics within a tradition were so uniform that they appear to be a form of religious ritual.[14]

A comparison of Nechaev's *Revolutionary Catechism* with Osama bin Laden's training manual, *Military Studies in the Jihad Against the Tyrants,* shows that they share one very significant feature: a paramount desire to become more *efficient* by learning from the experiences of friends and enemies alike.[15] The major difference in this respect is the role of women. Nechaev considers them "priceless assets," and indeed they were crucial leaders and participants in the first wave. Bin Laden dedicates his book to protecting the Muslim woman, but he ignores what experience can tell us about female terrorists.[16] Women do not participate in his forces and are virtually excluded in the fourth wave, except in Sri Lanka.

Each wave produces major technical works that reflect the special properties of that wave and contribute to a common modern effort to formulate a "science" of terror. Between Nechaev and bin Laden there were Georges Grivas, *Guerrilla War,* and Carlos Marighella, *Mini-Manual of the Urban Guerrilla,* in the second and third waves, respectively.

"Revolution" is the overriding aim in every wave, but revolution is understood in different ways.[17] Revolutionaries create a new source of political legitimacy, and more often than not that meant national self-determination. The anticolonial wave was dominated by this quest. The principle that a people should govern itself was bequeathed by the American and French revolutions. (The French Revolution also introduced the term *terror* to our vocabulary.)[18] Because the definition of "the people" has never been (and perhaps never can be) clear and fixed, however, it is a source of recurring conflict even when the sanctity of the principle is accepted everywhere. Revolution also can mean a radical reconstruction of authority to eliminate all forms of equality—a cardinal theme in the first wave and a significant one in the third wave. Fourth-wave groups use a variety of sacred texts or revelations for legitimacy.

This chapter treats the great events precipitating each wave and the aims and tactics of participating groups. The focus, however, is the international scene. I examine the interactions of the five principal actors: terrorist organizations; diaspora populations; states; sympathetic foreign publics; and, beginning with the second wave, supranational organizations.[19]

FIRST WAVE: CREATION OF A DOCTRINE

The creators of modern terrorism inherited a world in which traditional revolutionaries, who depended on pamphlets and leaflets to generate an uprising, suddenly seemed obsolete. The masses, Nechaev said, regarded them as "idle word-spillers."[20] A new form of communication (Peter Kropotkin named it "Propaganda by the Deed") was needed—one that would be heard and would command respect because the rebel took action that involved serious personal risks that signified deep commitment.

The anarchist analysis of modern society contained four major points. It noted that society had huge reservoirs of latent ambivalence and hostility and that the conventions society devised to muffle and diffuse antagonisms generated guilt and provided channels for settling grievances and securing personal amenities. By demonstrating that these conventions were simple historical creations, however, acts once declared immoral would be hailed by later generations as noble efforts to liberate humanity. In this view, terror was thought to be the quickest and most effective means to destroy conventions. By this reasoning, the perpetrators freed themselves from the paralyzing grip of guilt to become different kinds of people. They forced those who defended the government to respond in ways that undermined the rules the latter claimed to respect.[21] Dramatic action repeated again and again invariably would polarize the society, and the revolution inevitably would follow—or so the anarchists reasoned.

An incident that inspired the turbulent decades to follow illustrates the process. On January 24, 1878, Vera Zasulich wounded a Russian police commander who abused political prisoners. Throwing her weapon to the floor, she proclaimed that she was a "terrorist, *not* a killer."[22] The ensuing trial quickly became that of the police chief. When the court freed her, crowds greeted the verdict with thunderous applause.[23]

A successful campaign entailed learning how to fight and how to die, and the most admirable death occurred as a result of a court trial in which one accepted responsibility and used the occasion to indict the regime. Stepniak, a major figure in the history of Russian terrorism, described the Russian terrorist as "noble, terrible, irresistibly fascinating, uniting the two sublimities of human grandeur, the martyr and the hero."[24] Dynamite—a recent invention— was the weapon of choice because the assailant usually was killed too, so it was not a weapon a criminal would use.[25]

Terror was violence beyond the moral conventions used to regulate violence: the rules of war and punishment. The former distinguishes combatants from noncombatants, and the latter separates the guilty from the innocent. Invariably, most onlookers would label acts of terror atrocities or outrages.

The rebels described themselves as terrorists, not guerrillas, tracing their lineage to the French Revolution. They sought political targets or those that could affect public attitudes.[26] Terrorism was a strategy, not an end. The tactics used depended upon the group's political objective and on the specific context faced. Judging a context constantly in flux was both an art and a science.

The creators of this strategy took confidence from contemporary events. In the Russian case, as well as in all subsequent ones, major unexpected political events dramatized new government vulnerabilities. Hope was excited, and hope is always an indispensable lubricant of rebel activity.[27] The turn of events that suggested Russian vulnerability was the dazzling effort of the young Czar Alexander II to transform the system virtually overnight. In one stroke of the pen (1861) he freed the serfs (one-third of the population) and promised them funds to buy their land. Three years later he established limited local self-government, "westernized" the judicial system, abolished capital punishment, and relaxed censorship powers and control over education. Hopes were aroused but could not be fulfilled quickly enough, as indicated by the fact that the funds available for the serfs to buy land were insufficient. In the wake of inevitable disappointments, systematic assassination strikes against prominent officials began—culminating in the death of Alexander himself.

Russian rebels encouraged and trained other groups, even those with different political aims. Their efforts bore fruit quickly. Armenian and Polish nationalist groups committed to assassination emerged in Russia and used bank robbery to finance their activities. Then the Balkans exploded, as many groups found the boundaries of states recently torn out of the Ottoman Empire unsatisfactory.[28] In the West, where Russian anarchists fled and found refuge in Russian diaspora colonies and among other elements hostile to the czarist regime, a campaign of anarchist terror developed that influenced activities in India too.[29] The diaspora produced some surprising results for groups still struggling in Russia. The Terrorist Brigade in 1905 had its headquarters in Switzerland, launched strikes from Finland (an autonomous part of the Russian empire), got arms from an Armenian terrorist group Russians helped train, and were offered funds by the Japanese to be laundered through American millionaires.[30]

The high point of the first wave of international terrorist activity occurred in the 1890s, sometimes called the "Golden Age of Assassination"—when monarchs, prime ministers, and presidents were struck down, one after another, usually by assassins who moved easily across international borders.[31] The most immediately affected governments clamored for international police cooperation and for better border control, a situation President Theodore Roosevelt thought ideal for launching the first international effort to eliminate terrorism:

> Anarchy is a crime against the whole human race, and all mankind should band together against the Anarchist. His crimes should be made a crime against the law of nations . . . declared by treaties among all civilized powers.[32]

The consensus lasted only three years, however. The United States refused to send a delegation to a St. Petersburg conference to consider a German/Russian-sponsored protocol to meet these objectives. It feared that extensive involvement in European politics might be required, and it had no federal police force. Italy refused too, for a very different and revealing concern: If anarchists were returned to their original countries, Italy's domestic troubles might be worse than its international ones.

The first great effort to deal with international terrorism failed because the interests of states pulled them in different directions, and the divisions developed new expressions as the century developed. Bulgaria gave Macedonian nationalists sanctuaries and bases to aid operations in the Ottoman Empire. The suspicion that Serbia helped Archduke Franz Ferdinand's assassin precipitated World War I. An unintended consequence of the four terrible years that followed was a dampened enthusiasm for the strategy of assassination.

SECOND WAVE: MOSTLY SUCCESSFUL, AND A NEW LANGUAGE

A wave by definition is an international event; oddly, however, the first one was sparked by a domestic political situation. A monumental international event, the Versailles Peace Treaty that concluded World War I, precipitated the second wave. The victors applied the principle of national self-determination to break up the empires of the defeated states (mostly in Europe). The non-European portions of those defeated empires, which were deemed not yet ready for independence, became League of Nations "mandates" administered directly by individual victorious powers until the territories were ready for independence.

Whether the victors fully understood the implications of their decisions or not, they undermined the legitimacy of their own empires. The IRA achieved limited success in the 1920s,[33] and terrorist groups developed in all empires except the Soviet Union (which did not recognize itself as a colonial power) after World War II. Terrorist activity was crucial in establishing the new states of Ireland, Israel, Cyprus, and Algeria, among others. As empires dissolved, the wave receded.

Most terrorist successes occurred twenty-five years after Versailles, and the time lag requires explanation. World War II reinforced and enlarged the implications of Versailles. Once more the victors compelled the defeated to abandon empires; this time the colonial territories were overseas (Manchuria, Korea, Ethiopia, Libya, and so forth) and were not made mandates. The victors began liquidating their own empires as well, and in doing so they generally were not responding to terrorist activity, as in India, Pakistan, Burma, Ceylon, Tunisia, Egypt, Morocco, the Philippines, Ghana, and Nigeria—which indicated how firmly committed the Western world had become to the principle of self-determination. The United States had become the major Western power, and it pressed hardest for eliminating empires. As the cold war developed, the process was accelerated because the Soviets were always poised to help would-be rebels.[34]

The terror campaigns of the second wave were fought in territories where special political problems made withdrawal a less attractive option. Jews and Arabs in Palestine, for example, had dramatically conflicting versions of what the termination of British rule was supposed to mean. The considerable European population in Algeria did not want Paris to abandon its authority, and in Northern Ireland the majority wanted to remain British. In Cyprus, the Turkish community did not want to be put under Greek rule—the aim of Ethniki Organosis Kyprion Agoniston (EOKA)—and Britain wanted to retain Cyprus as a base for Middle East operations.

The problem of conflicting aspirations was reflected in the way the struggles were or were not settled. The terrorists did get the imperial powers to withdraw, but that was not the only purpose of the struggle. Menachem Begin's *Irgun* fought to gain the entire Palestine mandate but settled for partition.[35] IRA elements have never accepted the fact that Britain will not leave Northern Ireland without the consent of the territory's population. EOKA fought to unify Cyprus with Greece (*enosis*) but accepted an independent state that EOKA tried to subvert for the sake of an ever-elusive *enosis*. Algeria seems to be the chief exception because the Europeans all fled. The initial manifesto of the Front de Liberation Nationale, Algeria (FLN) proclaimed, however, that it wanted to retain that population and establish a democratic state; neither objective was achieved.[36]

Second-wave organizations understood that they needed a new language to describe themselves because the term *terrorist* had accumulated so many negative connotations that those who identified themselves as terrorists incurred enormous political liabilities. The Israeli group *Lehi* was the last self-identified terrorist group. Begin, leader of the *Irgun* (*Lehi's* Zionist rival)—which concentrated on purpose rather than mean—described his people as "freedom fighters" struggling against "government terror."[37] This self-description was so appealing that all subsequent terrorist groups followed suit; because the anticolonial struggle seemed more legitimate than the purposes served in the first wave, the "new" language became attractive to potential political supporters as well. Governments also appreciated the political value of "appropriate" language and began to describe all violent rebels as terrorists. The media, hoping to avoid being seen as blatantly partisan, corrupted language further. Major American newspapers, for example, often described the same individuals alternatively as terrorists, guerrillas, and soldiers in the same account.[38]

Terrorist tactics also changed in the second wave. Because diaspora sources contributed more money, bank robberies were less common. The first wave demonstrated that assassinating prominent political figures could be very counterproductive, and few assassinations occurred in the second wave. The

Balkans was an exception—an odd place especially when one considers where World War I started.[39] Elsewhere only *Lehi* (the British renamed it the Stern Gang) remained committed to a strategy of assassination. *Lehi* was much less effective than its two competitors, however, which may have been an important lesson for subsequent anticolonial movements. Martyrdom, often linked to assassination, seemed less significant as well.

The new strategy was more complicated than the old because there were more kinds of targets chosen, and it was important to strike them in proper sequence. Second-wave strategy sought to eliminate the police—a government's eyes and ears—first, through systematic assassinations of officers and/or their families. The military units replacing them, second-wave proponents reasoned, would prove too clumsy to cope without producing counter-atrocities that would increase social support for the cause. If the process of atrocities and counter-atrocities were well planned, it could favor those perceived to be weak and without alternatives.[40]

Major energies went into guerrilla-like (hit-and-run) actions against troops—attacks that still went beyond the rules of war because weapons were concealed and the assailants had no identifying insignia.[41] Some groups, such as the Irgun, made efforts to give warnings in order to limit civilian casualties. In some cases, such as Algeria, terror was one aspect of a more comprehensive rebellion that included extensive guerrilla forces.

Compared to terrorists in the first wave, those in the second wave used the four international ingredients in different and much more productive ways. Leaders of different national groups still acknowledged the common bonds and heritage of an international revolutionary tradition, but the heroes invoked in the literature of specific groups were overwhelmingly national heroes.[42] The underlying assumption seemed to be that if one strengthened ties with foreign terrorists, other international assets would become less useful.

Diaspora groups regularly displayed abilities not seen earlier. Nineteenth-century Irish rebels received money, weapons, and volunteers from the Irish-American community, but in the 1920s the exertions of the latter went further and induced the U.S. government to exert significant political influence on Britain to accept an Irish state.[43] Jewish diaspora communities, especially in the United States, exerted similar leverage as the horror of the Holocaust was finally revealed.

Foreign states with kindred populations also were active. Arab states gave the Algerian FLN crucial political support, and those adjacent to Algeria offered sanctuaries from which the group could stage attacks. Greece sponsored the Cypriot uprising against the British and against Cyprus when it became a state. Frightened Turkish Cypriots, in turn, looked to Turkey for aid. Turkish troops then invaded the island (1974) and are still there.

Outside influences obviously change when the purpose of the terrorist activity and the local context are perceived differently. The different Irish experiences illustrate the point well. The early effort in the 1920s was seen simply as an anticolonial movement, and the Irish-American community had its greatest or most productive impact.[44] The diaspora was less interested in the IRA's brief campaigns to bring Northern Ireland into the Republic during World War II or, later, during the cold war. Conflicting concerns weakened overseas enthusiasms and influences.

As the second wave progressed, a new, fifth ingredient—supranational organization—came into play. When Alexander I of Serbia was assassinated in Marseilles (1934), the League of Nations tried to contain international terror by drafting two conventions, including one for an international court (1937). Neither came into effect. Two League members (Hungary and Italy) apparently encouraged the assassination and blocked the antiterror efforts.[45] After World War II, the United Nations inherited the League's ultimate authority over the colonial mandates—territories that were now scenes of extensive terrorist activity. When Britain decided to withdraw from Palestine, the UN was crucial in legitimizing the partition; subsequently all anticolonial terrorists sought to interest the UN in their struggles. The new states admitted to the UN were nearly always former colonial territories, and they gave the anticolonial sentiment in that body more structure, focus, and opportunities. More and more participants in UN debates regularly used Begin's language to describe anticolonial terrorists as "freedom fighters."[46]

THIRD WAVE: EXCESSIVE INTERNATIONALISM?

The major political event stimulating the third, or "New Left," wave was the agonizing Vietnam War. The effectiveness of the Viet Cong's "primitive weapons" against the American goliath's modern technology rekindled radical hopes that the contemporary system was vulnerable. Groups developed in the Third World and in the Western heartland itself, where the war stimulated enormous ambivalence among the youth about the value of the existing system. Many Western groups—such as American Weather Underground, the West German Red Army Faction (RAF), the Italian Red Brigades, the Japanese Red Army, and the French Action Directe—saw themselves as vanguards for the Third World masses. The Soviet world encouraged the outbreaks and offered moral support, training, and weapons.

As in the first wave, radicalism and nationalism often were combined, as evidenced by the struggles of the Basques, Armenians, Corsicans, Kurds, and Irish.[47] Every first-wave nationalist movement had failed, but the linkage was renewed because ethnic concerns always have larger constituencies than radical aspirations have. Although self-determination ultimately obscured the radical programs and nationalist groups were much more durable than other groups in the third wave, none succeeded, and their survivors will fail too. The countries concerned—Spain, France, the United Kingdom, and Turkey—simply do not consider themselves to be colonial powers, and the ambivalence necessary for nationalist success is absent.

When the Vietnam War ended in 1975, the PLO replaced the Viet Cong as the heroic model. The PLO originated after the extraordinary collapse of three Arab armies in the six days of the 1967 Middle East war; its existence and persistence gave credibility to supporters who argued that only terror could remove Israel. Its centrality for other groups was strengthened because it got strong support from Arab states and the Soviet Union and made training facilities in Lebanon available to the other groups.

The first and third waves had some striking resemblances. Women in the second wave had been restricted to the role of messengers and scouts; now they became leaders and fighters once more.[48] "Theatrical targets," comparable to those of the first wave, replaced the second wave's military targets. International hijacking is one example. Terrorists understood that some foreign landing fields were accessible. Seven hundred hijackings occurred during the first three decades of the third wave.[49]

Planes were hijacked to secure hostages. There were other ways to generate hostage crises, however, and the hostage crisis became a third-wave characteristic. The most memorable episode was the 1979 kidnapping of former Italian Prime Minister Aldo Moro by the Red Brigades. When the government refused to negotiate, Moro was brutally murdered and his body dumped in the streets. The Sandinistas took Nicaragua's Congress hostage in 1978—an act so audacious that it sparked the popular insurrection that brought the Somoza regime down a year later. In Colombia the M–19 tried to duplicate the feat by seizing the Supreme Court on April 19, 1985, but the government refused to yield and in the struggle nearly 100 people were killed; the terrorists killed eleven justices.

Kidnappings occurred in seventy-three countries—especially in Italy, Spain, and Latin America. From 1968 to 1982 there were 409 international kidnapping incidents yielding 951 hostages.[50] Initially hostages gave their captors political leverage, but soon another concern became more dominant. Companies insured their executives, and kidnapping became lucrative. When money was the principal issue, kidnappers found that hostage negotiations were easier to consummate on their terms. Informed observers estimate the practice "earned" $350 million.[51]

The abandoned practice of assassinating prominent figures was revived. The IRA and its various splinter organizations, for example, assassinated the British ambassador to Ireland (1976) and Lord Mountbatten (1979) and attempted to kill prime ministers Thatcher (1984) and Major (1991).[52] The Palestinian Black September assassinated the Jordanian prime minister (1971) and attempted to assassinate Jordan's King Hussein (1974). Black September killed the American ambassador when it took the Saudi embassy in Khartoum (1973). Euskadi ta Askatasuna (Basque Nation and Liberty; ETA) killed the Spanish prime minister in the same year.

First- and third-wave assassinations had a different logic, however. A first-wave victim was assassinated because he or she held a public office. New Left-wave assassinations more often were "punishments." Jordan's prime minister and king had forced the PLO out of their country in a savage battle. Similarly, the attempt against British Prime Minister Margaret Thatcher occurred because she was "responsible" for the death of the nine IRA hunger strikers who refused to be treated as ordinary criminals.[53] Aldo Moro was assassinated because the Italian government refused to enter hostage negotiations. The German Red Army Faction provided a second typical pattern: 15 percent of its strikes involved assassination. Although the RAF did not seek the most prominent public figures, it did kill the head of the Berlin Supreme Court and a well-known industrialist.[54]

For good reason, the abandoned term "international terrorism" was revived. Again the revolutionary ethos created significant bonds between separate national groups—bonds that intensified when first Cuban and then PLO training facilities were made available. The targets chosen reflected international dimensions as well. Some groups conducted more assaults abroad than on their home territories; the PLO, for example, was more active in Europe than on the West Bank, and sometimes more active in Europe than many European groups themselves were. Different national groups cooperated in attacks such as the Munich Olympics massacre (1972) and the kidnapping of OPEC ministers (1975), among others.

On their own soil, groups often chose targets with international significance. Strikes on foreign embassies began when the PLO attacked the Saudi embassy in Khartoum (1973). The Peruvian group *Tupac Amaru*—partly to gain political advantage over its rival *Sendero Luminoso* (The Shining Path)—held seventy-two hostages in the Japanese Embassy for more than four months (1996–97) until a rescue operation killed every terrorist in the complex.

One people became a favorite target of most groups. One-third of the international attacks in the third wave involved American targets—a pattern reflecting the United States' new importance. American targets were visible in Latin America, Europe, and the Middle East, where the United States supported most governments under terrorist siege.[55]

Despite its preeminent status as a target, cold war concerns sometimes led the United States to ignore its stated distaste for terror. In Nicaragua, Angola, and elsewhere the United States supported terrorist activity—an indication of how difficult it was to forgo a purpose deemed worthwhile even when deplorable tactics had to be used.

Third-wave organizations discovered that they paid a large price for not being able to negotiate between the conflicting demands imposed by various international elements.[56] The commitment to a revolutionary ethos alienated domestic and foreign liberal elements, particularly during the cold war. The IRA forfeited significant Irish American diaspora support during the third wave. Its initial goal during the third wave was a united socialist Ireland, and its willingness to accept support from Libya and the PLO created problems. Most of all, however, the cold war had to end before the Irish diaspora and an American government showed sustained interest in the Irish issue again and assisted moves to resolve the conflict.

Involvement with foreign groups made some terrorist organizations neglect domestic constituencies. A leader of the 2nd of June, a German anarchist body, suggested that its obsession with the Palestinian cause induced it to attack a Jewish synagogue on the anniversary of *Kristall Nacht*—a date often considered the beginning of the Holocaust. Such "stupidity," he said, alienated potential German constituencies.[57] When the power of the cooperating terrorist entities was very unequal, the weaker found that its interest did not count. Thus, the German Revolutionary Cells, hijacking partners of the Popular Front for the Liberation of Palestine (PFLP), could not get help from their partners to release German prisoners. "(D)ependent on the will of Wadi Haddad and his group," whose agenda was very different from theirs after all, the Revolutionary Cells terminated the relationship and soon collapsed.[58]

The PLO, always a loose confederation, often found international ties expensive because they complicated serious existing divisions within the organization. In the 1970s Abu Iyad, PLO founding member and intelligence chief, wrote that the Palestinian cause was so important in Syrian and Iraqi domestic politics that those states felt it necessary to capture organizations within the PLO to serve their own ends. That made it even more difficult to settle for a limited goal, as the Irgun and EOKA had done earlier.

Entanglements with Arab states created problems for both parties. Raids from Egyptian-occupied Gaza helped precipitate a disastrous war with Israel (1956), and the *fidayeen* were prohibited from launching raids from that territory ever again. A Palestinian raid from Syria brought Syria into the Six-Day War, and ever afterward Syria kept a tight control on those operating from its territories. When a PLO faction hijacked British and American planes to Jordan (1970) in the first effort to target non-Israelis, the Jordanian army devastated the PLO, which then lost its home. Finally, an attempted assassination of an Israeli diplomat in Britain sparked the 1982 invasion of Lebanon and forced the PLO to leave a home that had given it so much significance among foreign terrorist groups. (Ironically, the assassination attempt was organized by Abu Nidal's renegade faction associated with Iraq—a group that had made two previous attempts to assassinate the PLO's leader Yasser Arafat.) Subsequently, Tunisia—the PLO's new host—prohibited the PLO from training foreign groups, and to a large extent the PLO's career as an effective terrorist organization seemed to be over. Paradoxically, the Oslo Accords demonstrated that the PLO could achieve more of its objectives when it was less dangerous.[59]

To maintain control over their own destiny, states again began to "sponsor" groups (a practice abandoned in the second wave), and once more the sponsors found the practice costly. In the 1980s Britain severed diplomatic relations with Libya and Syria for sponsoring terrorism on British soil, and France broke with Iran when it refused to let the French interrogate its embassy staff about assassinations of Iranian émigrés. Iraq's surprising restraint during the 1991 Gulf War highlighted the weakness of state-sponsored terror. Iraq did threaten to use terror—a threat that induced Western authorities to predict that terrorists would flood Europe.[60] If terror had materialized, however, it would have made bringing Saddam Hussein to trial for crimes a war aim, and the desire to avoid that result is the most plausible explanation for the Iraqi dictator's uncharacteristic restraint.

The third wave began to ebb in the 1980s. Revolutionary terrorists were defeated in one country after another. Israel's invasion of Lebanon (1982) eliminated PLO facilities to train terrorist groups, and international counter-terrorist cooperation became increasingly effective.

As in the first wave, states cooperated openly and formally in counter-terror efforts. The United States, with British aid, bombed Libya (1986) because of its role as a state sponsor, and the European Community imposed an arms embargo. The international cooperation of national police forces sought at St. Petersburg (1904) became more significant as Trevi—established in the mid-1970s—was joined in this mission by Europol in 1994. Differences between states remained, however; even close allies could not always cooperate. France refused to extradite PLO, Red Brigade, and ETA suspects to West Germany, Italy, and Spain, respectively. Italy spurned American requests to extradite a Palestinian suspect in the seizure of the *Achille Lauro* cruise ship (1984), and Italy refused to extradite a Kurd (1988) because Italian law forbids capital punishment whereas Turkish law does not. The United States has re-fused to extradite some IRA suspects. Events of this sort will not stop until that improbable day when the laws and interests of separate states are identical.

The UN's role changed dramatically in the third wave. Now "new states"—former colonial territories—found that terrorism threatened their in-terests, and they particularly shunned nationalist movements. Major UN con-ventions from 1970 through 1999 made hijacking, hostage taking, attacks on senior government officials, "terrorist bombing" of a foreign state's facilities, and financing of international activities crimes. A change of language is some indication of the changed attitude. "Freedom fighter" was no longer a popu-lar term in UN debates, and the term *terrorism* actually was used for the title of a document: "International Convention for the Suppression of Terrorist Bombing" (1997).[61] Evidence that Libya's agents were involved in the Pan Am Lockerbie crash produced a unanimous Security Council decision obliging Libya to extradite the suspects (1988), and a decade later when collective sanc-tions had their full effects Libya complied; this episode will continue to shape UN responses to Libya's terrorist activities.

Yet very serious ambiguities and conflicts within the UN remained, re-flecting the ever-present fact that terror serves different ends—and some of those ends are prized. Ironically, the most important ambiguity concerned the third wave's major organization: the PLO. It received official UN status and was recognized by more than 100 states as a state that is entitled to receive a share of the Palestine Mandate.

FOURTH WAVE: HOW UNIQUE AND HOW LONG?

As its predecessor began to ebb, the "religious wave" gathered force. Reli-gious elements have always been important in modern terror because religious and ethnic identities often overlap. The Armenian, Macedonian, Irish,

Cypriot, French Canadian, Israeli, and Palestinian struggles illustrate the point.[62] In these cases, however, the aim was to create secular states.

Today religion has a vastly different significance, supplying justifications and organizing principles for a state. The religious wave has produced an occasional secular group—a reaction to excessive religious zeal. Buddhists in Sri Lanka tried to transform the country, and a terrorist response among the largely Hindu Tamils aims at creating a separate secular state.

Islam is at the heart of the wave. Islamic groups have conducted the most significant, deadly, and profoundly international attacks. Equally significant, the political events providing the hope for the fourth wave originated in Islam, and the successes achieved apparently influenced religious terror groups elsewhere.[63]

Although there is no direct evidence for the latter connection, the chronology is suggestive. After Islam erupted, Sikhs sought a religious state in the Punjab. Jewish terrorists attempted to blow up Islam's most sacred shrine in Jerusalem and waged an assassination campaign against Palestinian mayors. One Jew murdered twenty-nine Muslim worshippers in Abraham's tomb (Hebron, 1994), and another assassinated Israeli Prime Minister Rabin (1995). Aum Shinrikyo—a group that combined Buddhist, Hindu, and Christian themes—released nerve gas on the Tokyo subway (1995), killing 12 people and injuring 3,000 and creating worldwide anxiety that various groups would soon use weapons of mass destruction.

Christian terrorism, based on racist interpretations of the Bible, emerged in the amorphous American "Christian Identity" movement. In true medieval millenarian fashion, armed rural communes composed of families withdrew from the state to wait for the Second Coming and the great racial war. Although some observers have associated Christian Identity with the Oklahoma City bombing (1995), the Christian level of violence has been minimal—so far.

Three events in the Islamic world provided the hope or dramatic political turning point that was vital to launch the fourth wave. In 1979 the Iranian Revolution occurred, a new Islamic century began, and the Soviets made an unprovoked invasion of Afghanistan.

Iranian street demonstrations disintegrated the Shah's secular state. The event also was clear evidence to believers that religion now had more political appeal than did the prevailing third-wave ethos because Iranian Marxists could only muster meager support against the Shah. "There are no frontiers in Islam," Ayatollah Khomeini proclaimed, and "his" revolution altered relationships among all Muslims as well as between Islam and the rest of the world. Most immediately, the Iranians inspired and assisted Shiite terror movements outside of Iran, particularly in Iraq, Saudi Arabia, Kuwait, and Lebanon. In Lebanon, Shiites—influenced by the self-martyrdom tactic of the medieval Assassins—introduced suicide bombing, with surprising results, ousting American and other foreign troops that had entered the country on a peace mission after the 1982 Israeli invasion.

The monumental Iranian revolution was unexpected, but some Muslims had always believed that the year would be very significant because it marked the beginning of a new Islamic century. One venerable Islamic tradition holds that a redeemer will come with the start of a new century—an expectation that regularly sparkled uprisings at the turn of earlier Muslim centuries.[64] Muslims stormed the Grand Mosque in Mecca in the first minutes of the new century in 1979, and 10,000 casualties resulted. Whatever the specific local causes, it is striking that so many examples of Sunni terrorism appeared at the same time in Egypt, Syria, Tunisia, Morocco, Algeria, the Philippines, and Indonesia.

The Soviet Union invaded Afghanistan in 1979. Resistance strengthened by volunteers from all over the Sunni world and subsidized by U.S. aid forced the Soviets out by 1989—a crucial step in the stunning and unimaginable disintegration of the Soviet Union itself. Religion had eliminated a secular superpower, an astonishing event with important consequences for terrorist activity[65] in that the third wave received a decisive blow. Lands with large Muslim populations that formerly were part of the Soviet Union—such as Chechnya, Uzbekistan, Kyrgyzstan, Tajiikistan, and Azerbijan—became important new fields for Islamic rebels. Islamic forces ignited Bosnia. Kashmir again became a critical issue, and the death toll since 1990 has been more than 50,000.[66] Trained and confident Afghan veterans were major participants in the new and ongoing conflicts.

"Suicide bombing," reminiscent of anarchist bomb-throwing efforts, was the most deadly tactical innovation. Despite the conventional wisdom that only a vision of rewards in paradise could inspire such acts, the secular Tamil Tigers were so impressed by the achievement in Lebanon that they used the tactic in Sri Lanka to give their movement new life. From 1983 to 2000 they used suicide bombers more than all Islamic groups combined, and Tamil suicide bombers often were women—a very unusual event in the fourth wave.[67] Partly to enhance their political leverage at home, Palestinian religious groups began to use suicide bombers, compelling secular PLO elements to emulate them.

The fourth wave has displayed other distinctive international features. The number of terrorist groups declined dramatically. About 200 were active in the 1980s, but in the next decade the number fell to 40.[68] The trend appears to be related to the size of the primary audiences (nation versus religion). A major religious community such as Islam is much larger than any national group. Different cultural traditions also may be relevant. The huge number of secular terrorist groups came largely from Christian countries, And the Christian tradition has always generated many more religious divisions that the Islamic tradition has.[69] Islamic groups are more durable than their third-wave predecessors; the major groups in Lebanon, Egypt, and Algeria have persisted for two decades and are still functioning.[70] These groups are large organizations, and bin Laden's al-Qaeda was the largest, containing perhaps 5,000 members with cells operating in seventy-two countries.[71] Larger terrorist groups earlier usually had nationalist aims—with a few hundred active members and a few thousand available for recruitment. The PLO was a special case at least in Lebanon, where it had about 25,000 members and was trying to transform itself into a regular army. Likewise, most al-Qaeda recruits served with the Taliban in the Afghan civil war.

The American role too changed. Iran called the United States the "Great Satan." Al-Qaeda regarded America as its chief antagonist immediately after the Soviet Union was defeated—a fact not widely appreciated until September 11.[72] From the beginning, Islamic religious groups sought to *destroy* their American targets, usually military or civilian installations, an unknown pattern in the third wave. The aim was U.S. military withdrawal from the Middle East. U.S. troops were driven out of Lebanon and forced to abandon a humanitarian mission in Somalia. Attacks on military posts in Yemen and Saudi Arabia occurred. The destroyer USS *Cole* experienced the first terrorist strike against a military vessel ever (2000). All of the attacks on the U.S. military in the Arabian Peninsula and Africa drew military responses; moreover, Americans did not withdraw after those incidents. The strikes against American embassies in Kenya and Tanzania (1998) inflicted heavy casualties, and futile cruise missile attacks were made against al-Qaeda targets—the first time missiles were used against a group rather than a state. As Peter Bergen has noted, "The attacks, however, had a major unintended consequence: They turned bin Laden from a marginal figure in the Muslim world to a global celebrity."[73] Strikes on American soil began in 1993 with a partially successful effort on the World Trade Center. A mission to strike on the millennial celebration night seven years later was aborted.[74] Then there was September 11.

Al-Qaeda was responsible for attacks in the Arabian Peninsula, Africa, and the American homeland. Its initial object was to force U.S. evacuation of military bases in Saudi Arabia, the land containing Islam's two holiest sites. The Prophet Muhammed had said that only one religion should be in the land, and Saudi Arabia became a land where Christians and Jews could reside only for temporary periods.[75] Al-Qaeda's aim resonates in the Sunni world and is reflected in its unique recruiting pattern. Most volunteers come from Arab states—especially Egypt, Saudi Arabia, and Algeria—and the Afghan training camps received Sunnis from at least sixty Muslim and non-Muslim countries. Every previous terrorist organization, including Islamic groups, drew its recruits from a single national base. The contrast between PLO and al-Qaeda training facilities reflects this fact; the former trained units from other organizations and the latter received individuals only.

Beyond the evacuation of bases in Islam's Holy Land, al-Qaeda later developed another objective—a single Islamic state under the Sharia. Bin Laden gave vigorous support to Islamic groups that were active in various states of the Sunni world—states that many Muslims understand to be residues of collapsed colonial influence. Just as the United States refused to leave Saudi Arabia, it helped to frustrate this second effort by aiding the attacked states. The United States avoided direct intervention that could inflame the Islamic world, however. The support given to states attacked had some success, and perhaps September 11 should be understood as a desperate attempt to rejuvenate a failing cause by triggering indiscriminate reactions.[76]

The response to September 11 was as unprecedented as the attack itself. Under UN auspices, more than 100 states (including Iran) joined the attack on Afghanistan in various ways. Yet no one involved expected the intervention to be so quick and decisive. Afghanistan had always been difficult for invaders. Moreover, terrorist history demonstrates that even when antiterrorist forces were very familiar with territories containing terrorists (this time they were not), entrenched terrorists still had considerable staying power.

There are many reasons why al-Qaeda collapsed so quickly in Afghanistan. It violated a cardinal rule for terrorist organizations, which is to stay underground always. Al-Qaeda remained visible to operate its extensive training operations,[77] and as the Israelis demonstrated in ousting the PLO from Lebanon, visible groups are vulnerable. Moreover, al-Qaeda and the PLO were foreign elements in lands uncomfortable with their presence. Finally, al-Qaeda did not plan for an invasion possibility. The reason is not clear, but there is evidence that its contempt for previous American reactions convinced it that the United States would avoid difficult targets and not go to Afghanistan.[78]

The PLO regrouped in Tunisia, on condition that it would abandon its extensive training mission. Could al-Qaeda accept such limits, and if it did, would any state risk playing Tunisia's role? Pakistan's revolving-door policy suggests a much more likely reaction. Once al-Qaeda's principal supporter, Pakistan switched under U.S. pressure to give the coalition indispensable aid.

As of this writing, the world does not know what happened to al-Qaeda's leadership, but even if the portion left can be reassembled, how can the organization function without a protected sanctuary? Al Zawahiri, bin Laden's likely successor, warned his comrades before the Afghan training grounds were lost that "the victory . . . against the international alliance will not be accomplished without acquiring a . . . base in the heart of the Islamic world."[79] Peter Bergen's admirable study of al-Qaeda makes the same point.[80]

The disruption of al-Qaeda in Afghanistan has altered the organization's previous routine. Typically, al-Qaeda sleeper cells remained inactive until the moment to strike materialized, often designated by the organization's senior leadership. It was an unusual pattern in terrorist history. Normally cells are active and, therefore, need more autonomy so that police penetration in one cell does not go beyond that unit. Cells of this sort have more freedom to strike. They generally will do so more quickly and frequently, but the numbers and resources available to a cell constantly in motion limit them to softer or less protected targets. If direction from the top can no longer be a feature of al-Qaeda, the striking patterns will necessarily become more "normal."[81] Since the Afghan rout, strikes have been against "softer," largely unprotected civilian targets. As the destruction of tourist sites—such as the ancient synagogue in Tunisia and the nightclubs in Bali, Indonesia—suggests, however, the organization displays its trademark by maximizing casualties.

CONCLUDING THOUGHTS AND QUESTIONS

Unlike crime or poverty, international terrorism is a recent phenomenon. Its continuing presence for 125 years means, however, that it is rooted in important features of our world. Technology and doctrine have played vital roles. The latter reflects a modern inclination to rationalize activity or make it efficient, which Max Weber declared a distinctive feature of modern life. A third briefly noted factor is the spread of democratic ideas, which shapes terrorist activity in different ways—as suggested by the fact that nationalism or separatism is the most frequently espoused cause.[82]

The failure of a democratic reform program inspired the first wave, and the main theme of the second was national self-determination. A dominant, however confused, third-wave theme was that existing systems were not truly democratic. The spirit of the fourth wave appears explicitly antidemocratic because the democratic idea is inconceivable without a significant measure of secularism.

For many reasons, terrorist organizations often have short lives; sometimes their future is determined by devastating tactical mistakes. A decision to become visible is rare in the history of terror, and the quick success of the coalition's Afghan military campaign demonstrates why. If al-Qaeda successfully reconstructs itself, it may discover that it must become an "ordinary" terrorist group living underground among a friendly local population. That also suggests but, alas, does not demonstrate that its strikes will become more "ordinary" too.

No matter what happens to al-Qaeda, this wave will continue, but for how long is uncertain. The life cycle of its predecessors may mislead us. Each was inspired by a secular cause, and a striking characteristic of religious communities is how durable some are. Thus, the fourth wave may last longer than its predecessors, but the course of the Iranian revolution suggests something else. If history repeats itself, the fourth wave will be over in two decades. That history also demonstrates, however, that the world of politics always produces large issues to stimulate terrorists who regularly invent new ways to deal with them. What makes the pattern so interesting and frightening is that the issues emerge unexpectedly—or, at least, no one has been able to anticipate their tragic course.

The coalition assembled after September 11 was extraordinary for several reasons. September 11 was not only an American catastrophe: The World Trade Center housed numerous large foreign groups, and there were many foreign casualties. The UN involvement climaxed a transformation; it is hard to see it as the same organization that regularly referred to terrorists as freedom fighters forty years ago.

The only other coalition against terrorism was initiated a century ago. It aimed to make waves impossible by disrupting vital communication and migration conditions. Much less was expected from its participants, but it still fell apart in three years (1904). Will the current coalition last longer? September 11 will not be forgotten easily,[83] and the effort is focused now on an organization—a much easier focus to sustain.

When the present campaign against al-Qaeda and the small groups in Asia loosely associated with it concludes, what happens next? No organization has been identified as the next target, and until that happens one suspects that the perennial inclination for different states to distinguish groups according to the ends sought rather than the means used may reappear. Kashmir and Palestine are the two most important active scenes for terrorist activity. In Kashmir, Islamic insurgents are seriously dividing two important members of the coalition. India considers them terrorists, but Pakistan does not. War between those states, both possessing nuclear weapons, will push the coalition's war against terror aside. Successful outside mediation may produce a similar result because that would require some acceptance of the insurgents' legitimacy. The Israeli-Palestinian conflict has a similar meaning; so many important states understand the issue of terror there differently.

Islam fuels terrorist activity in Kashmir, but the issue—as in Palestine, where religious elements are less significant—is a local one. To what extent are other organizations in the fourth wave local too? How deeply can the coalition afford to get involved in situations where it will be serving the interests of local governments? Our experience supporting governments dealing with "local" terrorists has not always served our interests well, especially in the Islamic world.

The efforts of Aum Shinrikyo to use weapons of mass destruction has made American officials feel that the most important lesson of this wave is that those ·weapons will be used by terrorists against us.[84] September 11 intensified this anxiety even though suicide bombers armed with box cutters produced that catastrophe, and the history of terrorism demonstrates that cheap, easy to produce, portable, and simple to use weapons have always been the most attractive.

The fourth wave's cheap and distinctive weapon is suicide bombing. The victory in Lebanon was impressive, and suicide bombers have been enormously destructive in Sri Lanka and Israel. Driving foreign troops out of a country is one thing, however; compelling a people to give up a portion of its own country (Sri Lanka) or leave its own land (Israel) is another. In the latter case, the bombers' supporters seem to be suffering a lot more than their enemies are.

How does September 11 affect our understanding of foreign threats? This is a serious question that needs more discussion than it has received. Nechaev emphasized that the fear and rage rebel terror produced undermined a society's traditional moral conventions and ways of thinking. He was thinking of the domestic context, and indeed the history of modern terrors shows that domestic responses frequently are indiscriminate and self-destructive.[85] Can the same pattern be observed on the international scene?

The 2003 invasion of Iraq suggests that Nechaev's observation is apt for the international scene as well. The justifications for the war were that Iraq might give terrorists weapons of mass destruction or use them itself against the West—considerations that are applicable to a variety of states, as the "axis of evil" language suggests. After September 11 the United States scrapped the deterrence doctrine, which we developed to help us cope with states possessing weapons of mass destruction and served us well for more than fifty years. Preemption seemed to fit the new age better. Deterrence worked because states knew that they were visible and could be destroyed if they used the dreaded weapons. Underground terrorist groups do not have this vulnerability, which is why preemption has been an important part of police counterterrorist strategy since the first wave. Deterrence is linked to actions, whereas preemption is more suitable when intentions have to be assessed—a task always shrouded in grave ambiguities. Is there any reason to think the crucial distinction between states and terrorist groups has disappeared, however, and that we should put decisions of war and peace largely in the hands of very imperfect intelligence agencies?

The significance of the Iraqi war for the war against terrorism remains unclear. The coalition's cohesion has been weakened, and the flagging fortunes of Islamic groups could be revived. Both possibilities are more likely if preemption is employed against another state or if the victory in Iraq ultimately is understood as an occupation.

NOTES

An earlier version of this essay was published in *Current History* (December 2001):419–25. Another version was delivered at the annual John Barlow Lecture, University of Indiana, Indianapolis. I am indebted to Jim Ludes, Lindsay Clutterbuck, Laura Donohue, Clark McCauley, Barbara Rapoport, and Sara Grdan for useful comments, even those I did not take. The problems in the essay are my responsibility.

1. On September 20, 2001, the president told Congress that "any nation that continues to harbor or support terrorism will be regarded as a hostile regime. [T]he war would not end until every terrorist group of global reach has been found, stopped, and defeated."

2. See Richard B. Jensen, "The United States, International Policing, and the War against Anarchist Terrorism," *Terrorism and Political Violence* (hereafter *TPV*) 13, no. 1 (spring 2001):5–46.

3. No good history of terrorism exists. Schmid and Jongman's monumental study of the terrorism literature does not even list a history of the subject. See *Political Terrorism: A New Guide to Actors, Authors, Concepts, Theories, DataBases, and Literature,* rev. ed. (New Brunswick, N.J.: Transaction Books, 1988).

4. I lack space to discuss the domestic sphere, which offers important parallels as well. The unusual character of terrorist activity made an enormous impact on national life in many countries beginning in the latter part of the nineteenth century. Every state affected in the first wave radically

transformed its police organizations as tools to penetrate underground groups. The Russian *Okhrana,* the British Special Branch, and the FBI are conspicuous examples. The new organizational form remains a permanent, perhaps indispensable, feature of modern life. Terrorist tactics, *inter alia,* aim at producing rage and frustration, often driving governments to respond in unanticipated, extraordinary, illegal, socially destructive, and shameful ways. Because a significant Jewish element, for example, was present in the several Russian terrorist movements, the *Okhrana* organized pogroms to intimidate Russian Jews, compelling many to flee to the West and to the Holy Land. *Okhrana* fabricated *The Protocols of Zion,* a book that helped stimulate a virulent anti-Semitism that went well beyond Russia. The influence of that fabrication continued for decades and still influences Christian and Islamic terrorist movements today.

Democratic states "overreacted" too. President Theodore Roosevelt proposed sending all anarchists back to Europe. Congress did not act, but more than a decade later President Wilson's Attorney General Palmer implemented a similar proposal and rounded up all anarchists to ship them back "home," regardless of whether they had committed crimes. That event produced the 1920 Wall Street bombing, which in turn became the justification for an immigration quota law that for decades made it much more difficult for persons from southern and eastern European states (the original home of most anarchists) to immigrate—a law Adolph Hitler praised highly. It is still too early to know what the domestic consequences of September 11 will be. The very first reactions suggested that we had learned from past mistakes. The federal government made special efforts to show that we were not at war with Islam, and it curbed the first expressions of vigilante passions. The significance of subsequent measures seems more problematic, however. Our first experience with terror led us to create important new policing arrangements. Now Congress has established a Department of Homeland Security with 170,000 employees—clearly the largest change in security policy in our history. No one knows what that seismic change means. One casualty could be the Posse Comitatus law, which prohibits the military forces from administering civil affairs—a law that ironically was passed because we were unhappy with military responses to KKK terrorist activity after the Civil War! A policy of secret detentions, a common reaction to serious terrorist activities in many countries, has been implemented. Extensive revisions of immigration regulations are being instituted. Prisoners taken in Afghanistan are not being prosecuted under the criminal law, reversing a long-standing policy in virtually all states including our own. Previous experiences suggest that it will take time for the changes to have their effect because so much depends on the scope, frequency, and duration of future terrorist activity.

5. David M. Chalmers, *Hooded Americanism: The History of the Ku Klux Klan,* 3d ed. (Durham, N.C.: Duke University Press, 1987), 19.

6. The activities of the Thugs and Assassins had international dimensions but were confined to specific regions; more important, there were no comparable groups operating at the same time in this region or elsewhere. See David C. Rapoport, "Fear and Trembling: Terror in Three Religious Traditions," *American Political Science Review* 78, no. 3 (1984):658–77.

7. The lineage of rebel terror is very ancient, going back at least to the first century. Hinduism, Judaism, and Islam produced the Thugs, Zealots, and Assassins, respectively; these names still are used to designate terrorists. Religion determined every purpose and each tactic of this ancient form. See Rapoport, "Fear and Trembling."

8. By far most published academic articles on terrorism deal with counterterrorism and with organizations. Judging by my experience as an editor of *TPV,* the proportions increase further in this direction if we also consider articles that are rejected.

9. See note 1.

10. The rebels fought in uniform and against soldiers. George Bernard Shaw said, "My own view is that the men who were shot in cold blood . . . after their capture were prisoners of war." Prime Minister Asquith said that by Britain's own standards, the rebels were honorable, that "they conducted themselves with great humanity . . . fought very bravely and did not resort to outrage." The *Manchester Guardian* declared that the executions were "atrocities." See my introduction to part III of David C. Rapoport and Yonah Alexander, eds., *The Morality of Terrorism: Religious Origins and Ethnic Implications,* 2d ed. (New York: Columbia University Press, 1989), 219–27.

11. Guerrillas carry weapons openly and wear an identifying emblem—circumstances that oblige a state to treat them as soldiers.

12. Anyone who has tried to explain the intensity of the 1960s experience to contemporary students knows how difficult it is to transmit a generation's experience.

13. Nechaev's "Revolutionary Catechism" is reprinted in David C. Rapoport, *Assassination and Terrorism* (Toronto: CBC, 1971). See Michael Bakunin and Peter Kropotkin, *Revolutionary Pamphlets* (New York: Benjamin Bloom, 1927); Nicholas Mozorov, *Terroristic Struggle* (London, 1880); Serge Stepniak, *Underground Russia: Revolutionary Profiles and Sketches from Life* (New York, 1892).

14. See Rapoport, "Fear and Trembling."

15. It took time for this attitude to develop in Islam. If one compares bin Laden's work with Faraj's *Neglected Duty*—a work primarily written at the beginning of the fourth wave to justify the assassination of Egyptian President Sadat (1981)—the two authors seem to be in different worlds. Faraj cites no experience outside the Islamic tradition, and his most recent historical reference is to Napoleon's invasion of Europe. See David C.

Rapoport, "Sacred Terror: A Case from Contemporary Islam," in *Origins of Terrorism,* ed. Walter Reich (Cambridge: Cambridge University Press, 1990), 103–30. I am grateful to Jerry Post for sharing his copy of the bin Laden treatise. An edited version appears on the Department of Justice website www.usdoj.gov/ag/trainingmanual.htm.

16. Bin Laden's dedication reads as follows:

Pledge, O Sister

To the sister believer whose clothes the criminals have stripped off:

To the sister believer whose hair the oppressors have shaved.

To the sister believer whose body has been abused by the human dogs.

. . .

Covenant, O Sister . . . to make their women widows and their children orphans. . . .

17. I ignore right-wing groups because more often than not they are associated with government reactions. I also ignore "single issue" groups such as the contemporary antiabortion and Green movements.

18. The term *terror* originally referred to actions of the Revolutionary government that went beyond the rules regulating punishment in order to "educate" a people to govern itself.

19. Vera Figner, the architect of Narodnaya Volya's foreign policy, identifies the first four ingredients. The fifth was created later. For a more extensive discussion of Figner, see David C. Rapoport, "The International World as Some Terrorists Have Seen It: A Look at a Century of Memoirs," in *Inside Terrorist Organizations,* 2d ed. (London: Frank Cass, 2001), 125*ff.*

20. Nechaev, "Revolutionary Catechism."

21. An equivalent for this argument in religious millennial thought is that the world must become impossibly bad before it could become unimaginably good.

22. Adam B. Ulam, *In the Name of the People* (New York: Viking Press, 1977), 269 (emphasis added).

23. Newspaper reports in Germany the next day interpreted the demonstrations to mean that a revolution was coming. See *New York Times,* 4 April 1878.

24. Stepniak, *Underground Russia,* 39–40.

25. The bomb was most significant in Russia. Women were crucial in Russian groups but sometimes were precluded from throwing the bomb, presumably because bombers rarely escaped. Other terrorists used the bomb extensively but chose other weapons as well.

26. A guerrilla force has political objectives, as any army does, but it aims to weaken or destroy the enemy's military forces first. The terrorist, on the

other hand, strikes directly at the political sentiments that sustain the enemy.

27. Thomas Hobbes may have been the first to emphasize hope as a necessary ingredient of revolutionary efforts. The first chapter of Menachem Begin's account of his experience in the Irgun contains the most moving description of the necessity of hope in terrorist literature. Menachem Begin, *The Revolt: Story of the Irgun* (Jerusalem: Steinmatzky's Agency, 1997).

28. There were many organizations: the Internal Macedonian Revolutionary Organization, Young Bosnia, and the Serbian Black Hand.

29. See Peter Heehs, *Nationalism, Terrorism, and Communalism: Essays in Modern Indian History* (Delhi: Oxford University Press, 1998), chap. 2.

30. The Japanese offer to finance Russian terrorists during the Russo-Japanese War (1905) encouraged Indian terrorists to believe that the Japanese would help them too. Heehs, *Nationalism, Terrorism, and Communalism,* 4. The Russians turned the Japanese offer down, fearing that knowledge of the transaction during a time of war would destroy their political credibility.

31. Italians were particularly active as international assassins, crossing borders to kill French President Carnot (1894), Spanish Premier Casnovas (1896), and Austrian Empress Elizabeth (1898). In 1900 an agent of an anarchist group in Patterson, New Jersey, returned to Italy to assassinate King Umberto.

32. Jensen, "The United States, International Policing, and the War against Anarchist Terrorism," 19.

33. The IRA's success in 1921 occurred when the British recognized the Irish state. Northern Ireland remained British, however, and the civil war between Irish factions over the peace settlement ended in defeat for those who wanted to continue until Northern Ireland joined the Irish state.

34. For an interesting and useful account of the decolonialization process, see Robert Hager, Jr., and David A. Lake, "Balancing Empires: Competitive Decolonization in International Politics," *Security Studies* 9, no. 3 (spring 2000): 108–48. Hager and Lake emphasize that the literature on decolonization "has ignored how events and politics within the core (metropolitan area) shaped the process" (145).

35. Begin said that his decision was determined by the fact that if he pursued it, a civil war among Jews would occur, indicating that most Jews favored partition. Begin, *The Revolt,* chapters 9 and 10.

36. Alistair Horne, *A Savage War of Peace* (London: Macmillan, 1977), 94–96.

37. Begin, *The Revolt.*

38. For a more detailed discussion of the definition problem, see David C. Rapoport, "Politics of Atrocity," in *Terrorism: Interdisciplinary Perspectives,*

ed. Yonah Alexander and Seymour Finger (New York: John Jay Press, 1987), 46.

39. Alexander I of Yugoslavia (1934) was the most prominent victim, and historians believe that Hungary and Italy were involved in providing help for Balkan terrorists. Begin points out in *The Revolt* that it was too costly to assassinate prominent figures.

40. The strategy is superbly described in the film "Battle of Algiers," based on the memoirs of Yaacev Saadi, who organized the battle. Attacks occur against the police, whose responses are limited by rules governing criminal procedure. In desperation, the police set a bomb off in the Casbah, inadvertently exploding an ammunition dump and killing Algerian women and children. A mob emerges screaming for revenge, and at this point the FLN has the moral warrant to attack civilians. There is another underlying element that often gives rebel terrorism in a democratic world special weight. The atrocities of the strong always seem worse than those of the weak because people believe that the latter have no alternatives.

41. See note 11.

42. See Rapoport, "The International World as Some Terrorists Have Seen It."

43. Irish Americans have always given Irish rebels extensive support. In fact, the Fenian movement was born in the American Civil War. Members attempted to invade Canada from the United States and then went to Ireland to spark rebellion there.

44. World War I, of course, increased the influence of the United States, and Wilson justified the war with the self-determination principle.

45. Martin David Dubin, "Great Britain and the Anti-Terrorist Conventions of 1937," *TPV* 5, no. 1 (spring 1993):1.

46. See John Dugard, "International Terrorism and the Just War," in Rapoport and Alexander, *Morality of Terrorism,* 77–78.

47. Basque Nation and Liberty (ETA), the Armenian Secret Army for the Liberation of Armenia (ASALA), the Corsican National Liberation Front (FNLC), and the IRA.

48. The periods of the first and third waves were times when the rights of women were asserted more strenuously in the general society.

49. Sean Anderson and Stephen Sloan, *Historical Dictionary of Terrorism* (Metuchen, N.J.: Transaction Press, 1995), 136.

50. Although bank robbing was not as significant as in the first wave, some striking examples materialized. In January 1976 the PLO, together with its bitter enemies the Christian Phalange, hired safe breakers to help loot the vaults of the major banks in Beirut. Estimates of the amount stolen range between $50 and a $100 million. "Whatever the truth the robbery

was large enough to earn a place in the *Guinness Book of Records* as the biggest bank robbery of all time"; James Adams, *The Financing of Terror* (New York: Simon and Schuster, 1986), 192.

51. Adams, *Financing of Terror*, 94.

52. The attack on Major actually was an attack on the cabinet, so it is not clear whether the prime minister was the principal target (Lindsay Clutterbuck, personal communication to author).

53. The status of political prisoner was revoked in March 1976. William Whitelaw, who granted it in the first place, ranked it as one of his "most regrettable decisions."

54. Anderson and Sloan, *Historical Dictionary of Terrorism*, 303.

55. Sometimes there was American support for terrorist activity (e.g., the Contras in Nicaragua).

56. When a disappointed office-seeker assassinated President Garfield, Figner's sympathy letter to the American people said that there was no place for terror in democratic states. The statement alienated elements of her radical constituency in other countries.

57. Michael Baumann, *Terror or Love* (New York: Grove Press, 1977), 61.

58. Interview with Hans J. Klein in Jean M. Bourguereau, *German Guerrilla: Terror, Rebel Reaction and Resistance* (Sanday, U.K.: Cienfuegos Press, 1981), 31.

59. Abu Nidal himself was on a PLO list of persons to be assassinated.

60. W. Andrew Terrill, "Saddam's Failed Counterstrike: Terrorism and the Gulf War," *Studies in Conflict and Terrorism* 16 (1993):219–32.

61. In addition to four UN conventions there are eight other major multilateral terrorism conventions, starting with The Tokyo Convention of 1963, dealing with the aircraft safety. See http://usinfo.state.gov/topical/pol/terror/conven.htm and http://untreaty.un.org/English/Terrorism.asp.

62. Khachig Tololyan, "Cultural Narrative and the Motivation of the Terrorist," in Rapoport, *Inside Terrorist Organizations*, 217–33.

63. See David C. Rapoport, "Comparing Militant Fundamentalist Movements and Groups," in *Fundamentalisms and the State*, ed. Martin Marty and Scott Appleby (Chicago: University of Chicago Press, 1993), 429–61.

64. To those in the West the most familiar was the nineteenth-century uprising in the Sudan, which resulted in the murder of legendary British General "Chinese" Gordon.

65. This was not the first time secular forces would help launch the careers of those who would become religious terrorists. Israel helped Hamas to get started, thinking it would compete to weaken the PLO. To check left-wing opposition, President Sadat released religious elements from prison that later assassinated him.

66. Peter Bergen, *Holy War Inc.: Inside the Secret World of Osama Bin Ladin* (New York: Free Press, 2001), 208.

67. In the period specified, Tamil suicide bombers struck 171 times; the combined total for all thirteen Islamic groups using the tactic was 117. Ehud Sprinzak cites the figures compiled by Yoram Schweitzer in "Rational Fanatics," *Foreign Policy* (October 2001):69. The most spectacular Tamil act was the assassination of Indian Prime Minister Rajiv Gandhi. (Religion did not motivate the notorious Kamikaze attacks during World War II either.) The example of the Tamils has other unusual characteristics. Efforts to make Sri Lanka a Buddhist state stimulated the revolt. Although Tamils largely come from India, there are several religious traditions represented in the population, and religion does not define the terrorists' prupose.

68. See Ami Pedahzur, William Eubank, and Leonard Weinberg, "The War on Terrorism and the Decline of Terrorist Group Formation," *TPV* 14, no. 3. (fall 2002):141–47.

69. The relationship between different religious terror groups is unusual. Groups from different mainstream traditions (Christianity, Islam, etc.) do not cooperate. Even traditional cleavages within a religion—as in Shiite and Sunni Islam, for example—sometimes are intensified. Shiite terror groups generally take their lead from Iran regarding aid to Sunnis. Iran has helped the Palestinians and is hostile to al-Qaeda and the Saudi religious state.

70. I have no statistical evidence on this point.

71. Rohan Gunaratna, *Inside Al Qaeda: Global Network of Terror* (New York: Columbia University Press, 2002), 97.

72. The stated object of al-Qaeda is to recreate a single Muslim state, and one could argue that if the United States had withdrawn military units from the Muslim world, the attacks would have ceased. What if the issue really was the impact of American secular culture on the world?

73. Bergen, *Holy War Inc.,* 225.

74. Those attacks, as well as the expected attacks that did not materialize, are discussed in a special volume of *TPV* 14, no. 1 (spring 2002) edited by Jeffrey Kaplan, titled *Millennial Violence*. The issue also was published as a book: *Millennial Violence: Past, Present, and Future* (London: Frank Cass, 2002).

75. Bernard Lewis, "License to Kill," *Foreign Affairs* (November/December 1998).

76. For a very interesting discussion of the circumstances that provoke American military responses to terrorist attacks, see Michelle Mavesti, "Explaining the United States' Decision to Strike Back at Terrorists," *TPV* 13, no. 2 (summer 2001):85–106.

77. If the organization understood its vulnerability, it might have thought that an attack on the sovereignty of the state protecting it was unlikely. One

reason the Taliban government refused a repeated UN demand to expel al-Qaeda was because without al-Qaeda support it could not survive local domestic opposition. Because most al-Qaeda recruits served in the Taliban forces in the ongoing civil war, the Taliban must have felt that it had no choice. Clearly, however, there must have been a failure to plan for an invasion possibility; the failure to resist is astonishing otherwise.

78. Gunaratna, *Inside Al Qaeda.*

79. Quoted by Nimrod Raphaeli, "Ayman Muhammad Rabi Al-Zawahri: The Making of an Arch-Terrorist," *TPV* 14, no. 4 (winter 2002):1–22.

80. Bergen, *Holy War Inc.,* 234.

81. The Spaniards conquered the Aztecs and Incas easily, but the United States had more difficulty with the less powerful but highly decentralized native Americans. Steven Simon and Daniel Benjamin make a different argument, contending that bin Laden's group is uniquely decentralized and therefore less likely to be disturbed by destroying the center. See "America and the New Terrorism," *Survival* 42, no. 2 (2000):156–57.

82. We lack a systematic comparison of the aims sought by organizations in the history of modern terror.

83. September 11 has had an impact on at least one terrorist group: The Tamils found diaspora financial support suddenly disappearing for suicide bombing—an opportunity the Norwegians seized to bring them to the bargaining table again.

84. See David C. Rapoport, "Terrorism and Weapons of the Apocalypse," *National Security Studies Quarterly* 5, no. 3 (summer 1999): 49–69, reprinted in Henry Sokolski and James Ludes, *Twenty-First Century Weapons Proliferation* (London: Frank Cass, 2001), 14–33.

85. See note 3.

3

"Misunderestimating" Terrorism

Alan B. Krueger and David D. Laitin

Although terrorism is a top U.S. concern, the State Department's annual terrorism report was riddled with errors. If Washington wants to win the war, it needs to get its facts straight.

As the war on terrorism continues, statistics on terrorist attacks are becoming as important as the unemployment rate or the GDP. Yet the terrorism reports produced by the U.S. government do not have nearly as much credibility as its economic statistics, because there are no safeguards to ensure that the data are as accurate as possible and free from political manipulation. The flap over the error-ridden 2003 Patterns of Global Terrorism report, which Secretary of State Colin Powell called "a big mistake" and which had to be corrected and re-released, recently brought these issues to the fore. But they still have not been adequately addressed.

Now-common practices used to collect and disseminate vital economic statistics could offer the State Department valuable guidance. Not long ago, economic statistics were also subject to manipulation. In 1971, President Richard Nixon attempted to spin unemployment data released by the Bureau of Labor Statistics (BLS) and transferred officials who defied him. This meddling prompted the establishment of a series of safeguards for collecting and disseminating economic statistics. Since 1971, the Joint Economic Committee of

Foreign Affairs, Sept–Oct 2004, v83, i5, p8.

Alan Krueger and David Laitin, "'Misunderestimating' Terrorism," *Foreign Affairs,* Sept.–Oct. 2004. Reprinted by permission.

Congress has held regular hearings at which the commissioner of the BLS discusses the unemployment report. More important, in the 1980s, the Office of Management and Budget issued a directive that permits a statistical agency's staff to "provide technical explanations of the data" in the first hour after principal economic indicators are released and forbids "employees of the Executive Branch" from commenting publicly on the data during that time.

The State Department should adopt similar protections in the preparation and dissemination of its reports. In addition to the global terrorism report, the State Department is required by Congress to report annually on international bribery, human rights practices, narcotics control, and religious freedom. Gathering and reporting data for congressional oversight is presently a low-level function at the State Department. The department rarely relies on high-quality, objective data or on modern diagnostic tests to distinguish meaningful trends from chance associations. Adopting safeguards against bias, both statistical and political, would enable Congress to better perform its constitutional role as the White House's overseer and allow the American public to assess the government's foreign policy achievements.

A PATTERN OF ERRORS

Congress requires that the State Department provide each year "a full and complete report" that includes "detailed assessments with respect to each foreign country . . . in which acts of international terrorism occurred which were, in the opinion of the Secretary, of major significance." The global terrorism reports are intended to satisfy this requirement, but, over time, they have become glossy advertisements of Washington's achievements in combating terrorism, aimed as much at the public and the press as at congressional overseers.

The 2003 global terrorism report was launched at a celebratory news conference in April. Deputy Secretary of State Richard Armitage and Ambassador J. Cofer Black, the State Department coordinator for counterterrorism, outlined some remaining challenges, but principally they announced the Bush administration's success in turning the terrorist tide. Black called the report "good news," and Armitage introduced it by saying, "You will find in these pages clear evidence that we are prevailing in the fight." The document's first paragraph claimed that worldwide terrorism dropped by 45 percent between 2001 and 2003 and that the number of acts committed last year "represents the lowest annual total of international terrorist attacks since 1969." The report was transmitted to Congress with a cover letter that interpreted the data as "an indication of the great progress that has been made in fighting terrorism" after the horrific events of September 11.

But we immediately spotted errors in the report and evidence contradicting the administration's claims. For example, the chronology in Appendix A, which lists each significant terrorist incident occurring in the year, stopped on

November 11—an unusual end to the calendar year. Clearly, this was a mistake, as four terrorist attacks occurred in Turkey between November 12 and the end of 2003. Yet it was impossible to tell whether the post–November 11 incidents were inadvertently dropped off the chronology and included in figures in the body of the report or completely overlooked.

More important, even with the incomplete data, the number of significant incidents listed in the chronology was very high. It tallied a total of 169 significant events for 2003 alone, the highest annual count in 20 years; the annual average over the previous five years was 131. How could the number of significant attacks be at a record high, when the State Department was claiming the lowest total number of attacks since 1969? The answer is that the implied number of "nonsignificant" attacks has declined sharply in recent years. But because nonsignificant events were not listed in the chronology, the drop could not be verified. And if, by definition, they were not significant, it is unclear why their decrease should merit attention.

On June 10, after a critical op-ed we wrote in *The Washington Post*, a follow-up letter to Powell from Representative Henry Waxman (D-Calif.), and a call for review from the Congressional Research Service, the State Department acknowledged errors in the report. "We did not check and verify the data sufficiently," spokesman Richard Boucher said. " . . . [T]he figures for the number of attacks and casualties will be up sharply from what was published."

At first, Waxman accused the administration of manipulating the data to "serve the Administration's political interests." Powell denied the allegation, insisting that "there's nothing political about it. It was a data collection and reporting error." Although there is no reason to doubt Powell's explanation, if the errors had gone in the opposite direction—making the rise in terrorism on President George W. Bush's watch look even greater than it has been—it is a safe bet that the administration would have caught them before releasing the report. And such asymmetric vetting is a form of political manipulation.

Critical deficiencies in the way the report was prepared and presented compromised its accuracy and credibility. Chief among these were the opaque procedures used to assemble the report, the inconsistent application of definitions, insufficient review, and the partisan release of the report. These deficiencies resulted in a misleading and unverifiable report that appeared to be tainted by political manipulation.

It is unclear exactly how the report was assembled. The report notes that the U.S. government's Incident Review Panel (IRP) is responsible for determining which terrorist events are significant. It says little, however, about the panel's members: how many there are, whether they are career employees or political appointees, or what affiliations they have. Nor does it describe how they decide whether an event is significant. Do they work by consensus or majority rule? What universe of events do they consider?

The State Department announced a decline in total terrorist attacks, which resulted from a decline in nonsignificant events. But without information about the nonsignificant events, readers were essentially asked to blindly trust the nameless experts who prepared it.

The report's broad definitions, moreover, are sometimes too blunt to help classification. Terrorism is defined as "premeditated, politically motivated violence perpetrated against noncombatant targets by subnational groups or clandestine agents, usually intended to influence an audience." The report specifies that an international terrorist attack is an act committed by substate actors from one nation against citizens or property of another. An incident "is judged significant if it results in loss of life or serious injury to persons, major property damage, and/or is an act or attempted act that could reasonably be expected to create the conditions noted."

But hardly any explanation was provided about how the IRP distinguishes significant from nonsignificant events. When is property damage too minor for an event to be significant? How are nonsignificant events identified? Is the IRP responsible for making these determinations too? Has the source and scope of their information changed over time? The corrected 2003 report, the first to list individual nonsignificant acts, defines as "major" property damage that exceeds $10,000. It does not indicate, however, whether that criterion applied to previous reports.

Admittedly, measuring international terrorism is no easy task. Even scholarly reckonings are not free from subjective judgment, and there are inevitably close calls to be made. The most one can hope for in many cases is consistent application of ambiguous definitions.

Unfortunately, in the global terrorism reports the rules have been applied inconsistently. Many cross-border attacks on civilians in Africa have not been included in the reports, for example, even though similar attacks in other regions have been. The report for 2002, moreover, counts as significant a suicide attack by Chechen shaheeds (Islamist martyrs) against a government building in Moscow that killed 72 people. Yet none of the numerous suicide attacks by the Chechen "black widows" that terrorized Russia and killed scores in 2003 was tallied as an international terrorist attack in the latest report. After one such attack, Russian President Vladimir Putin said, "Today, after a series of recent terrorist attacks, we can say that the bandits active in Chechnya are not just linked with international terrorism, they are an integral part of it." If the State Department considers such attacks domestic, rather than international, it should do so consistently from one year to the next.

Another problem is that the staff that prepared the 2003 global terrorism report did not participate in releasing it; in fact, they have yet to be identified. High-level Bush administration officials presented the report to the media, using it to support White House policies and take credit for the alleged decline in terrorism. Even after the report's flaws were recognized, they continued to spin the figures. When the corrected version was released, Black repeated that "we have made significant progress," despite being pressed to acknowledge that last year the number of significant attacks reached a 20-year high. Given the war on terrorism's central role in the upcoming presidential election, such presentation gives the appearance that the report is being manipulated for political gain.

The State Department has tried to explain the report's flaws using language eerily reminiscent of the Bush administration's justification of the failure to find weapons of mass destruction in Iraq. Spokesman Boucher told reporters that previous claims that the war on terrorism was succeeding had been based "on the facts as we had them at the time [and] the facts that we had were wrong." Even Powell partook in the spinning. On the one hand, he announced that "the [original] narrative is sound and we're not changing any of the narrative." On the other hand, he acknowledged, "We will change the narrative wherever the narrative relates to the data."

To his credit, Powell instructed those responsible for preparing the report to brief Waxman's staff on the procedures they had used and the origins of their mistakes. Based on a summary of the briefing by Waxman's staff, much has come to light. Authority for compiling the list of attacks was shifted from the CIA to the Terrorist Threat Integration Center (TTIC), an organization created in May 2003 to "merge and analyze all threat information in a single location." The TTIC provided information to the IRP, which, it was disclosed, consists of representatives from the CIA, the Defense Intelligence Agency, the National Security Agency, and the State Department's Bureau of Intelligence and Research. A TTIC representative chaired the meetings and could cast a vote to break ties on the classification of an event as significant or nonsignificant.

At least this year, chaos prevailed. The IRP's members changed from meeting to meeting—when they attended the meetings at all. The CIA employee responsible for the database left but was never replaced; in mid-process, an outside contractor who entered data was replaced by another contractor. Because of technical incompetence, the report relied on the wrong cutoff date.

Arithmetic errors were rampant. Larry Johnson, a retired CIA and State Department professional, discovered that the total number of fatalities in the chronology exceeded the number listed in the statistical review in Appendix G. According to Black, the errors resulted from "a combination of things: inattention, personnel shortages and database that is awkward and is antiquated and needs to have very proficient input be made in order for to be sure that the numbers will spill then to the different categories that are being captured [sic]." The debacle is more like an episode of the Keystone Kops than a chapter from Machiavelli, but even that analogy is not very comforting.

SETTING THE RECORD STRAIGHT

Despite the data's limitations, the chronology of significant events in the 2003 global terrorism report yields important information about terrorism's trends, its geographical characteristics, and its magnitude.

Time-series analysis, which seeks to discern trends in given phenomena over time, requires a consistent approach to collecting data. The State Department's terrorism report presents time-series analysis, but by focusing on the total number of attacks it misleadingly combines verifiable data on significant events with nonverifiable data on insignificant ones. And because, as TTIC director John Brennan admitted, "many nonsignificant events occur throughout the world that are not counted in the report," one must also be concerned about consistency in the measurement of the total number of terrorist events. Even if the nonsignificant events were listed (and thus could be verified), trends in significant events are more relevant because they track events that, by definition, are more important. Accurately measuring these trends is a prerequisite for understanding the factors that underlie them and the policies that shape them. In fact, an analysis of the revised report reveals that the number of significant attacks increased from 124 to 175, or by 41 percent, from 2001 to 2003—a significant fact indeed.

The detailed chronology also allows analysts to cumulate terrorist events for each country and cross-classify them according to the country where they occurred and the perpetrators' country of origin. These figures can then be related to the countries' characteristics, yielding information that can help policymakers devise strategies to address terrorism's root causes. Using the global terrorism reports for the years 1997–2002, the authors of this article have previously found that terrorists tend to come from nondemocratic countries, both rich and poor, and generally target nationals from rich, democratic countries.

The State Department has rightly emphasized that the threat of terrorism remains serious, but a close examination of its data helps put the magnitude of the threat in perspective. In 2003, a total of 625 people—including 35 Americans—were killed in international terrorist incidents worldwide. Meanwhile, 43,220 died in automobile accidents in the United States alone, and three million died from AIDS around the world. Comparative figures, particularly when combined with forecasts of future terrorism trends, can help focus debate on the real costs people are willing to bear—in foregone civil liberties and treasure-to reduce the risk posed by terrorism.

CHANGING TRACKS

The State Department currently uses, and Congress accepts, nineteenth-century methods to analyze a twenty-first-century problem. To prevent errors of the type that riddled the 2003 global terrorism report, Congress has two alternatives. It could reassign the State Department's reporting responsibilities to a neutral research agency, such as the GAO (the General Accounting Office, recently renamed the Government Accountability Office) which routinely uses appropriate statistical practices. The problem is that the GAO has little foreign policy expertise and does not necessarily have access to the (sometimes classified) information that goes into the reports. Alternatively, Congress could keep the reports within the State Department's purview but demand that its practices for data collection and analysis be improved and that the reports be insulated from partisan manipulation.

If responsibility remains within the State Department, Congress should establish a statistical bureau in the department to ensure that scientific standards are respected in all reports, thereby elevating the status of data-gathering and statistics there. The bureau would promote consistency, statistical rigor, and transparency. When appropriate, it could seek input from the scientific community. And, while respecting classified sources, it could also insist that sufficient information be released to independent analysts for verification.

To overcome conflicts of interest facing political appointees who issue government reports, the State Department should adopt rules similar to those that govern the production and dissemination of key economic indicators. Career staff who prepare the reports should be given an hour to brief the media on technical aspects of the data, during which time political appointees would be precluded from making public comments. (After the hour elapses, it is expected that political appointees would offer their interpretations.) Career staff should be protected so they can prepare mandated reports without interference from political appointees and then present them for review by the statistics bureau. Once the reports are finalized, but before they are publicly released, they should be circulated to designated political appointees who need to prepare for their release. Disclosure dates should be announced long in advance to prevent opportunistic timing by political appointees.

Last October, in a candid memorandum to top aides that was leaked to the press, Secretary of Defense Donald Rumsfeld admitted, "Today, we lack metrics to know if we are winning or losing the global war on terror. Are we capturing, killing, or deterring and dissuading more terrorists every day than the madrassas [Islamic schools] and the radical clerics are recruiting, training, and deploying against us?" The statement was a stinging acknowledgment that the government lacks both classified and unclassified data to make critical policy decisions. It is also a reminder that only accurate information, presented without political spin, can help the public and decision-makers know where the United States stands in the war on terrorism and how best to fight it.

4

The Other Evil

Strobe Talbott

The war on terrorism won't succeed without a war on poverty.

History has often boiled down to the word *versus:* Athens versus Sparta, Rome versus Carthage, Imperial Britain versus Napoleonic France or Czarist Russia. For most of the second half of the 20th century, the Great Versus was capitalism versus communism. During the first decade after the end of the Cold War, there were hints (sometimes gruesome and portentous, as in the Balkans and Africa) of what was coining next: the forces of integration versus those of disintegration; the effort to build a New World Order—a still-serviceable catchphrase from Bush I—versus the New Jihad, with its implicit doctrine of "worse is better" and its celebration of mayhem and slaughter.

Underlying the long-term challenge of the post-September 11 era is much more than Islamic defiance of the Great Satan. There is a growing divide between what we've traditionally thought of as the haves and the have-nots, but who might better be described as those who feel like winners in the process of globalization and modernization and those who feel like losers.

There are about 6 billion people on the earth today. About half of them are struggling to survive on less than $2 a day and have never seen a personal computer or, for that matter, ever made a telephone call. That fifty-fifty ratio is unstable. It's tipping in the wrong direction in two respects: The numbers of poor are growing faster than the numbers of rich, and the gap between rich and poor is widening. When self-perceived losers outnumber self-perceived winners, it's lose-lose for everyone.

We must distinguish between, on the one hand, the assassins and those who mastermind and abet their operations and, on the other hand, their

Foreign Policy, Nov–Dec 2001, p75.

Strobe Talbott, "The Other Evil (poverty and terrorism)," *Foreign Policy,* Nov.-Dec. 2001, p. 75–76. Reprinted by permission. www.foreignpolicy.com.

constituencies—those millions who feel so victimized by the modern world that they want us to be victims, too; those who see Osama bin Laden as a combination avenging angel and Robin Hood. As the mug shots and bios of the suicide pilots emerged, it became apparent that for the most part they did not come from the ranks of the world's desperate and aggrieved. Their fanaticism, like bin Laden's, was nurtured in privilege and in individual madness. During the immediate aftermath of the attacks on New York and Washington, the focus has rightly been on that species of menace, difficult to fathom, find, or deter, yet utterly deserving eradication.

However, the other set of images so memorable from September 11—Palestinians and Pakistanis dancing in the streets—is a reminder of a parallel challenge. Disease, overcrowding, undernourishment, political repression, and alienation breed despair, anger, and hatred. These are the raw materials of what we're up against, and they constitute a check on the willingness of Arab and other regimes to take effective action against networks of conspirators.

The principal way to address those conditions is through economic aid, refugee relief, public health campaigns, democracy promotion, and diplomacy as the first line of defense against communal and regional conflict. There will have to be not only more international development assistance but also better strategies for making the money work. That, in itself, will require urgent and concerted rethinking and reform. Throwing money at good causes has too often lined the pockets of bureaucrats and politicians—and not only in the countries receiving foreign aid. Traditional approaches must be supplemented, and in some cases replaced, by innovative ones, such as microcredit projects and programs aimed at empowering women as a force for social, economic, and political advancement.

In addition to rethinking and reform, there will have to be vastly increased commitments from treasuries, first and foremost that of the United States.

Yet exactly the opposite seems to be in prospect.

Programs that are instrumental in getting at the roots of terrorism are more in jeopardy now than they were two months ago. The blank check that Congress seems willing to write is for enhancing military defenses (including a national anti-missile system), improving intelligence-gathering and covert action, keeping airlines in business, and reinforcing airport and onboard security.

The United States will throw itself into meeting those priorities just as the nation says goodbye to its hard-won surplus and heads into what threatens to be a severe recession. In the budget crunch ahead, there will be a temptation to squeeze down the very programs that will allow us to move from reactive, defensive warfare against the terrorists to a proactive, prolonged offensive against the ugly, intractable realities that terrorists exploit and from which they derive popular support, foot soldiers, and political cover. That's why another phrase from America's political past needs to be dusted off, put back in service, and internationalized: the war on poverty. Only if the long struggle ahead is also fought on that front will it be winnable.

5

License to Kill

Bernard Lewis

Islamic call to kill Jews and Americans. An Arabic newspaper, in Feb 1998, published the "Declaration of the World Islamic Front for Jihad against the Jews and the Crusaders." The declaration, deplores the coming of the Jews and Crusaders to the Arabian peninsula, and calls for all Muslims to kill Americans and their allies. Such an action is called God's command. While most Americans will view the declaration as a harsh distortion of the facts, it nonetheless should be read. For in order to combat terrorism, it is necessary to understand it.

USAMA BIN LADIN'S
DECLARATION OF JIHAD

On February 23, 1998, *Al-Quds al-Arabi,* an Arabic newspaper published in London, printed the full text of a "Declaration of the World Islamic Front for Jihad against the Jews and the Crusaders." According to the paper, the statement was faxed to them under the signatures of Usama bin Ladin, the Saudi financier blamed by the United States for masterminding the August bombings of its embassies in East Africa, and the leaders of militant Islamist groups in Egypt, Pakistan, and Bangladesh. The statement—a magnificent piece of eloquent, at times even poetic Arabic prose—reveals a version of history that most Westerners will find unfamiliar. Bin Ladin's grievances are not quite what many would expect.

Bernard Lewis, "License to Kill," *Foreign Affairs,* Nov. 1998, p. 14. Reprinted by permission.

The declaration begins with an exordium quoting the more militant passages in the Quran and the sayings of the Prophet Muhammad, then continues:

> Since God laid down the Arabian peninsula, created its desert, and surrounded it with its seas, no calamity has ever befallen it like these Crusader hosts that have spread in it like locusts, crowding its soil, eating its fruits, and destroying its verdure; and this at a time when the nations contend against the Muslims like diners jostling around a bowl of food.

The statement goes on to talk of the need to understand the situation and act to rectify it. The facts, it says, are known to everyone and fall under three main headings:

> First—For more than seven years the United States is occupying the lands of Islam in the holiest of its territories, Arabia, plundering its riches, overwhelming its rulers, humiliating its people, threatening its neighbors, and using its bases in the peninsula as a spearhead to fight against the neighboring Islamic peoples.
>
> Though some in the past have disputed the true nature of this occupation, the people of Arabia in their entirety have now recognized it.
>
> There is no better proof of this; than the continuing American aggression against the Iraqi people, launched from Arabia despite its rulers, who all oppose the use of their territories for this purpose but are subjugated.
>
> Second—Despite the immense destruction inflicted on the Iraqi people at the hands of the Crusader-Jewish alliance and in spite of the appalling number of dead, exceeding a million, the Americans nevertheless, in spite of all this, are trying once more to repeat this dreadful slaughter. It seems that the long blockade following after a fierce war, the dismemberment and the destruction are not enough for them. So they come again today to destroy what remains of this people and to humiliate their Muslim neighbors.
>
> Third—While the purposes of the Americans in these wars are religious and economic, they also serve the petty state of the Jews, to divert attention from their occupation of Jerusalem and their killing of Muslims in it.
>
> There is no better proof of all this than their eagerness to destroy Iraq, the strongest of the neighboring Arab states, and their attempt to dismember all the states of the region, such as Iraq and Saudi Arabia and Egypt and Sudan, into petty states, whose division and weakness would ensure the survival of Israel and the continuation of the calamitous Crusader occupation of the lands of Arabia.

These crimes, the statement declares, amount to "a clear declaration of war by the Americans against God, his Prophet, and the Muslims." In such a situation, the declaration says, the ulema—authorities on theology and Islamic law, or sharia—throughout the centuries unanimously ruled that when enemies attack the Muslim lands, jihad becomes every Muslim's personal duty.

In the technical language of the ulema, religious duties may be collective, to be discharged by the community as a whole, or personal, incumbent on every individual Muslim. In an offensive war, the religious duty of jihad is collective and may be discharged by volunteers and professionals. When the Muslim community is defending itself, however, jihad becomes an individual obligation.

After quoting various Muslim authorities, the signatories then proceed to the final and most important part of their declaration, the fatwa, or ruling. It holds that

> To kill Americans and their allies, both civil and military, is an individual duty of every Muslim who is able, in any country where this is possible, until the Aqsa Mosque [in Jerusalem] and the Haram Mosque [in Mecca] are freed from their grip and until their armies, shattered and broken-winged, depart from all the lands of Islam, incapable of threatening any Muslim.

After citing some further relevant Quranic verses, the document continues:

> By God's leave, we call on every Muslim who believes in God and hopes for reward to obey God's command to kill the Americans and plunder their possessions wherever he finds them and whenever he can. Likewise we call on the Muslim ulema and leaders and youth and soldiers to launch attacks against the armies of the American devils and against those who are allied with them from among the helpers of Satan.

The declaration and fatwa conclude with a series of further quotations from Muslim scripture.

INFIDELS

Bin Ladin's view of the Gulf War as American aggression against Iraq may seem a little odd, but it is widely—though by no means universally—accepted in the Islamic world. For holy warriors of any faith, the faithful are always right and the infidels always wrong, whoever the protagonists and whatever the circumstances of their encounter.

The three areas of grievance listed in the declaration—Arabia, Iraq, and Jerusalem—will be familiar to observers of the Middle Eastern scene. What may be less familiar is the sequence and emphasis. For Muslims, as we in the West sometimes tend to forget but those familiar with Islamic history and literature know, the holy land par excellence is Arabia—Mecca, where the Prophet was born; Medina, where he established the first Muslim state; and the Hijaz, whose people were the first to rally to the new faith and become its standard-bearers. Muhammad lived and died in Arabia, as did the Rashidun caliphs, his immediate successors at the head of the Islamic community. There-after, except for a brief interlude in Syria, the center of the Islamic world and the scene of its major achievements was Iraq, the seat of the caliphate for half a millennium. For Muslims, no piece of land once added to the realm of Islam can ever be finally renounced, but none compares in significance with Arabia and Iraq.

Of these two, Arabia is by far the more important. The classical Arabic historians tell us that in the year 20 after the hijra (Muhammad's move from Mecca to Medina), corresponding to 641 of the Christian calendar, the Caliph Umar decreed that Jews and Christians should be removed from Arabia to fulfill an injunction the Prophet uttered on his deathbed: "Let there not be two religions in Arabia." The people in question were the Jews of the oasis of Khaybar in the north and the Christians of Najran in the south. Both were ancient and deep-rooted communities, Arab in their speech, culture, and way of life, differing from their neighbors only in their faith.

The saying attributed to the Prophet was impugned by some earlier Islamic authorities. But it was generally accepted as authentic, and Umar put it into effect. The expulsion of religious minorities is extremely rare in Islamic history—unlike medieval Christendom, where evictions compared with European expulsions, Umar's decree was both limited and compassionate. It did not include southern and southeastern Arabia, which were not seen as part of Islam's holy land. And unlike the Jews and Muslims driven out of Spain and other European countries to find what refuge they could elsewhere, the Jews and Christians of Arabia were resettled on lands assigned to them—the Jews in Syria, the Christians in Iraq. The process was also gradual rather than sudden, and there are reports of Jews and Christians remaining in Khaybar and Najran for some time after Umar's edict.

But the decree was final and irreversible, and from then until now the holy land of the Hijaz has been forbidden territory for non-Muslims. According to the Hanbali school of Islamic jurisprudence, accepted by both the Saudis and the declaration's signatories, for a non-Muslim even to set foot on the sacred soil is a major offense. In the rest of the kingdom, non-Muslims, while admitted as temporary visitors, were not permitted to establish residence or practice their religion.

The history of the Crusades provides a vivid example of the relative importance of Arabia and other places in Islamic perceptions. The Crusaders' capture of Jerusalem in 1099 was a triumph for Christendom and a disaster for the city's Jews. But to judge by the Arabic historiography of the period, it aroused scant interest in the region. Appeals for help by local Muslims to Damascus and Baghdad went unanswered, and the newly established Crusader principalities from Antioch to Jerusalem soon fitted into the game of Levantine politics, with cross-religious alliances forming a pattern of rivalries between and among Muslim and Christian princes.

The great counter-Crusade that ultimately drove the Crusaders into the sea did not begin until almost a century later. Its immediate cause was the activities of a freebooting Crusader leader, Reynald of Chatillon, who held the fortress of Kerak, in southern Jordan, between 1176 and 1187 and used it to launch a series of raids against Muslim caravans and commerce in the adjoining regions, including the Hijaz. Historians of the Crusades are probably right in saying that Reynald's motive was primarily economic—the desire for loot. But Muslims saw his campaigns as a provocation, a challenge directed against Islam's holy places. In 1182, violating an agreement between the Crusader king of Jerusalem and the Muslim leader Saladin, Reynald attacked and looted Muslim caravans, including one of pilgrims bound for Mecca. Even more heinous, from a Muslim point of view, was his threat to Arabia and a memorable buccaneering expedition in the Red Sea, featuring attacks on Muslim shipping and the Hijaz ports that served Mecca and Medina. Outraged, Saladin proclaimed a jihad against the Crusaders.

Even in Christian Europe, Saladin was justly celebrated and admired for his chivalrous and generous treatment of his defeated enemies. His magnanimity did not extend to Reynald of Chatillon. The great Arab historian Ibn al-Athir wrote, "Twice, [Saladin said,] I had made a vow to kill him if I had him in my hands; once when he tried to march on Mecca and Medina, and again when he treacherously captured the caravan." After Saladin's triumph, when many of the Crusader princes and chieftains were taken captive, he separated Reynald of Chattillon from the rest and beheaded him with his own hands.

After the success of the jihad and the recapture of Jerusalem, Saladin and his successors seem to have lost interest in the city. In 1229, one of them even ceded Jerusalem to the Emperor Frederick II as part of a general compromise agreement between the Muslim ruler and the Crusaders. Jerusalem was retaken in 1244 after the Crusaders tried to make it a purely Christian city, then eventually became a minor provincial town. Widespread interest in Jerusalem was reawakened only in the nineteenth century, first by the European powers' quarrels over custody of the Christian holy places and then by new waves of Jewish immigration after 1882.

In Arabia, however, the next perceived infidel threat came in the eighteenth century with the consolidation of European power in South Asia and the reappearance of Christian ships off the shores of Arabia. The resulting sense of outrage was at least one of the elements in the religious revival inspired in Arabia by the puritanical Wahhabi movement and led by the House of Saud, the founders of the modern Saudi state. During the period of Anglo-French domination of the Middle East, the imperial powers ruled Iraq, Syria, Palestine, Egypt, and Sudan. They nibbled at the fringes of Arabia, in Aden and the trucial sheikhdoms of the Gulf, but were wise enough to have no military and minimal political involvement in the affairs of the peninsula.

Oil made that level of involvement totally inadequate, and a growing Western presence, predominantly American, began to transform every aspect of Arabian life. The Red Sea port of Jiddah had long served as a kind of religious quarantine area in which foreign diplomatic, consular, and commercial representatives were allowed to five. The discovery and exploitation of oil—and the consequent growth of the Saudi capital, Riyadh, from small oasis town to major metropolis—brought a considerable influx of foreigners. Their presence, still seen by many as a desecration, planted the seeds for a growing mood of resentment.

As long as this foreign involvement was exclusively economic, and as long as the rewards were more than adequate to soothe every grievance, the alien presence could be borne. But in recent years both have changed. With the fall in oil prices and the rise in population and expenditure, the rewards are no longer adequate and the grievances have become more numerous and more vocal. Nor is the involvement limited to economic activities. The revolution in Iran and the wars of Saddam Hussein have added political and military dimensions to the foreign involvement and have lent some plausibility to the increasingly heard cries of "imperialism." Where their holy land is involved, many Muslims tend to define the struggle—and sometimes also the enemy— in religious terms, seeing the American troops sent to free Kuwait and save Saudi Arabia from Saddam Hussein as infidel invaders and occupiers. This perception is heightened by America's unquestioned primacy among the powers of the infidel world.

TRAVESTIES

To most Americans, the declaration is a travesty, a gross distortion of the nature and purpose of the American presence in Arabia. They should also know that for many—perhaps most—Muslims, the declaration is an equally grotesque travesty of the nature of Islam and even of its doctrine of jihad. The Quran speaks of peace as well as of war. The hundreds of thousands of traditions and sayings attributed with varying reliability to the Prophet, interpreted in various ways by the ulema, offer a wide range of guidance. The militant and violent interpretation is one among many. The standard juristic treatises on sharia normally contain a chapter on jihad, understood in the military sense as regular warfare against infidels and apostates. But these treatises prescribe correct behavior and respect for the rules of war in such matters as the opening and termination of hostilities and the treatment of noncombatants and prisoners, not to speak of diplomatic envoys. The jurists also discuss—and sometimes differ on—the actual conduct of war. Some permit, some restrict, and some disapprove of the use of mangonels, poisoned arrows, and the poisoning of enemy water supplies—the missile and chemical warfare of the Middle Ages— out of concern for the indiscriminate casualties that these weapons inflict. At no point do the basic texts of Islam enjoin terrorism and murder. At no point do they even consider the random slaughter of uninvolved bystanders.

Nevertheless, some Muslims are ready to approve, and a few of them to apply, the declaration's extreme interpretation of their religion. Terrorism requires only a few. Obviously, the West must defend itself by whatever means will be effective. But in devising strategies to fight the terrorists, it would surely be useful to understand the forces that drive them.

6

Rational Fanatics

Analysis of the Effects
of Suicide Bombers

Ehud Sprinzak

What makes suicide bombers tick? While most of the world sees them as lone zealots, they are, in fact, pawns of large terrorist networks that wage calculated psychological warfare. Contrary to popular belief, suicide bombers can be stopped—but only if governments pay more attention to their methods and motivations.

October 23, 1983, was one of the most horrific days in the history of modern terrorism. Two massive explosions destroyed the barracks of the U.S. and French contingents of the multinational peacekeeping force in Beirut, Lebanon, killing 241 American servicemen and 58 French paratroopers. Both explosions were carried out by Muslim extremists who drove to the heart of the target area and detonated bombs with no intention of escaping. Subsequent suicide attacks against Israeli and U.S. targets in Lebanon and Kuwait made it clear that a new type of killing had entered the repertoire of modern terrorism: a suicide operation in which the success of the attack depends on the death of the perpetrator.

This tactic stunned security experts. Two centuries of experience suggested that terrorists, though ready to risk their lives, wished to live after the terrorist act in order to benefit from its accomplishments. But this new terrorism defied that belief. It seemed qualitatively different, appearing almost supernatural, extremely lethal, and impossible to stop. Within six months,

Ehud Sprinzak, "Rational Fanatics," *Foreign Policy,* Sept. 2000, p. 66–73. Reprinted by permission. www.foreignpolicy.com.

French and U.S. Presidents Francois Mitterrand and Ronald Reagan pulled their troops out of Lebanon—a tacit admission that the new terrorism rendered all known counterterrorist measures useless. Government officials erected concrete barriers around the White House and sealed the Pentagon's underground bus tunnels. Nobody was reassured. As *Time* magazine skeptically observed in 1983: "No security expert thinks such defensive measures will stop a determined Islamic terrorist who expects to join Allah by killing some Americans."

Whereas the press lost no time in labeling these bombers irrational zealots, terrorism specialists offered a more nuanced appraisal, arguing that suicide terrorism has inherent tactical advantages over "conventional" terrorism: It is a simple and low-cost operation (requiring no escape routes or complicated rescue operations); it guarantees mass casualties and extensive damage (since the suicide bomber can choose the exact time, location, and circumstances of the attack); there is no fear that interrogated terrorists will surrender important information (because their deaths are certain); and it has an immense impact on the public and the media (due to the overwhelming sense of helplessness). Dr. Ramadan Shalah, secretary-general of the Palestinian Islamic Jihad, summarized the chilling logic of the new terror tactic: "Our enemy possesses the most sophisticated weapons in the world and its army is trained to a very high standard. . . . We have nothing with which to repel killing and thuggery against us except the weapon of martyrdom. It is easy and costs us only our lives . . . human bombs cannot be defeated, not even by nuclear bombs."

The prevalence of suicide terrorism during the last two decades testifies to its gruesome effectiveness. See table on opposite page. (All tables referenced can be found within the online version of this article, at http://www.infotrac-college.com.)

It has formed a vital part of several terror campaigns, including Hezbollah's successful operation against the Israeli invasion of Lebanon in the mid-1980s, the 1994–96 Hamas bus bombings aimed at stopping the Israeli-Palestinian peace process, and the 1995–99 Kurdistan Workers' Party (PKK) struggle against Turkey. The formation of special suicide units within the Liberation Tigers of Tamil Eelam (LTTE) army in Sri Lanka has added an atrocious dimension to the civil war on that devastated island. In addition to killing hundreds of civilians, soldiers, and high-ranking officers since 1987, LTTE suicide terrorists have assassinated two heads of state: Prime Minister Rajiv Gandhi of India in 1991 and President Ranasinghe Premadasa of Sri Lanka in 1993. Sri Lanka's current president, Chandrika Kumaratunga, recently lost sight in one eye following an assassination attempt that killed at least 24 people. The simultaneous 1998 bombings of the U.S. embassies in Kenya and Tanzania, which took the lives of nearly 300 civilians, were a brutal reprise of the 1983 tragedies in Lebanon.

Almost 20 years after its stunning modern debut, suicide terrorism continues to carry the image of the "ultimate" terror weapon. But is this tactic as unstoppable as it seems? The experiences of the last two decades have yielded important insights into the true nature of suicide bombers—insights that demystify their motivations and strategies, expose their vulnerabilities, and suggest ways to defeat what a senior State Department official once called a "frightening" problem to which there are "no answers."

AVERAGE, EVERYDAY MARTYRS

A long view of history reveals that suicide terrorism existed many years before "truck bombs" became part of the global vernacular. As early as the 11th century, the Assassins, Muslim fighters living in northern Persia, adopted suicide terrorism as a strategy to advance the cause of Islam. In the 18th century the Muslim communities of the Malabar Coast in India, Atjeh in Sumatra, and Mindanao and Sulu in the southern Philippines resorted to suicide attacks when faced with European colonial repression. These perpetrators never perceived their deaths as suicide. Rather, they saw them as acts of martyrdom in the name of the community and for the glory of God.

Moreover, suicide terrorism, both ancient and modern, is not merely the product of religious fervor, Islamic or otherwise. Martha Crenshaw, a leading terrorism scholar at Wesleyan University, argues that the mind-set of a suicide bomber is no different from those of Tibetan self-immolators, Irish political prisoners ready to die in a hunger strike, or dedicated terrorists worldwide who wish to live after an operation but know their chances of survival are negligible. Seen in this light, suicide terrorism loses its demonic uniqueness. It is merely one type of martyrdom venerated by certain cultures or religious traditions but rejected by others who favor different modes of supreme sacrifice.

Acts of martyrdom vary not only by culture, but also by specific circumstances. Tel Aviv University psychologist Ariel Merari has conducted the most comprehensive study of individuals who commit acts of suicide terrorism. After profiling more than 50 Muslim suicide bombers serving in Hezbollah, Amal, and secular pro-Syrian organizations in Lebanon, as well as Mamas and the Palestinian Islamic Jihad in Israel, he concluded that there is no single psychological or demographic profile of suicide terrorists. His findings suggest that intense struggles produce several types of people with the potential willingness to sacrifice themselves for a cause. Furthermore, Merari maintains that no organization can create a person's basic readiness to die. The task of recruiters is not to produce but rather to identify this predisposition in candidates and reinforce it. Recruiters will often exploit religious beliefs when indoctrinating would-be bombers, using their subjects' faith in a reward in paradise to strengthen and solidify preexisting sacrificial motives. But other powerful motives reinforce tendencies toward martyrdom, including patriotism, hatred of the enemy, and a profound sense of victimization.

Since suicide terrorism is an organizational phenomenon, the struggle against it cannot be conducted on an individual level. Although profiling suicide bombers may be a fascinating academic challenge, it is less relevant in the real-world struggle against them than understanding the modus operandi and mind-set of terrorist leaders who would never consider killing themselves, but opt for suicide terrorism as a result of cold reasoning.

THE CARE AND FEEDING
OF A SUICIDE BOMBER

A suicide terrorist is almost always the last link in a long organizational chain that involves numerous actors. Once the decision to launch a suicide attack has been made, its implementation requires at least six separate operations: target selection, intelligence gathering, recruitment, physical and "spiritual" training, preparation of explosives, and transportation of the suicide bombers to the target area. Such a mission often involves dozens of terrorists and accomplices who have no intention of committing suicide, but without whom no suicide operation could take place.

A careful survey of all the organizations that have resorted to suicide terrorism since 1983 suggests that the most meaningful distinction among them involves the degree to which suicide bombing is institutionalized. At the simplest level are groups that neither practice suicide terrorism on a regular basis nor approve of its use as a tactic. Local members or affiliates of such organizations, however, may initiate it on their own for a variety of reasons, such as imitating the glorious acts of others, responding to a perception of enormous humiliation and distress, avenging the murder of comrades and relatives, or being presented with a special opportunity to strike.

Within such a context, it is important to take into account what might be called "pre-suicide terrorism." Hamas and Palestinian Islamic Jihad suicide operations in Israel during the 1990s were preceded by a wave of knifings in the late 1980s. These attackers never planned an escape route and were often killed on the spot. The knifings did not involve any known organization and were mostly spontaneous. But they expressed a collective mood among young Palestinians of jihad (holy war) against Israel that helped create an atmosphere for the institutionalized suicide terrorism of the next decade.

Many terrorist groups are skeptical of suicide terrorism's strategic value but resort to this tactic in exceptional circumstances. Within this category are the bombings of the U.S. embassies in Kenya and Tanzania (allegedly executed by Osama bin Laden's Qaida organization) and similar irregular attacks conducted over the years by the Egyptian Islamic Group, the Egyptian Islamic Jihad, the Kuwaiti Dawa, and the Algerian Armed Islamic Group, among others. Such suicide bombings, though carefully planned, are irregular and unsystematic.

At another level are groups that formally adopt suicide terrorism as a temporary strategy. The leaders of these movements obtain (or grant) ideological or theological legitimization for its use, recruit and train volunteers, and then send them into action with a specific objective in mind. The most spectacular operations of Hezbollah between 1983 and 1985, of Hamas between 1994 and 1996, and of the PKK between 1995 and 1999 fall within this category. More recently, Chechen rebels suddenly launched a campaign of suicide bombings following nine months of inconclusive fighting against the Russian military; one of the first bombers, a cousin of noted rebel leader Arbi Barayev, had reportedly declared: "I am going willingly to my death in the name of Allah and the freedom of the Chechen people."

In such cases, the institutionalization of suicide terrorism has been temporary and conditional. Leaders who opt for this type of terrorism are usually moved by an intense sense of crisis, a conviction in the effectiveness of this new tactic, endorsement by the religious or ideological establishment, and the enthusiastic support of their community. At the same time, they are fully aware of the changeable nature of these conditions and of the potential costs associated with suicide terrorism (such as devastating military retaliation). They consequently have little difficulty in suspending suicide bombing or calling it off entirely.

A case in point is Hezbollah's decision to begin suicide bombings in 1983. It is known today that several leaders of the organization were extremely uneasy about the practice. Insisting that Islam does not approve of believers taking their own lives, clerics such as Sheikh Fadlallah raised legal objections and were unwilling to allow the use of this new tactic. However, suicide terrorism became so effective in driving foreigners out of Lebanon that there was no motivation to stop it. The result was theological hairsplitting that characterized suicide bombers as exceptional soldiers who risked their lives in a holy war. But following the Israeli withdrawal from Lebanon in 1985 and the decreasing effectiveness of this tactic, Hezbollah's clerics ordered the end of systematic suicide bombing. The organization's fighters were instructed to protect their lives and continue the struggle against the Zionists through conventional guerrilla methods. Only rarely, and on an irregular basis, has Hezbollah allowed suicide bombing since.

It is not exactly clear when the commanders of Hamas decided to turn their anti-Israel suicide attacks into a strategic struggle against the peace process. Their campaign, started haphazardly in 1992 against Israeli military and settler targets in the occupied territories, failed to produce glaring results. The 1994 Hebron Massacre, when Israeli doctor Baruch Goldstein murdered 29 praying Palestinians, changed everything. Determined to avenge the deaths of their countrymen, Hamas operators resorted to suicide bus bombings inside Israeli cities. In a matter of weeks, the new wave of terrorism had eroded Israel's collective confidence in the peace process and had played right into the hands of extremist Hamas clerics who opposed negotiations with Israel. Yet, in 1995 these attacks suddenly came to a complete halt. Several factors convinced Hamas leaders to back off: the growing Palestinian resentment against the costs of the bus bombings (expressed in massive Israeli economic sanctions), the increasing cooperation between Israeli and Palestinian security services, and the effectiveness of Israeli counterterrorism.

Ironically, Israel unintentionally pushed the organization to resume the bus bombings when, in 1996, then Prime Minister Shimon Peres ordered the assassination of Yehiya Ayash (known as "the Engineer")—a Hamas operative who masterminded many of the previous suicide bombings. Humiliated and angered, Hamas temporarily resumed bus bombings in Israel. A series of three successful attacks by Hamas and one by the Palestinian Islamic Jihad changed Israel's political mood about the peace process and led to the 1996 electoral defeat of Peres and his pro-peace government.

In the cases of Hezbollah and Hamas, no permanent suicide units were formed, and bombers were recruited and trained on an ad hoc, conditional basis. But, in rare instances, some organizations adopt suicide terrorism as a legitimate and permanent strategy, harkening back to the Japanese kamikaze pilots of the Second World War. Currently, the Sri Lankan Tamil Tigers are the only example of this phenomenon. The "Black Tigers" launched their first attack in July 1987, and since then suicide bombings have become an enduring feature of the LTTE's ruthless struggle. During the last 13 years, 171 attacks have killed hundreds of civilians and soldiers and wounded thousands more. The assassinations of two heads of state, political leaders, and high-ranking military officers have made it clear that no politician or public figure is immune to these attacks.

The Black Tigers constitute the most significant proof that suicide terrorism is not merely a religious phenomenon and that under certain extreme political and psychological circumstances secular volunteers are fully capable of martyrdom. The Tamil suicide bombers are not the product of a religious cult, but rather a cult of personality: Velupillai Prabhakaran, the brutal and charismatic LTTE leader who initiated the practice, appears to have been greatly influenced by the spectacular successes of Hezbollah in Lebanon. Fiercely determined to fight the repressive Sinhalese government until the Tamils achieve independence, Prabhakaran created the suicide units largely by the strength of his personality and his unlimited control of the organization.

The formation of the Black Tigers was greatly facilitated by an early practice of the organization's members: Since the early 1980s, all LTTE fighters—male and female alike—have been required to carry potassium cyanide capsules. A standard LTTE order makes it unequivocally clear that soldiers are to consume the capsule's contents if capture is imminent. The LTTE suicide units are essentially an extension of the organization's general culture of supreme martyrdom; the passage from ordinary combat soldier to suicide bomber is a short and tragic journey.

MAKING SUICIDE TERRORISTS PAY

The perceived strength of suicide bombers is that they are lone, irrational fanatics who cannot be deterred. The actual weakness of suicide bombers is that they are nothing more than the instruments of terrorist leaders who expect their organizations to gain tangible benefits from this shocking tactic. The key to countering suicide bombers, therefore, is to make terrorist organizations aware that this decision will incur painful costs. While no simple formula for countering suicide terrorism exists, the experiences of the last two decades suggest two complementary political and operational strategies.

Organizations only implement suicide terrorism systematically if their community (and, in some cases, a foreign client state) approves of its use. Thus, political and economic sanctions against the terrorists' community, combined with effective coercive diplomacy against their foreign patrons, may help reduce or end suicide terrorism. The problem with political counterterrorism, however, is that it takes a long time to implement and the results are never certain. The Taliban in Afghanistan, for instance, continue to host Osama bin Laden (who was indicted by the United States in November 1998 for the bombings of the two U.S. embassies in East Africa) despite international sanctions, a unanimously adopted United Nations Security Council Resolution demanding that he stand trial, and a threat from the United States that the Taliban will be held responsible for any terrorist acts undertaken while Bin Laden is under their protection.

The leaders of organizations that resort to suicide terrorism are evidently ready to take great risks. Consequently, the political battle against suicide bombers must always be enhanced by an aggressive operational campaign. Governments do not have to invent entirely new tactics when waging a war against suicide terrorists. Instead, they must adapt and intensify existing counterterrorism strategies to exploit the vulnerabilities of suicide bombers.

The Achilles' heel of suicide terrorists is that they are part of a large, operational infrastructure. It may not be possible to profile and apprehend would-be suicide bombers, but once it has been established that an organization has resolved to use suicide terrorism, security services can strike against the commanders and field officers who recruit and train the assailants and then plan the attacks. This counterterrorism effort calls for the formation of effective networks of informers, the constant monitoring of potential collaborators, and close cooperation among international intelligence services. Counterterrorist operatives must apply consistent pressure on the terrorist infrastructure through harassment and attacks. They must also seek ways to cut off the terrorists' sources of funding by depriving organizations of their financial resources (such as international bank accounts or "front" businesses). Regardless of the presence or absence of hard evidence for planned operations, it is essential to put potential terrorists on the run.

The physical protection of potential target areas is another essential tactic. The idea of erecting concrete barriers against a martyr driving a truck loaded with tons of explosives might strike some as ludicrously inadequate. But such physical protection serves two essential objectives: It reduces the effect of the suicide bombing if and when the terrorist hits the target area, and it serves as a deterrent against potential suicide strikes. For the terrorist field officers, who may never know when they will be caught or killed, each suicide squad is precious. When faced with highly protected areas, they are unlikely to send squads into action. Roadblocks, guards at special checkpoints, inspection teams in public places, and the use of dogs and artificial sniffing devices may drive suicide terrorism down significantly.

Such security measures also reassure the public. Governments must never forget that terrorism constitutes a form of psychological warfare, and that suicide terrorism is the ultimate expression of this struggle. Terrorism must always be fought psychologically—a battle that often takes place in the minds of ordinary people. Even if governments do not have an immediate operational solution to suicide terrorism, they must convince their citizens that they are not sitting ducks and that the authorities are doing everything they can to protect them. Ordinary people should, in fact, be informed that psychological warfare is being waged against them. Free people who are told that they are being subjected to psychological manipulation are likely to develop strong terrorism antibodies.

In fighting suicide bombers, it is important not to succumb to the idea that they are ready to do anything and lose everything. This is the same sort of simplistic reasoning that has fueled the widespread hysteria over terrorists acquiring weapons of mass destruction (WMD). The perception that terrorists are undeterrable fanatics who are willing to kill millions indiscriminately just to sow fear and chaos belies the reality that they are cold, rational killers who employ violence to achieve specific political objectives. Whereas the threat of WMD terrorism is little more than overheated rhetoric, suicide bombing remains a devastating form of terrorism whose complete demise is unlikely in the 21st century. The ongoing political instability in the Middle East, Russia, and South Asia—including Iran, Afghanistan, Chechnya, and possibly India and Pakistan—suggests that these regions will continue to be high-risk areas, with irregular suicide bombings occasionally extending to other parts of the globe. But the present understanding of the high costs of suicide terrorism and the growing cooperation among intelligence services worldwide gives credence to the hope that in the future only desperate organizations of losers will try to use this tactic on a systematic basis.

TINKER, TAILOR, SOLDIER, BOMBER

What sort of person is willing to become a suicide terrorist? Psychological profiles reveal that the personalities of suicide bombers are as varied as the causes for which they fight:

- Harnas and the Palestinian Islamic Jihad use shahids (martyrs) in their campaign to destroy Israel and replace it with an Islamic Palestinian state. Boaz Ganor, director of Israel's International Policy Institute for Counter-Terrorism, characterizes the typical shahid as a male, religious, unmarried, and unemployed high school graduate between the ages of 18 and 27. Many have had a relative or close friend killed, injured, or brutalized by the Israelis. Ganor observes that shahids do not volunteer, but rather are identified and recommended by their religious teachers. Once skilled field officers have selected and recruited the shahids, they begin a highly regimented process of mental purification and military preparation. The suicide candidates are also showered with rewards that help cement their sacrificial dedication. Often coming from a modest social background, most of them know that the suicide act will instantly upgrade their social status—and that of their families. (Indeed, the shah id's family is consistently awarded honors and praises and often receives a generous sum of money.) The martyr himself is guaranteed eternal life in paradise.

- The Black Tigers are the suicide battalions of the Liberation Tigers of Tamil Eelam (LTTE), which has waged an armed conflict against the Sri Lankan government since 1976 in hopes of establishing an independent Tamil state. Similar to the Palestinian shahids, Black Tiger recruits tend to be young, unemployed, and unmarried. However, they are not trained to become mere "human bombs." According to Rohan Gunaratna of Saint Andrews University, male and female volunteers come from the organization's toughest combat battalions and must bring with them a superb fighting record. The LTTE has fully integrated its suicide units with the organization's secular nationalist army, whose recruitment process employs neither religious rites nor clerical oversight. Just like other LTTE fighters, members of suicide squads are socialized into a culture of supreme sacrifice that glorifies death in action and reveres a long list of dead heroes. The recruitment process involves a tough military program aimed at selecting the most stable and devoted soldiers. Although designated to die in kamikaze-like attacks, many of these volunteers are often called upon to carry out sophisticated commando operations that do not require suicide.

- Between 1995 and 1999, 15 individuals conducted suicide bombings on behalf of the Kurdistan Workers' Party (PKK), which seeks to create an independent Kurdish state in southeastern Turkey. All but four of these perpetrators were young women. According to Dogu Ergil of Ankara University, these female suicide bombers were between the ages of 17 and 27, possessed no professional skills, generally came from large, poor families, and in some cases had lost relatives and loved ones in the struggle against Turkey. Coming from a rural traditional society that discriminates against women, most of the volunteers appear to have been motivated by a combination of devotion to PKK leader Abdullah Ocalan and the communal prestige bestowed on them as a result of their supreme sacrifice.

The PKK preferred female bombers because they could easily equip them with explosives and dress them to appear pregnant—thereby reducing the chance that they would be frisked by male police officers and soldiers. Also, according to captured PKK members, suicide missions were an effective means of "thinning their ranks" since women were not always able to keep up with the men in the treks across the mountains of southeastern

Turkey. The suicide bombings reached their peak following the arrest of Ocalan in February 1999, but stopped five months later when it had become clear that he would not be sentenced to death.

WANT TO KNOW MORE?

Bernard Lewis' classic book, *The Assassins* (New York: Oxford University Press, 1967), remains the most valuable study of this mysterious, 11th-century religious order. For a useful overview of Hezbollah, Lebanon's militant "Party of God," see Magnus Ranstorp's *Hizb'Allah in Lebanon: The Politics of the Western Hostage Crisis* (New York: St. Martin's Press, 1997). An informative description of the debate among Hezbollah's clerics on the question of suicide terrorism can be found in Martin Kramer's "Sacrifice and Fratricide in Shiite Lebanon," in *Violence and the Sacred in the Modern World,* Mark Juergensmeyer, ed. (London: Frank Cass, 1992). For general background on Hamas and the Palestinian Islamic Jihad, consult Ziad Abu Amr's *Islamic Fundamentalism in the West Bank and Gaza: Muslim Brotherhood and Islamic Jihad* (Bloomington: Indiana University Press, 1994) and Ely Karmon's "Hamas Terrorism Strategy: Operational Limitations and Political Constraints" (*Meria Journal,* March 2000).

For a valuable analysis of the Liberation Tigers of Tamil Eelam (LTTE), consult Manoj Joshi's "On the Razor's Edge: The Liberation Tigers of Tamil Eelam" (*Studies in Conflict and Terrorism,* January 1996). On LTTE's suicide modus operandi, see Rohan Gunaratna's "The LTTE and Suicide Terrorism" (*Frontline,* February 5–8, 2000).

For an early discussion of profiling suicide bombers in Lebanon, see Ariel Merari's "The Readiness to Kill and Die," in *Origins of Terrorism,* Walter Reich, ed. (Cambridge: Cambridge University Press, 1990). See also Harvey W. Kushner's "Suicide Bombers: What Makes Them Tick?" (*Counterterrorism & Security International,* Summer 1996). Ehud Sprinzak scrutinizes the motivations of terrorist organizations and casts doubt on their willingness to use weapons of mass destruction in "The Great Superterrorism Scare" (*Foreign Policy,* Fall 1998).

This article is based on a number of studies recently presented in Israel at the International Conference on Countering Suicide Terrorism. The conference was organized by the International Policy Institute for Counter-Terrorism (ICT) of the Interdisciplinary Center in Herzliya, Israel. The author wishes to thank Martha Crenshaw, Ariel Merari, Dogu Ergil, Ely Karmon, Shaul Shai, Rohan Gunaratna, Reuven Paz, Boaz Ganor, and Yoram Schweitzer for their informative papers. The proceedings of the conference are available from ICT.

*For links to relevant Web sites, as well as a comprehensive index of related *Foreign Policy* articles, access www.foreignpolicy.com.

7

The Strategic Logic of Suicide Terrorism

Robert A. Pape

Suicide terrorism is rising around the world, but the most common explanations do not help us understand why. Religious fanaticism does not explain why the world leader in suicide terrorism is the Tamil Tigers in Sri Lanka, a group that adheres to a Marxist/ Leninist ideology, while existing psychological explanations have been contradicted by the widening range of socio-economic backgrounds of suicide terrorists. To advance our understanding of this growing phenomenon, this study collects the universe of suicide terrorist attacks worldwide from 1980 to 2001, 187 in all. In contrast to the existing explanations, this study shows that suicide terrorism follows a strategic logic, one specifically designed to coerce modern liberal democracies to make significant territorial concessions. Moreover, over the past two decades, suicide terrorism has been rising largely because terrorists have learned that it pays. Suicide terrorists sought to compel American and French military forces to abandon Lebanon in 1983, Israeli forces to leave Lebanon in 1985, Israeli forces to quit the Gaza Strip and the West Bank in 1994 and 1995, the Sri Lankan government to create an independent Tamil state from 1990 on, and the Turkish government to grant autonomy to the Kurds in the late 1990s. In all but the case of Turkey, the terrorist political cause made more gains after the resort to suicide operations than it had before. Thus, Western democracies should pursue policies that teach terrorists that the lesson of the 1980s and 1990s no longer holds, policies which in practice may have more to do with improving homeland security than with offensive military action.

Robert Pape, "The Strategic Logic of Suidice Terrorism," *American Political Science Review* 97(3):343–361. Reprinted by permission of Cambridge University Press.

errorist organizations are increasingly relying on suicide attacks to achieve major political objectives. For example, spectacular suicide terrorist attacks have recently been employed by Palestinian groups in attempts to force Israel to abandon the West Bank and Gaza, by the Liberation Tigers of Tamil Eelam to compel the Sri Lankan government to accept an independent Tamil homeland, and by Al Qaeda to pressure the United States to withdraw from the Saudi Arabian Peninsula. Moreover, such attacks are increasing both in tempo and location. Before the early 1980s, suicide terrorism was rare but not unknown (Lewis 1968; O'Neill 1981; Rapoport 1984). However, since the attack on the U.S. embassy in Beirut in April 1983, there have been at least 188 separate suicide terrorist attacks worldwide, in Lebanon, Israel, Sri Lanka, India, Pakistan, Afghanistan, Yemen, Turkey, Russia and the United States. The rate has increased from 31 in the 1980s, to 104 in the 1990s, to 53 in 2000-2001 alone (Pape 2002). The rise of suicide terrorism is especially remarkable, given that the total number of terrorist incidents worldwide fell during the period, from a peak of 666 in 1987 to a low of 274 in 1998, with 348 in 2001 (Department of State 2001).

What accounts for the rise in suicide terrorism, especially, the sharp escalation from the 1990s onward? Although terrorism has long been part of international politics, we do not have good explanations for the growing phenomenon of suicide terrorism. Traditional studies of terrorism tend to treat suicide attack as one of many tactics that terrorists use and so do not shed much light on the recent rise of this type of attack (e.g., Hoffman 1998; Jenkins 1985; Laqueur 1987). The small number of studies addressed explicitly to suicide terrorism tend to focus on the irrationality of the act of suicide from the perspective of the individual attacker. As a result, they focus on individual motives—either religious indoctrination (especially Islamic Fundamentalism) or psychological predispositions that might drive individual suicide bombers (Kramer 1990; Merari 1990; Post 1990).

The first-wave explanations of suicide terrorism were developed during the 1980s and were consistent with the data from that period. However, as suicide attacks mounted from the 1990s onward, it has become increasingly evident that these initial explanations are insufficient to account for which individuals become suicide terrorists and, more importantly, why terrorist organizations are increasingly relying on this form of attack (Institute for Counter-Terrorism 2001). First, although religious motives may matter, modern suicide terrorism is not limited to Islamic Fundamentalism. Islamic groups receive the most attention in Western media, but the world's leader in suicide terrorism is actually the Liberation Tigers of Tamil Eelam (LTTE), a group who recruits from the predominantly Hindu Tamil population in northern and eastern Sri Lanka and whose ideology has Marxist/Leninist elements— The LTTE alone accounts for 75 of the 186 suicide terrorist attacks from 1980 to 2001. Even among Islamic suicide attacks, groups with secular orientations account for about a third of these attacks (Merari 1990; Sprinzak 2000).

Second, although study of the personal characteristics of suicide attackers may someday help identify individuals terrorist organizations are likely to recruit for this purpose, the vast spread of suicide terrorism over the last two decades suggests that there may not be a single profile. Until recently, the leading experts in psychological profiles of suicide terrorists characterized them as uneducated, unemployed, socially isolated, single men in their late teens and early 20s (Merari 1990; Post 1990). Now we know that suicide terrorists can be college educated or uneducated, married or single, men or women, socially isolated or integrated, from age 13 to age 47 (Sprinzak 2000). In other words, although only a tiny number of people become suicide terrorists, they come from a broad cross section of lifestyles, and it may be impossible to pick them out in advance.

In contrast to the first-wave explanations, this article shows that suicide terrorism follows a strategic logic. Even if many suicide attackers are irrational or fanatical, the leadership groups that recruit and direct them are not. Viewed from the perspective of the terrorist organization, suicide attacks are designed to achieve specific political purposes: to coerce a target government to change policy, to mobilize additional recruits and financial support, or both. Crenshaw (1981) has shown that terrorism is best understood in terms of its strategic function; the same is true for suicide terrorism. In essence, suicide terrorism is an extreme form of what Thomas Schelling (1966) calls "the rationality of irrationality," in which an act that is irrational for individual attackers is meant to demonstrate credibility to a democratic audience that still more and greater attacks are sure to come. As such, modern suicide terrorism is analogous to instances of international coercion. For states, air power and economic sanctions are often the preferred coercive tools (George et al. 1972; Pape 1996, 1997). For terrorist groups, suicide attacks are becoming the coercive instrument of choice.

To examine the strategic logic of suicide terrorism, this article collects the universe suicide terrorist attacks worldwide from 1980 to 2001, explains how terrorist organizations have assessed the effectiveness of these attacks, and evaluates the limits on their coercive utility.

Five principal findings follow. First, suicide terrorism is strategic. The vast majority of suicide terrorist attacks are not isolated or random acts by individual fanatics but, rather, occur in clusters as part of a larger campaign by an organized group to achieve a specific political goal. Groups using suicide terrorism consistently announce specific political goals and stop suicide attacks when those goals have been fully or partially achieved.

Second, the strategic logic of suicide terrorism is specifically designed to coerce modern democracies to make significant concessions to national self determination. In general, suicide terrorist campaigns seek to achieve specific territorial goals, most often the withdrawal of the target state's military forces from what the terrorists see as national homeland. From Lebanon to Israel to Sri Lanka to Kashmir to Chechnya, every suicide terrorist campaign from 1980 to 2001 has been waged by terrorist groups whose main goal has been to establish or maintain self determination for their community's homeland by compelling an enemy to withdraw. Further, every suicide terrorist campaign since 1980 has been targeted against a state that had a democratic form of government.

Third, during the past 20 years, suicide terrorism has been steadily rising because terrorists have learned that it pays. Suicide terrorists sought to compel American and French military forces to abandon Lebanon in 1983, Israeli forces to leave Lebanon in 1985, Israeli forces to quit the Gaza Strip and the West Bank in 1994 and 1995, the Sri Lankan government to create an independent Tamil state from 1990 on, and the Turkish government to grant autonomy to the Kurds in the late 1990s. Terrorist groups did not achieve their full objectives in all these cases. However, in all but the case of Turkey, the terrorist political cause made more gains after the resort to suicide operations than it had before. Leaders of terrorist groups have consistently credited suicide operations with contributing to these gains. These assessments are hardly unreasonable given the timing and circumstances of many of the concessions and given that other observers within the terrorists' national community, neutral analysts, and target government leaders themselves often agreed that suicide operations accelerated or caused the concession. This pattern of making concessions to suicide terrorist organizations over the past two decades has probably encouraged terrorist groups to pursue even more ambitious suicide campaigns.

Fourth, although moderate suicide terrorism led to moderate concessions, these more ambitious suicide terrorist campaigns are not likely to achieve still greater gains and may well fail completely. In general, suicide terrorism relies on the threat to inflict low to medium levels of punishment on civilians. In other circumstances, this level of punishment has rarely caused modern nation states to surrender significant political goals, partly because modern nation states are often willing to countenance high costs for high interests and partly because modern nation states are often able to mitigate civilian costs by making economic and other adjustments. Suicide terrorism does not change a nation's willingness to trade high interests for high costs, but suicide attacks can overcome a country's efforts to mitigate civilian costs. Accordingly, suicide terrorism may marginally increase the punishment that is inflicted and so make target nations somewhat more likely to surrender modest goals, but it is unlikely to compel states to abandon important interests related to the physical security or national wealth of the state. National governments have in fact responded aggressively to ambitious suicide terrorist campaigns in recent years, events which confirm these expectations.

Finally, the most promising way to contain suicide terrorism is to reduce terrorists' confidence in their ability to carry out such attacks on the target society. States that face persistent suicide terrorism should recognize that neither offensive military action nor concessions alone are likely to do much good and should invest significant resources in border defenses and other means of homeland security.

THE LOGIC OF SUICIDE TERRORISM

Most suicide terrorism is undertaken as a strategic effort directed toward achieving particular political goals; it is not simply the product of irrational individuals or an expression of fanatical hatreds. The main purpose of suicide terrorism is to use the threat of punishment to coerce a target government to change policy, especially to cause democratic states to withdraw forces from territory terrorists view as their homeland. The record of suicide terrorism from 1980 to 2001 exhibits tendencies in the timing, goals, and targets of attack that are consistent with this strategic logic but not with irrational or fanatical behavior: (1) timing—nearly all suicide attacks occur in organized, coherent campaigns, not as isolated or randomly timed incidents; (2) nationalist goals—suicide terrorist campaigns are directed at gaining control of what the terrorists see as their national homeland territory, specifically at ejecting foreign forces from that territory; and (3) target selection—all suicide terrorist campaigns in the last two decades have been aimed at democracies, which make more suitable targets from the terrorists' point of view.

Defining Suicide Terrorism

Terrorism involves the use of violence by an organization other than a national government to cause intimidation or fear among a target audience (Department of State 1983.2001; Reich 1990; Schmid and Jongman 1988). Although one could broaden the definition of terrorism so as to include the actions of a national government to cause terror among an opposing population, adopting such a broad definition would distract attention from what policy makers would most like to know: how to combat the threat posed by subnational groups to state security. Further, it could also create analytic confusion. Terrorist organizations and state governments have different levels of resources, face different kinds of incentives, and are susceptible to different types of pressures. Accordingly, the determinants of their behavior are not likely to be the same and, thus, require separate theoretical investigations.

In general, terrorism has two purposes—to gain supporters and to coerce opponents. Most terrorism seeks both goals to some extent, often aiming to affect enemy calculations while simultaneously mobilizing support or the terrorists cause and, in some cases, even gaining an edge over rival groups in the same social movement (Bloom 2002). However, there are trade-offs between these objectives and terrorists can strike various balances between them. These choices represent different forms of terrorism, the most important of which are demonstrative, destructive, and suicide terrorism.

Demonstrative terrorism is directed mainly at gaining publicity, for any or all of three reasons: to recruit more activists, to gain attention to grievances from softliners on the other side, and to gain attention from third parties who might exert pressure on the other side. Groups that emphasize ordinary, demonstrative terrorism include the Orange Volunteers (Northern Ireland), National

Liberation Army (Columbia), and Red Brigades (Italy) (Clutterbuck 1975; Edler Baumann 1973; St. John 1991). Hostage taking, airline hijacking, and explosions announced in advance are generally intended to use the possibility of harm to bring issues to the attention of the target audience. In these cases, terrorists often avoid doing serious harm so as not to undermine sympathy for the political cause. Brian Jenkins (1975, 4) captures the essence of demonstrative terrorism with his well-known remark, "Terrorists want a lot of people watching, not a lot of people dead."

Destructive terrorism is more aggressive, seeking to coerce opponents as well as mobilize support for the cause. Destructive terrorists seek to inflict real harm on members of the target audience at the risk of losing sympathy for their cause. Exactly how groups strike the balance between harm and sympathy depends on the nature of the political goal. For instance, the Baader-Meinhoft group selectively assassinated rich German industrialists, which alienated certain segments of German society but not others. Palestinian terrorists in the 1970s often sought to kill as many Israelis as possible, fully alienating Jewish society but still evoking sympathy from Muslim communities. Other groups that emphasize destructive terrorism include the Irish Republican Army, the Revolutionary Armed Forces of Colombia (FARC), and the nineteenth-century Anarchists (Elliott 1998; Rapoport 1971; Tuchman 1966).

Suicide terrorism is the most aggressive form of terrorism, pursuing coercion even at the expense of losing support among the terrorists' own community. What distinguishes a suicide terrorist is that the attacker does not expect to survive a mission and often employs a method of attack that requires the attacker's death in order to succeed (such as planting a car bomb, wearing a suicide vest, or ramming an airplane into a building). In essence, a suicide terrorist kills others at the same time that he kills himself.[1] In principle, suicide terrorists could be used for demonstrative purposes or could be limited to targeted assassinations.[2] In practice, however, suicide terrorists often seek simply to kill the largest number of people. Although this maximizes the coercive leverage that can be gained from terrorism, it does so at the greatest cost to

---

[1] A suicide attack can be defined in two ways, a narrow definition limited to situations in which an attacker kills himself and a broad definition that includes any instance when an attacker fully expects to be killed by others during an attack. An example that fits the broad definition is Baruch Goldstein, who continued killing Palestinians at the February 1994 Hebron Massacre until he himself was killed, who had no plan for escape, and who left a note for his family indicating that he did not expect to return. My research relies on the narrow definition, partly because this is the common practice in the literature and partly because there are so few instances in which it is clear that an attacker expected to be killed by others that adding this category of events would not change my findings.

[2] Hunger strikes and self-immolation are not ordinarily considered acts of terrorism, because their main purpose is to evoke understanding and sympathy from the target audience, and not to cause terror (Niebuhr 1960).

the basis of support for the terrorist cause. Maximizing the number of enemy killed alienates those in the target audience who might be sympathetic to the terrorists' cause, while the act of suicide creates a debate and often loss of support among moderate segments of the terrorists' community, even if also attracting support among radical elements. Thus, while coercion is an element in all terrorism, coercion is the paramount objective of suicide terrorism.

The Coercive Logic of Suicide Terrorism

At its core, suicide terrorism is a strategy of coercion, a means to compel a target government to change policy. The central logic of this strategy is simple: Suicide terrorism attempts to inflict enough pain on the opposing society to overwhelm their interest in resisting the terrorists demands and, so, to cause either the government to concede or the population to revolt against the government. The common feature of all suicide terrorist campaigns is that they inflict punishment on the opposing society, either directly by killing civilians or indirectly by killing military personnel in circumstances that cannot lead to meaningful battlefield victory. As we shall see, suicide terrorism is rarely a one-time event but often occurs in a series of suicide attacks. As such, suicide terrorism generates coercive leverage both from the immediate panic associated with each attack and from the risk of civilian punishment in the future.

Suicide terrorism does not occur in the same circumstances as military coercion used by states, and these structural differences help to explain the logic of the strategy. In virtually all instances of international military coercion, the coercer is the stronger state and the target is the weaker state; otherwise, the coercer would likely be deterred or simply unable to execute the threatened military operations (Pape 1996). In these circumstances, coercers have a choice between two main coercive strategies, punishment and denial. Punishment seeks to coerce by raising the costs or risks to the target society to a level that overwhelms the value of the interests in dispute. Denial seeks to coerce by demonstrating to the target state that it simply cannot win the dispute regardless of its level of effort, and therefore fighting to a finish is pointless—for example, because the coercer has the ability to conquer the disputed territory. Hence, although coercers may initially rely on punishment, they often have the resources to create a formidable threat to deny the opponent victory in battle and, if necessary, to achieve a brute force military victory if the target government refuses to change its behavior. The Allied bombing of Germany in World War II, American bombing of North Vietnam in 1972, and Coalition attacks against Iraq in 1991 all fit this pattern.

Suicide terrorism (and terrorism in general) occurs under the reverse structural conditions. In suicide terrorism, the coercer is the weaker actor and the target is the stronger. Although some elements of the situation remain the same, flipping the stronger and weaker sides in a coercive dispute has a dramatic change on the relative feasibility of punishment and denial. In these circumstances, denial is impossible, because military conquest is ruled out by relative weakness. Even though some groups using suicide terrorism have received important support from states and some have been strong enough to wage guerrilla military campaigns as well as terrorism, none have been strong enough to have serious prospects of achieving their political goals by conquest. The suicide terrorist group with the most significant military capacity has been the LTTE, but it has not had a real prospect of controlling the whole of the homeland that it claims, including Eastern and Northern Provinces of Sri Lanka.

As a result, the only coercive strategy available to suicide terrorists is punishment. Although the element of "suicide" is novel and the pain inflicted on civilians is often spectacular and gruesome, the heart of the strategy of suicide terrorism is the same as the coercive logic used by states when they employ air power or economic sanctions to punish an adversary: to cause mounting civilian costs to overwhelm the target state's interest in the issue in dispute and so to cause it to concede the terrorists' political demands. What creates the coercive leverage is not so much actual damage as the expectation of future damage. Targets may be economic or political, military or civilian, but in all cases the main task is less to destroy the specific targets than to convince the opposing society that they are vulnerable to more attacks in the future. These features also make suicide terrorism convenient for retaliation, a tit-for-tat interaction that generally occurs between terrorists and the defending government (Crenshaw 1981).

The rhetoric of major suicide terrorist groups reflects the logic of coercive punishment. Abdel Karim, a leader of Al Aksa Martyrs Brigades, a militant group linked to Yasir Arafat's Fatah movement, said the goal of his group was "to increase losses in Israel to a point at which the Israeli public would demand a withdrawal from the West Bank and Gaza Strip" (Greenberg 2002). The infamous fatwa signed by Osama Bin Laden and others against the United States reads, "The ruling to kill the Americans and their allies—civilians and military—is an individual duty for every Muslim who can do it in any country in which it is possible to do it, in order to liberate the al-Aqsa Mosque and the holy mosque [Mecca] from their grip, and in order for their armies to move out of all the lands of Islam, defeated and unable to threaten any Muslim" (World Islamic Front 1998).

Suicide terrorists' willingness to die magnifies the coercive effects of punishment in three ways. First, suicide attacks are generally more destructive than other terrorist attacks. An attacker who is willing to die is much more likely to accomplish the mission and to cause maximum damage to the target. Suicide attackers can conceal weapons on their own bodies and make last-minute adjustments more easily than ordinary terrorists. They are also better able to infiltrate heavily guarded targets because they do not need escape plans or rescue teams. Suicide attackers are also able to use certain especially destructive tactics such as wearing "suicide vests" and ramming vehicles into targets. The 188 suicide terrorist attacks from 1980 to 2001 killed an average of 13 people each, not counting the unusually large number of fatalities on September 11 and also not counting the attackers themselves. During the same period, there were about 4,155 total terrorist incidents worldwide, which killed 3,207 people (also excluding September 11), or less than one person per incident. Overall, from 1980 to 2001, suicide attacks amount to 3% of all terrorist attacks but account for 48% of total deaths due to terrorism, again excluding September 11 (Department of State 1983, 2001).

Second, suicide attacks are an especially convincing way to signal the likelihood of more pain to come, because suicide itself is a costly signal, one that suggests that the attackers could not have been deterred by a threat of costly retaliation. Organizations that sponsor suicide attacks can also deliberately orchestrate the circumstances around the death of a suicide attacker to increase further expectations of future attacks. This can be called the "art of martyrdom" (Schalk 1997). The more suicide terrorists justify their actions on the basis of religious or ideological motives that match the beliefs of a broader national community, the more the status of terrorist martyrs is elevated, and the more plausible it becomes that others will follow in their footsteps. Suicide terrorist organizations commonly cultivate "sacrificial myths" that include elaborate sets of symbols and rituals to mark an individual attacker's death as a contribution to the nation. Suicide attackers' families also often receive material rewards both from the terrorist organizations and from other supporters. As a result, the art of martyrdom elicits popular support from the terrorists' community, reducing the moral backlash that suicide attacks might otherwise produce, and so establishes the foundation for credible signals of more attacks to come.

Third, suicide terrorist organizations are better positioned than other terrorists to increase expectations about escalating future costs by deliberately violating norms in the use of violence. They can do this by crossing thresholds of damage, by breaching taboos concerning legitimate targets, and by broadening recruitment to confound expectations about limits on the number of possible terrorists. The element of suicide itself helps increase the credibility of future attacks, because it suggests that attackers cannot be deterred. Although the capture and conviction of Timothy McVeigh gave reason for some confidence that others with similar political views might be deterred, the deaths of the September 11 hijackers did not, because Americans would have to expect that future Al Qaeda attackers would be equally willing to die.

The Record of Suicide Terrorism, 1980 to 2001

To characterize the nature of suicide terrorism, this study identified every suicide terrorist attack from 1980 to 2001 that could be found in Lexis Nexis's on-line database of world news media (Pape 2002).[3] Examination of the universe shows that suicide terrorism has three properties that are consistent with the above strategic logic but not with irrational or fanatical behavior: (1) timing—nearly all suicide attacks occur in organized, coherent campaigns, not as isolated or randomly timed incidents; (2) nationalist goals—suicide terrorist campaigns are directed at gaining control of what the terrorists see as their national homeland territory, specifically at ejecting foreign forces from that territory; and (3) target selection—all suicide terrorist campaigns in the last two decades have been aimed at democracies, which make more suitable targets from the terrorists' point of view. Nationalist movements that face nondemocratic opponents have not resorted to suicide attack as a means of coercion.

Timing

As Table 1 indicates, there have been 188 separate suicide terrorist attacks between 1980 and 2001. Of these, 179, or 95%, were parts of organized, coherent campaigns, while only nine were isolated or random events. Seven separate disputes have led to suicide terrorist campaigns: the presence of American and French forces in Lebanon, Israeli occupation of West Bank and Gaza, the independence of the Tamil regions of Sri Lanka, the independence of the Kurdish region of Turkey, Russian occupation of Chechnya, Indian occupation of Kashmir, and the presence of American forces on the Saudi Arabian Peninsula. Overall, however, there have been 16 distinct campaigns, because in certain disputes the terrorists elected to suspend operations one or more times either in response to concessions or for other reasons. Eleven of the campaigns have ended and five were ongoing as of the end of 2001. The attacks comprising each campaign were organized by the same terrorist group (or, sometimes, a set of cooperating groups as in the ongoing "second intifada" in Israel/Palestine), clustered in time, publicly justified in terms of a specified political goal, and directed against targets related to that goal.

The most important indicator of the strategic orientation of suicide terrorists is the timing of the suspension of campaigns, which most often

---

[3] This survey sought to include every instance of a suicide attack in which the attacker killed himself except those explicitly authorized by a state and carried out by the state government apparatus (e.g., Iranian human wave attacks in the Iran–Iraq war were not counted). The survey is probably quite reliable, because a majority of the incidents were openly claimed by the sponsoring terrorist organizations. Even those that were not were, in nearly all cases, reported multiple times in regional news media, even if not always in the U.S. media. To probe for additional cases, I interviewed experts and officials involved in what some might consider conflicts especially prone to suicide attacks, such as Afghanistan in the 1980s, but this did not yield more incidents. According to the CIA station chief for Pakistan from 1986 to 1988 (Bearden 2002), "I cannot recall a single incident where an Afghan launched himself against a Soviet target with the intention of dying in the process. I don't think these things ever happened, though some of their attacks were a little hare-brained and could have been considered suicidal. I think it's important that Afghans never even took their war outside their borders—for example they never tried to blow up the Soviet Embassy in Pakistan."

Table 1. Suicide Terrorist Campaigns, 1980–2001

Date	Terrorist Group	Terrorists' Goal	No. of Attacks	No. Killed	Target Behavior
		Completed Campaigns			
1. Apr–Dec 1983	Hezbollah	U.S./France out of Lebanon	6	384	Complete withdrawal
2. Nov 1983–Apr 1985	Hezbollah	Israel out of Lebanon	6	96	Partial withdrawal
3. June 1985–June 1986	Hezbollah	Israel out of Lebanon security zone	16	179	No change
4. July 1990–Nov 1994	LTTE	Sri Lanka accept Tamil state	14	164	Negotiations
5. Apr 1995–Oct 2000	LTTE	Sri Lanka accept Tamil state	54	629	No change
6. Apr 1994	Hamas	Israel out of Palestine	2	15	Partial withdrawal from Gaza
7. Oct 1994–Aug 1995	Hamas	Israel out of Palestine	7	65	Partial withdrawal from West Bank
8. Feb–Mar 1996	Hamas	Retaliation for Israeli assassination	4	58	No change
9. Mar–Sept 1997	Hamas	Israel out of Palestine	3	24	Hamas leader released
10. June–Oct 1996	PKK	Turkey accept Kurd autonomy	3	17	No change
11. Mar–Aug 1999	PKK	Turkey release jailed leader	6	0	No change
		Ongoing Campaigns, as of December 2001			
12. 1996–	Al Qaeda	U.S. out of Saudi Peninsula	5	3,329	TBD[a]
13. 2000–	Chechnen Rebels	Russia out of Chechnya	4	53	TBD
14. 2000–	Kashmir Rebels	India out of Kashmir	3	45	TBD
15. 2001–	LTTE	Sri Lanka accept Tamil state	6	51	TBD
16. 2000–	Several	Israel out of Palestine	39	177	TBD
Total incidents	188				
No. in campaigns	179				
No. isolated	9				

Source: Pape (2002).
[a]To be determined.

73

occurs based on a strategic decision by leaders of the terrorist organizations that further attacks would be counterproductive to their coercive purposes— for instance, in response to full or partial concessions by the target state to the terrorists' political goals. Such suspensions are often accompanied by public explanations that justify the decision to opt for a "cease-fire." Further, the terrorist organizations' discipline is usually fairly good; although there are exceptions, such announced cease-fires usually do stick for a period of months at least, normally until the terrorist leaders take a new strategic decision to resume in pursuit of goals not achieved in the earlier campaign. This pattern indicates that both terrorist leaders and their recruits are sensitive to the coercive value of the attacks.

As an example of a suicide campaign, consider Hamas's suicide attacks in 1995 to compel Israel to withdraw from towns in the West Bank Hamas leaders deliberately withheld attacking during the spring and early summer in order to give PLO negotiations with Israel an opportunity to finalize a withdrawal. However, when in early July, Hamas leaders came to believe that Israel was backsliding and delaying withdrawal, Hamas launched a series of suicide attacks. Israel accelerated the pace of its withdrawal, after which Hamas ended the campaign. Mahmud al-Zahar, a Hamas leader in Gaza, announced, following the cessation of suicide attacks in October 1995:

> We must calculate the benefit and cost of continued armed operations.
> If we can fulfill our goals without violence, we will do so. Violence is a
> means, not a goal. Hamas's decision to adopt self-restraint does not contra-
> dict our aims, which include the establishment of an Islamic state instead of
> Israel. . . . We will never recognize Israel, but it is possible that a truce could
> prevail between us for days, months, or years. (Mishal and Sela 2000, 71)

If suicide terrorism were mainly irrational or even disorganized, we would expect a much different pattern in which either political goals were not artic- ulated (e.g., references in news reports to "rogue" attacks) or the stated goals varied considerably even within the same conflict. We would also expect the timing to be either random or, perhaps, event-driven, in response to particularly provocative or infuriating actions by the other side, but little if at all related to the progress of negotiations over issues in dispute that the terrorists want to influence.

Nationalist Goals

Suicide terrorism is a high-cost strategy, one that would only make strategic sense for a group when high interests are at stake and, even then, as a last re- sort. The reason is that suicide terrorism maximizes coercive leverage at the expense of support among the terrorists' own community and so can be sus- tained over time only when there already exists a high degree of commitment among the potential pool of recruits. The most important goal that a commu- nity can have is the independence of its homeland (population, property, and way of life) from foreign influence or control. As a result, a strategy of suicide terrorism is most likely to be used to achieve nationalist goals, such as gaining control of what the terrorists see as their national homeland territory and expelling foreign military forces from that territory.

In fact, every suicide campaign from 1980 to 2001 has had as a major objective—or as its central objective—coercing a foreign government that has military forces in what they see as their homeland to take those forces out. Table 2 summarizes the disputes that have engendered suicide terrorist campaigns. Since 1980, there has not been a suicide terrorist campaign directed mainly against domestic opponents or against foreign opponents who did not have military forces in the terrorists' homeland. Although attacks against civilians are often the most salient to Western observers, actually every suicide terrorist campaign in the past two decades has included attacks directly against the foreign military forces in the country, and most have been waged by guerrilla organizations that also use more conventional methods of attack against those forces.

Even Al Qaeda fits this pattern. Although Saudi Arabia is not under American military occupation per se and the terrorists have political objectives against the Saudi regime and others, one major objective of Al Qaeda is the expulsion of U.S. troops from the Saudi Peninsula and there have been attacks by terrorists loyal to Osama Bin Laden against American troops in Saudi Arabia. To be sure, there is a major debate among Islamists over the morality of suicide attacks, but within Saudi Arabia there is little debate over Al Qaeda's objection to American forces in the region and over 95% of Saudi society reportedly agrees with Bin Laden on this matter (Sciolino 2002).

Still, even if suicide terrorism follows a strategic logic, could some suicide terrorist campaigns be irrational in the sense that they are being waged for unrealistic goals? The answer is that some suicide terrorist groups have not been realistic in expecting the full concessions demanded of the target, but this is normal for disputes involving overlapping nationalist claims and even for coercive attempts in general. Rather, the ambitions of terrorist leaders are realistic in two other senses. First, suicide terrorists' political aims, if not their methods, are often more mainstream than observers realize; they generally reflect quite common, straightforward nationalist self-determination claims of their community. Second, these groups often have significant support for their policy goals versus the target state, goals that are typically much the same as those of other nationalists within their community. Differences between the terrorists and more "moderate" leaders usually concern the usefulness of a certain level of violence and—sometimes—the legitimacy of attacking additional targets besides foreign troops in the country, such as attacks in other countries or against third parties and civilians. Thus, it is not that the terrorists pursue radical goals and then seek others' support. Rather, the terrorists are simply the members of their societies who are the most optimistic about the usefulness of violence for achieving goals that many, and often most, support.

The behavior of Hamas illustrates the point. Hamas terrorism has provoked Israeli retaliation that has been costly for Palestinians, while pursuing the— apparently unrealistic—goal of abolishing the state of Israel. Although prospects

Table 2. Motivation and Targets of Suicide Terrorist Campaigns, 1980–2001

Region Dispute	Homeland Status	Terrorist Goal	Target a Democracy?
Lebanon, 1983–86	U.S./F/IDF military presence	U.S./F/IDF withdrawal	Yes
West Bank/Gaza, 1994–	IDF military presence	IDF withdrawal	Yes
Tamils in Sri Lanka, 1990–	SL military presence	SL withdrawal	Yes (1950)[a]
Kurds in Turkey, 1990s	Turkey military presence	Turkey withdrawal	Yes (1983)[a]
Chechnya, 2000–	Russia military presence	Russian withdrawal	Yes (1993)[a]
Kashmir, 2000–	Indian military presence	Indian withdrawal	Yes
Saudi Peninsula, 1996–	U.S. military presence	U.S. withdrawal	Yes

Sources: Pape (2002). Przeworski et al. 2000 identifies four simple rules for determining regime type: (1) The chief executive must be elected, (2) the legislature must be elected, (3) there must be more than one party, and (4) there must be at least one peaceful transfer of power. By these criteria all the targets of suicide terrorism were and are democracies. Przeworski et al. codes only from 1950 to 1990 and is updated to 1999 by Boix and Rosato 2001. Freedom House also rates countries as "free," "partly free," and "not free," using criteria for degree of political rights and civil liberties. According to Freedom House's measures, Sri Lanka, Turkey, and Russia were all partly free when they were the targets of suicide terrorism, which puts them approximately in the middle of all countries, a score that is actually biased against this study since terrorism itself lowers a country's civil liberties rating (freedomhouse.org).
[a]Date established as a democracy (if not always a democracy).

of establishing an Arab state in all of "historic Palestine" may be poor, most Palestinians agree that it would be desirable if possible. Hamas's terrorist violence was in fact carefully calculated and controlled. In April 1994, as its first suicide campaign was beginning, Hamas leaders explained that "martyrdom operations" would be used to achieve intermediate objectives, such as Israeli withdrawal from the West Bank and Gaza, while the final objective of creating an Islamic state from the Jordan River to the Mediterranean may require other forms of armed resistance (Shiqaqi 2002; Hroub 2000; Nusse 1998).

Democracies as the Targets

Suicide terrorism is more likely to be employed against states with democratic political systems than authoritarian governments for several reasons. First, democracies are often thought to be especially vulnerable to coercive punishment. Domestic critics and international rivals, as well as terrorists, often view democracies as "soft," usually on the grounds that their publics have low thresholds of cost tolerance and high ability to affect state policy. Even if there is little evidence that democracies are easier to coerce than other regime types (Horowitz and Reiter 2001), this image of democracy matters. Since terrorists can inflict only moderate damage in comparison to even small interstate wars, terrorism can be expected to coerce only if the target state is viewed as especially vulnerable to punishment. Second, suicide terrorism is a tool of the weak, which means that, regardless of how much punishment the terrorists inflict, the target state almost always has the capacity to retaliate with far more extreme punishment or even by exterminating the terrorists' community. Accordingly, suicide terrorists must not only have high interests at stake, they must also be confident that their opponent will be at least somewhat restrained. While there are infamous exceptions, democracies have generally been more restrained in their use of force against civilians, at least since World War II. Finally, suicide attacks may also be harder to organize or publicize in authoritarian police states, although these possibilities are weakened by the fact that weak authoritarian states are also not targets.

In fact, the target state of every modern suicide campaign has been a democracy. The United States, France, Israel, India, Sri Lanka, Turkey, and Russia were all democracies when they were attacked by suicide terrorist campaigns, even though the last three became democracies more recently than the others. To be sure, these states vary in the degree to which they share "liberal" norms that respect minority rights Freedom House rates Sri Lanka, Turkey, and Russia as "partly free" (3.5.4.5 on a seven-point scale) rather than "free" during the relevant years, partly for this reason and partly because terrorism and civil violence themselves lowers the freedom rating of these states. Still, all these states elect their chief executives and legislatures in multiparty elections and have seen at least one peaceful transfer of power, making them solidly democratic by standard criteria (Boix and Rosato 2001; Huntington 1991; Przeworski et al. 2000).

The Kurds, which straddle Turkey and Iraq, illustrate the point that suicide terrorist campaigns are more likely to be targeted against democracies than authoritarian regimes. Although Iraq has been far more brutal toward its Kurdish population than has Turkey, violent Kurdish groups have used suicide attacks exclusively against democratic Turkey and not against the authoritarian regime in Iraq. There are plenty of national groups living under authoritarian regimes with grievances that could possibly inspire suicide terrorism, but none have. Thus, the fact that rebels have resorted to this strategy only when they face the more suitable type of target counts against arguments that suicide terrorism is a nonstrategic response, motivated mainly by fanaticism or irrational hatreds.

TERRORISTS' ASSESSMENTS OF SUICIDE TERRORISM

The main reason that suicide terrorism is growing is that terrorists have learned that it works. Even more troubling, the encouraging lessons that terrorists have learned from the experience of 1980s and 1990s are not, for the most part, products of wild-eyed interpretations or wishful thinking. They are, rather, quite reasonable assessments of the outcomes of suicide terrorist campaigns during this period.

To understand how terrorists groups have assessed the effectiveness of suicide terrorism requires three tasks: (1) explanation of appropriate standards for evaluating the effectiveness of coercion from the standpoint of coercers; (2) analysis of the 11 suicide terrorist campaigns that have ended as of 2001 to determine how frequently target states made concessions that were, or at least could have been, interpreted as due to suicide attack; and (3) close analysis of terrorists' learning from particular campaigns. Because some analysts see suicide terrorism as fundamentally irrational (Kramer 1990; Merari 1990; Post 1990), it is important to assess whether the lessons that the terrorists drew were reasonable conclusions from the record. The crucial cases are the Hamas and Islamic Jihad campaigns against Israel during the 1990s, because they are most frequently cited as aimed at unrealistic goals and therefore as basically irrational.

Standards of Assessment

Terrorists, like other people, learn from experience. Since the main purpose of suicide terrorism is coercion, the learning that is likely to have the greatest impact on terrorists' future behavior is the lessons that they have drawn from past campaigns about the coercive effectiveness of suicide attack.

Most analyses of coercion focus on the decision making of target states, largely to determine their vulnerability to various coercive pressures (George 1972; Pape 1996). The analysis here, however, seeks to determine why terrorist coercers are increasingly attracted to a specific coercive strategy. For this purpose, we must develop a new set of standards, because assessing the value of coercive pressure for the coercer is not the same problem as assessing its impact on the target.

From the perspective of a target state, the key question is whether the value of the concession that the coercer is demanding is greater than the costs imposed by the coercive pressure, regardless of whether that pressure is in the form of lives at risk, economic hardship, or other types of costs. However, from the perspective of the coercer, the key question is whether a particular coercive strategy promises to be more effective than alternative methods of influence and, so, warrants continued (or increased) effort. This is especially true for terrorists who are highly committed to a particular goal and so willing to exhaust virtually any alternative rather than abandoning it. In this search for an effective strategy, coercers' assessments are likely to be largely a function of estimates of the success of past efforts; for suicide terrorists, this means assessments of whether past suicide campaigns produced significant concessions.

A glance at the behavior of suicide terrorists reveals that such trade-offs between alternative methods are important in their calculations. All of the organizations that have resorted to suicide terrorism began their coercive efforts with more conventional guerrilla operations, nonsuicide terrorism, or both. Hezbollah, Hamas, Islamic Jihad, the PKK, the LTTE, and Al Qaeda all used demonstrative and destructive means of violence long before resorting to suicide attack. Indeed, looking at the trajectory of terrorist groups over time, there is a distinct element of experimentation in the techniques and strategies used by these groups and distinct movement toward those techniques and strategies that produce the most effect. Al Qaeda actually prides itself for a commitment to even tactical learning over time—the infamous "terrorist manual" stresses at numerous points the importance of writing "lessons learned" memoranda that can be shared with other members to improve the effectiveness of future attacks.

The most important analytical difficulty in assessing outcomes of coercive efforts is that successes are more ambiguous than failures. Whenever a suicide terrorist campaign, or any coercive effort, ends without obtaining significant concessions, presumably the coercers must judge the effort as a failure. If, however, the target state does make policy changes in the direction of the terrorists' political goals, this may or may not represent a coercive success for suicide attack in the calculations of the terrorists. The target government's decision could have been mainly or partly a response to the punishment inflicted by the suicide attacks, but it also could be a response to another type of pressure (such as an ongoing guerrilla campaign), or to pressure from a different actor (such as one of the target state's allies) or a different country, or the target's policy decision may not even have been intended as a concession but could have been made for other reasons that only coincidently moved in a direction desired by the terrorists. Different judgments among these alternatives yield different lessons for future usefulness of suicide attack.

Standard principles from social psychology suggest how terrorists are likely to resolve these ambiguities. Under normal conditions, most people tend to interpret ambiguous information in ways that are consistent with their prior beliefs, as well as in ways that justify their past actions (Jervis 1976; Lebow 1981). Suicide terrorists, of course, are likely to have at least some initial confidence in the efficacy of suicide attack or else they would not resort to it, and of course, the fact of having carried out such attacks gives them an interest in justifying that choice. Thus, whenever targets of suicide terrorism make a real or apparent concession and it is a plausible interpretation that it was due to the coercive pressure of the suicide campaign, we would expect terrorists to favor that interpretation even if other interpretations are also plausible.

This does not mean that we should simply expect terrorists to interpret virtually all outcomes, regardless of evidence, as encouraging further terrorism; that would not constitute learning and would make sense only if the terrorists were deeply irrational. To control for this possibility, it is crucial to consider the assessments of the same events by other well-informed people. If we find that when suicide terrorist leaders claim credit for coercing potential concessions, their claims are unique (or nearly so), then it would be appropriate to dismiss them as irrational. If, on the other hand, we find that their interpretations are shared by a significant portion of other observers, across a range of circumstances and interests—from target state leaders, to others in the terrorists' community, to neutral analysts—then we should assume that their assessments are as rational as anyone else's and should take the lessons they draw seriously. In making these judgments, the testimony of target state leaders is often especially telling; although states like the United States and Israel virtually never officially admit making concessions to terrorism, leaders such as Ronald Reagan and Yitzhak Rabin have at times been quite open about the impact of suicide terrorism on their own policy decisions, as we see below.

Finally, understanding how terrorists' assess the effectiveness of suicide terrorism should also be influenced by our prior understanding of the fanatical nature of the specific terrorists at issue. If the most fanatical groups also make what appear to be reasonable assessments, then this would increase our confidence in the finding that most terrorists would make similar calculations. Hamas and Islamic Jihad are the most crucial case, because these groups have been considered to be fanatical extremists even among terrorists (Kramer 1996). Thus, detailed examination of how Hamas and Islamic Jihad leaders assessed the coercive value of suicide attacks during the 1990s is especially important.

The Apparent Success of Suicide Terrorism

Perhaps the most striking aspect of recent suicide terrorist campaigns is that they are associated with gains for the terrorists' political cause about half the time. As Table 1 shows, of the 11 suicide terrorist campaigns that were completed during 1980–2001, six closely correlate with significant policy changes by the target state toward the terrorists' major political goals. In one case, the terrorists' territorial goals were fully achieved (Hezbollah v. US/F, 1983); in three cases, the terrorists' territorial aims were partly achieved (Hezbollah v. Israel, 1983.85; Hamas v. Israel, 1994; and Hamas v. Israel, 1994–95); in one case, the target government to entered into sovereignty negotiations with the terrorists (LTTE v. Sri Lanka, 1993–94); and in one case, the terrorist organization's top leader was released from prison (Hamas v. Israel, 1997). Five campaigns did not lead to noticeable concessions (Hezbollah's second effort against Israel in Lebanon, 1985–86; a Hamas campaign in 1996 retaliating for an Israeli assassination; the LTTE v. Sri Lanka, 1995–2002; and both PKK campaigns). Coercive success is so rare that even a 50% success rate is significant, because international military and economic coercion, using the same standards as above, generally works less than a third of the time (Art and Cronin 2003).

There were limits to what suicide terrorism appeared to gain in the 1980s and 1990s. Most of the gains for the terrorists' cause were modest, not involving interests central to the target countries' security or wealth, and most were potential revocable. For the United States and France, Lebanon was a relatively minor foreign policy interest. Israel's apparent concessions to the Palestinians from 1994 to 1997 were more modest than they might appear. Although Israel withdrew its forces from parts of Gaza and the West Bank and released Sheikh Yassin, during the same period Israeli settlement in the occupied territories almost doubled, and recent events have shown that the Israel is not deterred from sending force back in when necessary. In two disputes, the terrorists achieved initial success but failed to reach greater goals. Although Israel withdrew from much of Lebanon in June 1985, it retained a six-mile security buffer zone along the southern edge of the country for another 15 years from which a second Hezbollah suicide terrorist campaign failed to dislodge it. The Sri Lankan government did conduct apparently serious negotiations with the LTTE from November 1994 to April 1995, but did not concede the Tamil's main demand, for independence, and since 1995, the government has preferred to prosecute the war rather than consider permitting Tamil secession.

Still, these six concessions, or at least apparent concessions, help to explain why suicide terrorism is on the rise. In three of the cases, the target government policy changes are clearly due to coercive pressure from the terrorist group. The American and French withdrawal was perhaps the most clear-cut coercive success for suicide terrorism. In his memoirs, President Ronald Reagan (1990, 465) explained the U.S. decision to withdraw from Lebanon:

> The price we had to pay in Beirut was so great, the tragedy at the barracks was so enormous . . . We had to pull out. . . . We couldn't stay there and run the risk of another suicide attack on the Marines.

The IDF withdrawal from most of southern Lebanon in 1985 and the Sri Lankan government decision to hold negotiations with the LTTE were also widely understood to be a direct result of the coercive punishment imposed by Hezbollah and LTTE respectively. In both cases, the concessions followed periods in which the terrorists had turned more and more to suicide attacks, but since Hezbollah and the LTTE employed a combination of suicide attack and conventional attack on their opponents, one can question the relative weight of suicide attack in coercing these target states. However, there is little question in either case that punishment pressures inflicted by these terrorist organizations were decisive in the outcomes. For instance, as a candidate in the November 9, 1994, presidential election of Sri Lanka, Mrs. Chandrika Kumaratunga explicitly asked for a mandate to redraw boundaries so as to appease the Tamils in their demand for a separate homeland in the island's northeast provinces, often saying, "We definitely hope to begin discussions with the Tamil people, with their representatives— including the Tigers—and offer them political solutions to end the war... [involving] extensive devolution." This would, Kumaratunga said, "create an environment in which people could live without fear." (Sauvagnargues 1994; "Sri Lanka" 1994).

The other three concessions, or arguable concessions, are less clear-cut. All three involve Hamas campaigns against Israel. Not counting the ongoing second intifada, Hamas waged four separate suicide attack campaigns against Israel, in 1994, 1995, 1996, and 1997.One, in 1996, did not correspond with Israeli concessions. This campaign was announced as retaliation for Israel's assassination of a Hamas leader; no particular coercive goal was announced, and it was suspended by Hamas after four attacks in two weeks. The other three all do correspond with Israeli concessions. In April 1994, Hamas begin a series of suicide bombings in relation for the Hebron Massacre. After two attacks, Israel decided to accelerate its withdrawal from Gaza, which was required under the Oslo Agreement but which had been delayed. Hamas then suspended attacks for five months. From October 1994 to August 1995, Hamas (and Islamic Jihad) carried out a total of seven suicide attacks against Israel. In September 1995, Israel agreed to withdraw from certain West Bank towns that December, which it earlier had claimed could not be done before April 1996 at the soonest. Hamas then suspended attacks until its retaliation campaign during the last week of February and first week of March 1996. Finally, in March 1997, Hamas began a suicide attack campaign that included an attack about every two months until September 1997. In response Israeli Prime Minister Netanyahu authorized the assassination of a Hamas leader. The attempt, in Amman, Jordan, failed and the Israeli agents were captured. To get them back Israel agreed to release Sheikh Ahmed Yassin, spiritual leader of Hamas. While this was not a concession to the terrorists' territorial goals, there is no evidence that Hamas interpreted this in anyway different from the standard view that this release was the product of American and Jordanian pressure. Accordingly the key Hamas campaigns that might have encouraged the view that suicide terrorism pays were the 1994 and 1995 campaigns that were associated with Israel's military withdrawals from Gaza and the West Banks. Terrorists' assessments of these events are evaluated in detail.

The Crucial Case of Hamas

The Hamas and Islamic Jihad suicide campaigns against Israel in 1994 and 1995 are crucial tests of the reasonableness of terrorists' assessments. In each case, Israel made significant concessions in the direction of the terrorists' cause and terrorist leaders report that these Israeli concessions increased their confidence in the coercive effectiveness of suicide attack. However, there is an important alternative explanation for Israel's concessions in these cases—the Israeli government's obligations under the Oslo Accords. Accordingly, evaluating the reasonableness of the terrorists' assessments of these cases is crucial because many observers characterize Hamas and Islamic Jihad as fanatical, irrational groups, extreme both within Palestinian society and among terrorists groups in general (Kramer 1996). Further, these campaigns are also of special interest because they helped to encourage the most intense ongoing campaign, the second intifada against Israel, and may also have helped to encourage Al Qaeda's campaign against the United States.

Examination of these crucial cases demonstrates that the terrorist groups came to the conclusion that suicide attack accelerated Israeli's withdrawal in both cases. Although the Oslo Accords formally committed to withdrawing the IDF from Gaza and the West Bank, Israel routinely missed key deadlines, often by many months, and the terrorists came to believe that Israel would not have withdrawn when it did, and perhaps not at all, had it not been for the coercive leverage of suicide attack. Moreover, this interpretation of events was hardly unique. Numerous other observers and key Israeli government leaders themselves came to the same conclusion. To be clear, Hamas may well have had motives other than coercion for launching particular attacks, such as retaliation (De Figueredo and Weingast 1998), gaining local support (Bloom 2002), or disrupting negotiated outcomes it considered insufficient (Kydd and Walter 2002). However, the experience of observing how the target reacted to the suicide campaigns appears to have convinced terrorist leaders of the coercive effectiveness of this strategy.

To evaluate these cases, we need to know (1) the facts of each case, (2) how others interpreted the events, and (3) how the terrorists interpreted these events. Each campaign is discussed in turn.

Israel's Withdrawal from Gaza, May 1994

The Facts. Israel and the Palestinian Liberation Organization signed the Oslo Accords on September 13, 1993. These obligated Israel to withdraw its military forces from the Gaza Strip and West Bank town of Jericho beginning on December 13 and ending on April 13, 1994. In fact, Israel missed both deadlines. The major sticking points during the implementation negotiations in Fall and Winter of 1993–94 were the size of the Palestinian police force (Israel proposed a limit of 1,800, while the Palestinians demanded 9,000) and jurisdiction for certain criminal prosecutions, especially whether Israel could retain a right of hot pursuit to prosecute Palestinian attackers who might flee into Palestinian ruled zones. As of April 5, 1994, these issues were unresolved. Hamas then launched two suicide attacks, one on April 6 and another on April 13, killing 15 Israeli civilians. On April 18, the Israeli Knesset voted to withdraw, effectively accepting the Palestinian positions on both disputed issues. The suicide attacks then stopped and the withdrawal was actually conducted in a few weeks starting on May 4, 1994.[4]

These two suicide attacks may not originally have been intended as coercive, since Hamas leaders had announced them in March 1994 as part of a planned series of five attacks in retaliation for the February 24th Hebron massacre in which an Israeli settler killed 29 Palestinians and had strong reservations about negotiating a compromise settlement with Israel (Kydd and Walter 2002). However, when Israel agreed to withdraw more promptly than expected, Hamas decided to forgo the remaining three planned attacks. There is thus a circumstantial case that these attacks had the effect of coercing the Israelis into being more forthcoming in the withdrawal negotiations and both Israeli government leaders and Hamas leaders publically drew this conclusion.

Israeli and Other Assessments. There are two main reasons to doubt that terrorist pressure accelerated Israel's decision to withdraw. First, one might think that Israel would have withdrawn in any case, as it had promised to do in the Oslo Accords of September 1993. Second, one might argue that Hamas was opposed to a negotiated settlement with Israel. Taking both points together, therefore, Hamas' attacks could not have contributed to Israel's withdrawal.

The first of these arguments, however, ignores the facts that Israel had already missed the originally agreed deadline and, as of early April 1994, did not appear ready to withdraw at all if that meant surrendering on the size of the Palestinian police force and legal jurisdiction over terrorists. The second argument is simply illogical. Although Hamas objected to surrendering claims to all of historic Palestine, it did value the West Bank and Gaza as an intermediate goal, and certainly had no objection to obtaining this goal sooner rather than later.

Most important, other observers took explanations based on terrorist pressure far more seriously, including the person whose testimony must count most, Israeli Prime Minister Yitzhak Rabin. On April 13, 1994, Rabin said,

> I can't recall in the past any suicidal terror acts by the PLO. We have seen by now at least six acts of this type by Hamas and Islamic Jihad. . . . The only response to them and to the enemies of peace on the part of Israel is to accelerate the negotiations. (Makovsky and Pinkas 1994).

---

[4] There were no suicide attacks from April to October 1994.

On April 18, 1994, Rabin went further, giving a major speech in the Knesset explaining why the withdrawal was necessary:

> Members of the Knessett: I want to tell the truth. For 27 years we have been dominating another people against its will. For 27 years Palestinians in the territories . . . get up in the morning harboring a fierce hatred for us, as Israelis and Jews. Each morning they get up to a hard life, for which we are also, but not solely responsible. We cannot deny that our continuing control over a foreign people who do not want us exacts a painful price. . . . For two or three years we have been facing a phenomenon of extremist Islamic terrorism, which recalls Hezbollah, which surfaced in Lebanon and perpetrated attacks, including suicide missions. . . . There is no end to the targets Hamas and other terrorist organizations have among us. Each Israeli, in the territories and inside sovereign Israel, including united Jerusalem, each bus, each home, is a target for their murderous plans. Since there is no separation between the two populations, the current situation creates endless possibilities for Hamas and the other organizations.

Independent Israeli observers also credited suicide terrorism with considerable coercive effectiveness. The most detailed assessment is by Efraim Inbar (1999, 141–42):

> A significant change occurred in Rabin's assessment of the importance of terrorist activities. . . . Reacting to the April 1994 suicide attack in Afula, Rabin recognized that terrorists activities by Hamas and other Islamic radicals were "a form of terrorism different from what we once knew from the PLO terrorist organizations. . . ." Rabin admitted that there was no "hermitic" solution available to protect Israeli citizens against such terrorist attacks. . . .He also understood that such incidents intensified the domestic pressure to freeze the Palestinian track of the peace process. Islamic terrorism thus initially contributed to the pressure for accelerating the negotiations on his part.

Arab writers also attributed Israeli accommodation to the suicide attacks. Mazin Hammad wrote in an editorial in a Jordanian newspaper:

> It is unprecedented for an Israeli official like Y. Rabin to clearly state that there is no future for the settlements in the occupied territories. . . . He would not have said this [yesterday] if it was not for the collapse of the security Israel. . . . The martyrdom operation in Hadera shook the faith of the settlers in the possibility of staying in the West Bank and Gaza and increased their motivation to pack their belongings and dismantle their settlements. ("Hamas Operations" 1994)

Terrorists' Assessments. Even though the favorable result was apparently unexpected by Hamas leaders, given the circumstances and the assessments voiced by Rabin and others, it certainly would have been reasonable for them to conclude that suicide terrorism had helped accelerate Israeli withdrawal, and they did.

Hamas leader Ahmed Bakr (1995) said that "what forced the Israelis to withdraw from Gaza was the intifada and not the Oslo agreement," while Imad al-Faluji judged that

> all that has been achieved so far is the consequence of our military actions. Without the so-called peace process, we would have gotten even more. . . . We would have got Gaza and the West Bank without this agreement. . . . Israel can beat all Arab Armies. However, it can do nothing against a youth with a knife or an explosive charge on his body. Since it was unable to guarantee security within its borders, Israel entered into negotiations with the PLO. . . . If the Israelis want security, they will have to abandon their settlements . . . in Gaza, the West Bank, and Jerusalem. ("Hamas Leader" 1995)

Further, these events appear to have persuaded terrorists that future suicide attacks could eventually produce still greater concessions. Fathi al-Shaqaqi (1995), leader of Islamic Jihad, said,

> Our jihad action has exposed the enemy weakness, confusion, and hysteria. It has become clear that the enemy can be defeated, for if a small faithful group was able to instill all this horror and panic in the enemy through confronting it in Palestine and southern Lebanon, what will happen when the nation confronts it with all its potential. . . . Martyrdom actions will escalate in the face of all pressures . . . [they] are a realistic option in confronting the unequal balance of power. If we are unable to effect a balance of power now, we can achieve a balance of horror.

Israel's Withdrawal from West Bank Towns, December 1995
The second Hamas case, in 1995, tells essentially the same story as the first. Again, a series of suicide attacks was associated with Israeli territorial concessions to the Palestinians, and again, a significant fraction of outside observers attributed the concessions to the coercive pressure of suicide terrorism, as did the terrorist leaders themselves.

The Facts. The original Oslo Accords scheduled Israel to withdraw from the Palestinian populated areas of the West Bank by July 13, 1994, but after the delays over Gaza and Jericho all sides recognized that this could not be met. From October 1994 to April 1995, Hamas, along with Islamic Jihad, carried out a series of seven suicide terrorist attacks that were intended to compel Israel to make further withdrawals and suspended attacks temporarily at the request of the Palestinian Authority after Israel agreed on March 29, 1995 to begin withdrawals by July 1. Later, however, the Israelis announced that withdrawals could not begin before April 1996 because bypass roads needed for the security of Israeli settlements were not ready. Hamas and Islamic Jihad then mounted new suicide attacks on July 24 and August 21, 1995, killing 11

Israeli civilians. In September, Israel agreed to withdraw from the West Bank towns in December (Oslo II) even though the roads were not finished. The suicide attacks then stopped and the withdrawal was actually carried out in a few weeks starting on December 12, 1995.[5]

Israeli and Other Assessments. Although Israeli government spokesmen frequently claimed that suicide terrorism was delaying withdrawal, this claim was contradicted by, among others, Prime Minister Rabin. Rabin (1995) explained that the decision for the second withdrawal was, like the first in 1994, motivated in part by the goal of reducing suicide terrorism:

> *Interviewer:* Mr. Rabin, what is the logic of withdrawing from towns and villages when you know that terror might continue to strike at us from there?
>
> *Rabin:* What is the alternative, to have double the amount of terror? As for the issue of terror, take the suicide bombings. Some 119 Israelis . . . have been killed or murdered since 1st January 1994, 77 of them in suicide bombings perpetrated by Islamic radical fanatics. . . . All the bombers were Palestinians who came from areas under our control.

Similarly, an editorial in the Israeli daily *Yediot Aharonot* ("Bus Attack" 1995) explained,

> If the planners of yesterday's attack intended to get Israel to back away from the Oslo accord, they apparently failed. In fact, Prime Minister Y. Rabin is leaning toward expediting the talks with the Palestinians. . . . The immediate conclusion from this line of thinking on Rabin's part— whose results we will witness in the coming days—will be to instruct the negotiators to expedite the talks with the Palestinians with the aim of completing them in the very near future.

Terrorists' Assessments. As in 1994, Hamas and Islamic Jihad came to the conclusion that suicide terrorism was working. Hamas's spokesman in Jordan explained that new attacks were necessary to change Israel's behavior:

> Hamas, leader Muhammad Nazzal said, needed military muscle in order to negotiate with Israel from a position of strength. Arafat started from a position of weakness, he said, which is how the Israelis managed to push on him the solution and get recognition of their state and settlements without getting anything in return. (Theodoulou 1995)

After the agreement was signed, Hamas leaders also argued that suicide operations contributed to the Israeli withdrawal. Mahmud al-Zahhar (1996), a spokesman for Hamas, said,

> The Authority told us that military action embarrasses the PA because it obstructs the redeployment of the Israeli's forces and implementation of the agreement. . . . We offered many martyrs to attain freedom. . . . Any

---

[5] There were no suicide attacks from August 1995 to February 1996. There were four suicide attacks in response to an Israeli assassination from February 25 to March 4, 1996, and then none until March 1997.

fair person knows that the military action was useful for theAuthority during negotiations.

Moreover, the terrorists also stressed that stopping the attacks only discouraged Israel from withdrawing. An early August Hamas communique (No. 125, 1995) read,

> They said that the strugglers' operations have been the cause of the delay in widening the autonomous rule in the West Bank, and that they have been the reason for the deterioration of the living and economic conditions of our people. Now the days have come to debunk their false claims . . . and to affirm that July 1 [a promised date for IDF withdrawal] was no more than yet another of the "unholy" Zionist dates. . . . Hamas has shown an utmost degree of self-restraint throughout the past period. . . . but matters have gone far enough and the criminals will reap what their hands have sown.

Recent Impact of Lessons Learned. In addition to the 1994 and 1995 campaigns, Palestinian terrorist leaders have also cited Hezbollah experience in Lebanon as a source of the lesson that suicide terrorism is an effective way of coercing Israel. Islamic Jihad leader Ramadan Shallah (2001) argued that:

> The shameful defeat that Israel suffered in southern Lebanon and which caused its army to flee it in terror was not made on the negotiations table but on the battlefield and through jihad and martyrdom, which achieved a great victory for the Islamic resistance and Lebanese People. . . . We would not exaggerate if we said that the chances of achieving victory in Palestine are greater than in Lebanon. . . . If the enemy could not bear the losses of the war on the border strip with Lebanon, will it be able to withstand a long war of attrition in the heart of its security dimension and major cities?

Palestinian terrorists are now applying the lessons they have learned. In November 2000, Khalid Mish'al explained Hamas's strategy for the second *intifada,* which was then in its early stages:

> Like the intifada in 1987, the current intifada has taught us that we should move forward normally from popular confrontation to the rifle to suicide operations. This is the normal development. . . . We always have the Lebanese experiment before our eyes. It was a great model of which we are proud.

Even before the second *intifada* began, other Hamas statements similarly expressed,

> The Zionist enemy . . . only understands the language of Jihad, resistance and martyrdom, that was the language that led to its blatant defeat in South Lebanon and it will be the language that will defeat it on the land of Palestine. (Hamas Statement 2000)

The bottom line is that the ferocious escalation of the pace of suicide terrorism that we have witnessed in the past several years cannot be considered irrational or even surprising. Rather, it is simply the result of the lesson that terrorists have quite reasonably learned from their experience of the previous two decades: Suicide terrorism pays.

THE LIMITS OF SUICIDE TERRORISM

Despite suicide terrorists' reasons for confidence in the coercive effectiveness of this strategy, there are sharp limits to what suicide terrorism is likely to accomplish in the future. During the 1980s and 1990s, terrorist leaders learned that moderate punishment often leads to moderate concessions and so concluded that more ambitious suicide campaigns would lead to greater political gains. However, today's more ambitious suicide terrorist campaigns are likely to fail. Although suicide terrorism is somewhat more effective than ordinary coercive punishment using air power or economic sanctions, it is not drastically so.

Suicide Terrorism Is Unlikely to Achieve
Ambitious Goals

In international military coercion, threats to inflict military defeat often generate more coercive leverage than punishment. Punishment, using anything short of nuclear weapons, is a relatively weak coercive strategy because modern nation states generally will accept high costs rather than abandon important national goals, while modern administrative techniques and economic adjustments over time often allow states to minimize civilian costs. The most punishing air attacks with conventional munitions in history were the American B-29 raids against Japan's 62 largest cities from March to August 1945. Although these raids killed nearly 800,000 Japanese civilians—almost 10% died on the first day, the March 9, 1945, fire-bombing of Tokyo, which killed over 85,000—the conventional bombing did not compel the Japanese to surrender.

Suicide terrorism makes adjustment to reduce damage more difficult than for states faced with military coercion or economic sanctions. However, it does not affect the target state's interests in the issues at stake. As a result, suicide terrorism can coerce states to abandon limited or modest goals, such as withdrawal from territory of low strategic importance or, as in Israel's case in 1994 and 1995, a temporary and partial withdrawal from a more important area. However, suicide terrorism is unlikely to cause targets to abandon goals central to their wealth or security, such as a loss of territory that would weaken the economic prospects of the state or strengthen the rivals of the state.

Suicide terrorism makes punishment more effective than in international military coercion. Targets remain willing to countenance high costs for important goals, but administrative, economic, or military adjustments to prevent suicide attack are harder, while suicide attackers themselves are unlikely to be deterred by the threat of retaliation. Accordingly, suicide attack is likely to present a threat of continuing limited civilian punishment that the target government cannot completely eliminate, and the upper bound on what punishment can gain for coercers is recognizably higher in suicidal terrorism than in international military coercion.

The data on suicide terrorism from 1980 to 2001 support this conclusion. While suicide terrorism has achieved modest or very limited goals, it has so far failed to compel target democracies to abandon goals central to national wealth or security. When the United States withdrew from Lebanon in 1984, it had no important security, economic, or even ideological interests at stake. Lebanon was largely a humanitarian mission and not viewed as central to the national welfare of the United States. Israel withdrew from most of Lebanon in June 1985 but remained in a security buffer on the edge of southern Lebanon for more than a decade afterward, despite the fact that 17 of 22 suicide attacks occurred in 1985 and 1986. Israel's withdrawals from Gaza and the West Bank in 1994 and 1995 occurred at the same time that settlements increased and did little to hinder the IDF's return, and so these concessions were more modest than they may appear. Sri Lanka has suffered more casualties from suicide attack than Israel but has not acceded to demands that it surrender part of its national territory. Thus, the logic of punishment and the record of suicide terrorism suggests that, unless suicide terrorists acquire far more destructive technologies, suicide attacks for more ambitious goals are likely to fail and will continue to provoke more aggressive military responses.

Policy Implications for Containing Suicide Terrorism

While the rise in suicide terrorism and the reasons behind it seem daunting, there are important policy lessons to learn. The current policy debate is misguided. Offensive military action or concessions alone rarely work for long. For over 20 years, the governments of Israel and other states targeted by suicide terrorism have engaged in extensive military efforts to kill, isolate, and jail suicide terrorist leaders and operatives, sometimes with the help of quite good surveillance of the terrorists' communities. Thus far, they have met with meager success. Although decapitation of suicide terrorist organizations can disrupt their operations temporarily, it rarely yields long-term gains. Of the 11 major suicide terrorist campaigns that had ended as of 2001, only one—the PKK versus Turkey—did so as a result of leadership decapitation, when the leader, in Turkish custody, asked his followers to stop. So far, leadership decapitation has also not ended Al Qaeda's campaign. Although the United States successfully toppled the Taliban in Afghanistan in December 2001, Al Qaeda launched seven successful suicide terrorist attacks from April to December 2002, killing some 250

Western civilians, more than in the three years before September 11, 2001, combined.

Concessions are also not a simple answer. Concessions to nationalist grievances that are widely held in the terrorists' community can reduce popular support for further terrorism, making it more difficult to recruit new suicide attackers and improving the standing of more moderate nationalist elites who are in competition with the terrorists. Such benefits can be realized, however, only if the concessions really do substantially satisfy the nationalist or self-determination aspirations of a large fraction of the community.

Partial, incremental, or deliberately staggered concessions that are dragged out over a substantial period of time are likely to become the worst of both worlds. Incremental compromise may appear—or easily be portrayed—to the terrorists' community as simply delaying tactics and, thus, may fail to reduce, or actually increase, their distrust that their main concerns will ever be met. Further, incrementalism provides time and opportunity for the terrorists to intentionally provoke the target state in hopes of derailing the smooth progress of negotiated compromise in the short term, so that they can reradicalize their own community and actually escalate their efforts toward even greater gains in the long term.[6] Thus, states that are willing to make concessions should do so in a single step if at all possible.

Advocates of concessions should also recognize that, even if they are successful in undermining the terrorist leaders' base of support, almost any concession at all will tend to encourage the terrorist leaders further about their own coercive effectiveness. Thus, even in the aftermath of a real settlement with the opposing community, some terrorists will remain motivated to continue attacks and, for the medium term, may be able to do so, which in term would put a premium on combining concessions with other solutions.

Given the limits of offense and of concessions, homeland security and defensive efforts generally must be a core part of any solution. Undermining the feasibility of suicide terrorism is a difficult task. After all, a major advantage of suicide attack is that it is more difficult to prevent than other types of attack. However, the difficulty of achieving perfect security should not keep us from taking serious measures to prevent would be terrorists from easily entering their target society. As Chaim Kaufmann (1996) has shown, even intense ethnic civil wars can often be stopped by demographic separation because it greatly reduces both means and incentives for the sides to attack each other. This logic may apply with even more force to the related problem of suicide terrorism, since, for suicide attackers, gaining physical access to the general area of the target is the only genuinely demanding part of an operation, and as

---

[6] The Bush administration's decision in May 2003 to withdraw most U.S. troops from Saudi Arabia is the kind of partial concession likely to backfire. Al Qaeda may well view this as evidence that the United States is vulnerable to coercive pressure, but the concession does not satisfy Al Qaeda's core demand to reduce American military control over the holy areas on the Arab peninsula. With the conquest and long term military occupation of Iraq, American military capabilities to control Saudi Arabia have substantially increased even if there are no American troops on Saudi soil itself.

we have seen, resentment of foreign occupation of their national homeland is a key part of the motive for suicide terrorism.

The requirements for demographic separation depend on geographic and other circumstances that may not be attainable in all cases. For example, much of Israel's difficulty in containing suicide terrorism derives from the deeply intermixed settlement patterns of the West Bank and Gaza, which make the effective length of the border between Palestinian and Jewish settled areas practically infinite and have rendered even very intensive Israeli border control efforts ineffective (Kaufmann 1998). As a result, territorial concessions could well encourage terrorists leaders to strive for still greater gains while greater repression may only exacerbate the conditions of occupation that cultivate more recruits for terrorist organizations. Instead, the best course to improve Israel's security may well be a combined strategy: abandoning territory on the West Bank along with an actual wall that physically separates the populations.

Similarly, if Al Qaeda proves able to continue suicide attacks against the American homeland, the United States should emphasize improving its domestic security. In the short term, the United States should adopt stronger border controls to make it more difficult for suicide attackers to enter the United States. In the long term, the United States should work toward energy independence and, thus, reduce the need for American troops in the Persian Gulf countries where their presence has helped recruit suicide terrorists to attack America. These measures will not provide a perfect solution, but they may make it far more difficult for Al Qaeda to continue attacks in the United States, especially spectacular attacks that require elaborate coordination.

Perhaps most important, the close association between foreign military occupations and the growth of suicide terrorist movements in the occupied regions should give pause to those who favor solutions that involve conquering countries in order to transform their political systems. Conquering countries may disrupt terrorist operations in the short term, but it is important to recognize that occupation of more countries may well increase the number of terrorists coming at us.

ACKNOWLEDGMENTS

I thank Robert Art, Steven Cicala, Alex Downs, Daniel Drezner, Adria Lawrence, Sean Lynn-Jones, John Mearsheimer, Michael O'Connor, Sebastian Rosato, Lisa Weeden, the anonymous reviewers, and the members of the program on International Security Policy at the University of Chicago for their superb comments. I especially thank James K. Feldman and Chaim D. Kaufmann for their excellent comments on multiple drafts. I would also like to acknowledge encouragement from the committee for the Combating Political Violence paper competition sponsored by the Institute for War and Peace Studies at Columbia University, which selected an earlier version as a winning paper.

Appendix: Suicide Terrorist Campaigns, 1980–2001

	Weapon	Target	Killed*
		Completed Campaigns	
Campaign #1: Hezbollah vs. US, France			
1. April 18, 1983	car bomb	US embassy, Beirut	63
2. Oct 23, 1983	car bomb	US Marine barracks	241
3. Oct 23, 1983	car bomb	French barracks	58
4. Dec 12, 1983	grenades	US Embassy, Kuwait	7
5. Dec 21, 1983	car bomb	French HQ, Beirut	1
6. Sept 7, 1984	truck bomb	US Beirut embassy	14
Campaign #2: Hezbollah vs. Israel			
1. Nov 4, 1983	car bomb	IDF post in Tyre, Lebanon	50
2. Jun 16, 1984	car bomb	IDF post, southern Lebanon	5
3. Mar 8, 1985:	truck bomb	IDF post	12
4. Apr 9, 1985:	car bomb	IDF post	4
5. May 9, 1985:	suitcase bomb	SLA checkpoint	2
6. June 15, 1985:	car bomb	IDF post in Beirut	23
Campaign #3: Hezbollah vs. Israel and South Lebanon Army			
1. July 9, 1985	car bombs	2 SLA outposts	22
2. July 15, 1985	car bomb	SLA outpost	10
3. July 31, 1985	car bomb	IDF patrol, south Lebanon	2
4. Aug 6, 1985	mule bomb	SLA outpost	0
5. Aug 29, 1985	car bomb	SLA outpost	15
6. Sept 3, 1985	car bomb	SLA outpost	37
7. Sept 12, 1985	car bomb	SLA outpost	21

(continued)

Appendix: (*Continued*)

	Weapon	Target	Killed*
Completed Campaigns			
Campaign #3: Hezbollah vs. Israel and South Lebanon Army			
8. Sept 17, 1985	car bomb	SLA outpost	30
9. Sept 18, 1985	car bomb	SLA outpost	0
10. Oct 17, 1985	grenades	SLA radio station	6
11. Nov 4, 1985	car bomb	SLA outpost	0
12. Nov 12, 1985	car bomb	Christ. militia leaders, Beirut	5
13. Nov 26, 1985	car bomb	SLA outpost	20
14. April 7, 1986	car bomb	SLA outpost	1
15. July 17, 1986	car bomb	Jezzine, S. Lebanon	7
16. Nov 20, 1986:	car bomb	SLA outpost	3
Campaign #4: Liberation Tigers of Tamil Eelam vs. Sri Lanka			
1. Jul 12, 1990	boat bomb	naval vessel, Trincomalee	6
2. Nov 23, 1990	???	army camp, Manakulam	0
3. Mar 2, 1991	car bomb	defense minister, Colombo	18**
4. Mar 19, 1991	truck bomb	army camp, Silavathurai	5
5. May 5, 1991	boat bomb	naval vessel	5
6. May 21, 1991	belt bomb	Rajiv Gandhi, Madras, India	1**
7. June 22, 1991	car bomb	defense ministry, Colombo	27
8. Nov 16, 1992	motorcycle bomb	navy commander, Colombo	1**
9. May 1, 1993	belt bomb	President Premadasa, Colombo	23**
10. Nov 11, 1993	boat bomb	naval base, Jaffna Lagoon	0
11. Aug 2, 1994	grenades	air force helicopter, Palali	0
12. Sept 19, 1994	mines	naval vessel, Sagarawardene	25

Date	Weapon	Target	Killed
13. Oct 24, 1994	belt bomb	Presidential candidate, Colombo	53**
14. Nov 8, 1994	mines	naval vessel, Vettilaikerny	0

Campaign #5: LTTE vs. Sri Lanka

Date	Weapon	Target	Killed
1. Apr 18, 1995	scuba divers	naval vessel, Trincomalee	11
2. Jul 16, 1995	scuba divers	naval vessel, Jaffna peninsula	0
3. Aug 7, 1995	belt bomb	government bldg, Colombo	22
4. Sep 3, 1995	scuba divers	naval vessel, Trincomalee	0
5. Sep 10, 1995	scuba divers	naval vessel, Kankesanthurai	0
6. Sep 20, 1995	scuba divers	naval vessel, Kankesanthurai	0
7. Oct 2, 1995	scuba divers	Naval vessel, Kankesanthurai	0
8. Oct 17, 1995	scuba divers	naval vessel, Trincomalee	9
9. Oct 20, 1995	mines	2 oil depots, Colombo	23
10. Nov 11, 1995	belt bombs	army HQ, crowd, Colombo	23
11. Dec 5, 1995	truck bomb	police camp, Batticaloa	23
12. Jan 8, 1996	belt bomb	market, Batticaloa	0
13. Jan 31, 1996	truck bomb	bank, Colombo	91
14. Apr 1, 1996	boat bomb	navy vessel, Vettilaikerni	10
15. Apr 12, 1996	scuba divers	port building, Colombo	0
16. Jul 3, 1996	belt bomb	gov motorcade, Jaffna	37
17. Jul 18, 1996	mines	naval gunboat, Mullaittivu	35
18. Aug 6, 1996	boat bomb	naval ship, north coast	0
19. Aug 14, 1996	bicycle bomb	public rally, Kalmunai	0
20. Oct 25, 1996	boat bomb	gunboat, Trincomalee	12
21. Nov 25, 1996	belt bomb	police chief vehicle, Trincomalee	0
22. Dec 17, 1996	motorcycle bomb	police unit jeep, Ampara	1
23. Mar 6, 1997	grenades	China Bay air base	0

(continued)

Appendix: (Continued)

	Weapon	Target	Killed*
		Completed Campaigns	
Campaign #5: LTTE vs. Sri Lanka			
24. Oct 15, 1997	truck bomb	World Trade Centre, Colombo	18
25. Oct 19, 1997	boat bomb	naval gunboat, northeastern coast	7
26. Dec 28, 1997	truck bomb	chief Cecil Tissera, south Sri Lanka	0
27. Jan 25, 1998	truck bomb	Buddhist shrine, Kandy	11
28. Feb 5, 1998	belt bomb	Air Force headquarters, Colombo	8
29. Feb 23, 1998	boat bombs	2 landing ships off Point Pedru	47
30. Mar 5, 1998	bus bomb	train station, Colombo	38
31. May 15, 1998	belt bomb	army brigadier, Jaffna peninsula	1
32. Sep 11, 1998	belt bomb	new mayor of Jaffna	20**
33. Mar 15, 1999	belt bomb	police station, Colombo	5
34. May 29, 1999	belt bomb	Tamil rival leader, Batticaloa	2
35. Jul 25, 1999	belt bomb	passenger ferry, Trincomalee	1
36. Jul 29, 1999	belt bomb	Tamil politician, Colombo	1
37. Aug 4, 1999	bicycle bomb	police vehicle, Vavuniya	12
38. Aug 9, 1999	belt bomb	military commander, Vakarai	1
39. Sep 2, 1999	belt bomb	Tamil rival, Vavuniya,	3
40. Dec 18, 1999	2 belt bombs	Pres C. Kumaratunga, Colombo	38***
41. Jan 5, 2000	belt bomb	PM S. Bandaranaike, Colombo	11***
42. Feb 4, 2000	sea diver	naval vessel, Trincomalee	0
43. Mar 2, 2000	belt bomb	military commander, Trincomalee	1***
44. Mar 10, 2000	belt bomb	government motorcade Colombo	23

#	Date	Group	Weapon	Target/Location	Casualties
45.	Jun 5, 2000		scuba diver	ammunition ship, northeast coast	5
46.	Jun 7, 2000		belt bomb	Industries Minister Colombo	26**
47.	Jun 14, 2000		bicycle bomb	air force bus, Wattala town	2
48.	Jun 26, 2000		boat bomb	merchant vessel, north coast	7
49.	Aug 16, 2000		belt bomb	military vehicle, Vavuniya	1
50.	Sep 15, 2000		belt bomb	hospital, Colombo	7
51.	Oct 2, 2000		belt bomb	SLMC leader, Trincomalee	22**
52.	Oct 5, 2000		belt bomb	People's Alliance rally, Medawachchiya	12
53.	Oct 19, 2000		belt bomb	Cabinet ceremony, Colombo	0
54.	Oct 23, 2000		boat bombs	gunboat/troop carrier, Trincomalee	2

Campaign #6: Hamas vs. Israel

#	Date	Group	Weapon	Target/Location	Casualties
1.	Apr 6, 1994	Hamas	car bomb	Afula, Israel	9
2.	Apr 13, 1994	Hamas	belt bomb	Hadera, Israel	6

Campaign #7: Hamas/Islamic Jihad vs. Israel

#	Date	Group	Weapon	Target/Location	Casualties
1.	Oct 19, 1994	Hamas	belt bomb	Tel Aviv	22
2.	Nov 11, 1994	Islamic Jihad	belt bomb	Netzarim, Gaza	3
3.	Dec 25, 1994	Hamas	belt bomb	Jerusalem	0
4.	Jan 22, 1995	Islamic Jihad	belt bomb	Tel Aviv	21
5.	Apr 9, 1995	Islamic Jihad	belt bomb	Netzarim, Gaza	8
6.	July 24, 1995	Hamas	belt bomb	Tel Aviv	6
7.	Aug 21, 1995	Hamas	belt bomb	Jerusalem	5

Campaign #8: Hamas vs. Israel

#	Date	Group	Weapon	Target/Location	Casualties
1.	Feb 25, 1996	Hamas	belt bomb	Jerusalem	25
2.	Feb 25, 1996	Hamas	belt bomb	Ashkelon	1
3.	Mar 3, 1996	Hamas	belt bomb	Jerusalem	19
4.	Mar 4, 1996	Hamas	belt bomb	Tel Aviv	13

(continued)

	Group	Weapon	Target	Killed*
Completed Campaigns				
Campaign #9: Hamas vs. Israel				
1. Mar 21, 1997	Hamas	belt bomb	café, Tel Aviv	3
2. Jul 30, 1997	Hamas	belt bomb	Jerusalem	14
3. Sept 7, 1997	Hamas	belt bomb	Jerusalem	7
Campaign #10: Kurdistan Workers Party (PKK) vs. Turkey				
1. Jun 30, 1996		belt bomb	Tunceli, Turkey	9
2. Oct 25, 1996		belt bomb	Adana, Turkey	4
3. Oct 29, 1996		belt bombs	Sivas, Turkey	4
Campaign #11: PKK vs. Turkey				
1. Mar 4, 1999		belt bomb	Batman, Turkey	0
2. Mar 27, 1999		grenade	Istanbul	0
3. Apr 5, 1999		belt bomb	governor, Bingol, Turkey	0
4. Jul 5, 1999		belt bomb	Adana, Turkey	0
5. Jul 7, 1999		grenades	Iluh, Turkey	0
6. Aug 28, 1999		bomb	Tunceli, Turkey	0
Ongoing Campaigns				
Campaign #12: Al Qaeda vs. United States				
1. Nov 13, 1995		car bomb	US military base, Riyadh, SA	5
2. Jun 25, 1996		truck bomb	US military base, Dhahran SA	19
3. Aug 7, 1998		truck bombs	US embassies, Kenya/Tanzania	250
4. Oct 12, 2000		boat bomb	USS Cole, Yemen	17

#	Date	Organization	Weapon	Target	Killed
5.	Sep 9, 2001		camera bomb	Ahmed Shah Masood, Afghanistan	1
6.	Sep 11, 2001		hijacked airplanes	WTC/Pentagon	3037

Campaign #13: Chechen Separatists vs. Russia

#	Date	Weapon	Target	Killed
1.	Jun 7, 2000	truck bomb	Russian police, Chech.	2
2.	Jul 3, 2000	truck bomb	Argun, Russia	30
3.	Mar 24, 2001	car bomb	Chechnya	20
4.	Nov 29, 2001	belt bomb	military commander, Chechnya	1

Campaign #14: Kashmir Separatists vs. India

#	Date	Weapon	Target	Killed
1.	Dec 25, 2000	car bomb	Srinagar, Kashmir	8
2.	Oct 1, 2001	car bomb	Legislative assembly	30
3.	Dec 13, 2001	gunmen	Parliament, New Delhi	7

Campaign #15: LTTE vs. Sri Lanka

#	Date	Weapon	Target	Killed
1.	Jul 24, 2001	belt bomb	international airport, Colombo	12
2.	Sep 16, 2001	boat bomb	navel vessel, north	29
3.	Oct 29, 2001	belt bomb	PM Wickremanayake, Colombo	3***
4.	Oct 30, 2001	boat bomb	oil tanker, northern coast	4
5.	Nov 9, 2001	belt bomb	police jeep, Batticaloa	0
6.	Nov 15, 2001	belt bomb	crowd, Batticaloa	3

Compaign #16: Hamas/Islamic Jihad vs. Israel

#	Date	Organization	Weapon	Target	Killed
1.	Oct 30, 2000	Hamas	belt bomb	Jerusalem	15
2.	Nov 2, 2000	Al Aqsa			2
3.	Nov 20, 2000	Hamas	car bomb	Hadera, Israel	2
4.	Dec 22, 2000	Al Aqsa	belt bomb	West Bank	3
5.	Jan 1, 2001	Hamas	belt bomb	Netanya, Israel	10
6.	Feb 8, 2001	Hamas			4

(continued)

Appendix: (Continued)

Ongoing Compaigns

Campaign #16: Hamas/Islamic Jihad vs. Israel

	Group	Weapon	Target	Killed*
7. Feb 14, 2001	Hamas	bus driver	Tel Aviv	8
8. Mar 1, 2001	Hamas	belt bomb		1
9. Mar 4, 2001	Hamas	belt bomb	Netanya, Israel	3
10. Mar 27, 2001	Hamas	belt bomb	Jerusalem	1
11. Mar 27, 2001	Hamas	belt bomb	Jerusalem (2nd attack)	0
12. Mar 28, 2001	Hamas	belt bomb	Kfar Saba, Israel	3
13. Apr 22, 2001	Hamas	belt bomb	Kfar Saba, Israel	3
14. Apr 23, 2001	PFLP	car bomb	Yehuda, Israel	8
15. Apr 29, 2001	Hamas	belt bomb	West Bank	0
16. May 18, 2001	Hamas	belt bomb	Netanya, Israel	5
17. May 25, 2001	Islamic Jihad	truck bomb	Netzarim, Gaza	2
18. May 27, 2001	Hamas	car bomb	Netanya, Israel	1
19. May 30, 2001	Islamic Jihad			8
20. Jun 1, 2001	Hamas	belt bomb	nightclub, Tel Aviv	22
21. Jun 22, 2001	Hamas	belt bomb	Gaza	2
22. Jul 2, 2001	Hamas	car bomb	IDF checkpt, Gaza	0
23. Jul 9, 2001	Hamas	car bomb	Gaza	0
24. Jul 16, 2001	Islamic Jihad	belt bomb	Jerusalem	5
25. Aug 8, 2001	Al Aqsa	car bomb	Jerusalem	8
26. Aug 9, 2001	Islamic Jihad	belt bomb	Haifa, Israel	15
27. Aug 12, 2001	Islamic Jihad	belt bomb	Haifa, Israel	0
28. Aug 21, 2001	Al Aqsa		Jerusalem	0

#	Date	Group	Weapon	Location	Killed
29.	Sept 4, 2001	Hamas	belt bomb	Jerusalem	0
30.	Sept 9, 2001	Hamas	belt bomb	Nahariya, Israel	3
31.	Oct 1, 2001	???			1
32.	Oct 7, 2001	Islamic Jihad	car bomb	Israel	2
33.	Nov 26, 2001	Hamas	car bomb	Gaza	0
34.	Nov 29, 2001	Islamic Jihad	belt bomb	Gaza	3
35.	Dec 1, 2001	Hamas	belt bomb	Haifa, Israel	11
36.	Dec 2, 2001	Hamas	belt bomb	Jerusalem	15
37.	Dec 5, 2001	Islamic Jihad	belt bomb	Jerusalem	0
38.	Dec 9, 2001	???	belt bomb	Haifa, Israel	0
39.	Dec 12, 2001	???	belt bomb	Gaza	0

Isolated Attacks

#	Date	Group	Weapon	Location	Killed
1.	Dec 15, 1981	???	car bomb	Iraqi embassy, Beirut	30
2.	May 25, 1985	Hezbollah	car bomb	ruler, Kuwait	0***
3.	Jul 5, 1987	LTTE	truck bomb	army camp, Jaffna Penin	20
4.	Aug 15, 1993	???	motorcycle bomb	Egyptian Interior Minister	3
5.	Jan 30, 1995	AIG****	truck bomb	crowd, Algiers	42
6.	Nov 19, 1995	Islamic Group	truck bomb	Egyptian embassy, Pakistan	16
7.	Oct 29, 1998	Hamas	belt bomb	Gaza	1
8.	Nov 17, 1998	???	belt bomb	Yuksekova, Turkey	0
9.	Dec 29, 1999	Hezbollah	grenades	Lebanon	1

Note: Several reports of PKK suicide in May and June 1997 during fighting between PKK and Kurdish militias in Iraq, but coverage insufficient to distinguish suicide attack from suicide to avoid capture.

*Not including attacker.

**Assassination target killed.

***Assassination target survived.

??? = unclaimed.

****Armed Islamic Group.

REFERENCES

al-Shaqaqi, Fathi. 1995. "Interview with Secretary General of Islamic Jihad." *Al-Quds,* 11 April. FBIS-NES-95-70, 12 April 1995.

al-Zahhar, Mahmud. 1996. "Interview." *Al-Dustur* (Amman), 19 February. FBIS-NES-96-034, 20 February 1996.

Art, Robert J., and Patrick M. Cronin. 2003. *The United States and Coercive Diplomacy.* Washington, DC: United States Institute of Peace.

Bakr, Ahmed. 1995. "Interview." *The Independent* (London), 14 March. FBIS-NES-95-086, 4 May 1995.

Bearden, Milton. 2002. Personal correspondence. University of Chicago, March 26.

Bloom, Mia. 2002. "Rational Interpretations of Palestinian Suicide Bombing." Paper presented at the Program on International Security Policy, University of Chicago.

Boix, Carlos, and Sebastian Rosato. 2001. "A Complete Dataset of Regimes, 1850–1999." University of Chicago. Typescript. "Bus Attack Said to Spur Rabin to Speed Talks." 1995. *Yediot Aharonot,* July 25. FBIS-NES-94-142, 25 July 1995.

Clutterbuck, Richard. 1975. *Living with Terrorism.* London: Faber& Faber.

Crenshaw, Martha. 1981. "The Causes of Terrorism." *Comparative Politics* 13 (July): 397–99.

De Figueiredo, Rui, and Barry R. Weingast. 1998. "Vicious Cycles: Endogenous Political Extremism and Political Violence." Paper presented at the annual meeting of the American Political Science Association.

Department of State. 1983–2001. *Patterns of Global Terrorism.* Washington, DC: DOS.

Edler Baumann, Carol. 1973. *Diplomatic Kidnapings: A Revolutionary Tactic of Urban Terrorism.* The Hague: Nijhoff.

Elliott, Paul. 1998. *Brotherhoods of Fear.* London: Blandford.

George, Alexander, et al. 1972. *Limits of Coercive Diplomacy.* Boston: Little, Brown.

Greenberg, Joel. 2002. "Suicide Planner Expresses Joy Over His Missions," *New York Times,* 9 May.

Hamas Communique No. 125. 1995. *Filastin al-Muslimah* (London), August. FBIS-NES-95-152, 8 August 1995.

"Hamas Leader Discusses Goals." 1995. *Frankfurter Runschau,* 3 May. FBIS-NES-95-086, 4 May 1995.

"Hamas Operations Against Israel Said to Continue." 1994. *Al-Dustur* (Amman, Jordan), 14 April. FBIS-NES-94-072, 14 April 1994.

Hamas Statement. 2000. *BBC Summary of World Broadcasts,* 23 July.

Hoffman, Bruce. 1998. *Inside Terrorism.* New York: Columbia University Press.

Horowitz, Michael, and Dan Reiter. 2001. "When Does Aerial Bombing Work? Quantitative Empirical Tests, 1917–1999." *Journal of Conflict Resolution* 45 (April): 147–73.

Hroub, Khaled. 2000. *Hamas: Political Thought and Practice.* Washington, DC: Institute for Palestine Studies.

Huntington, Samuel P. 1991. *The Third Wave: Democratization in the Twentieth Century.* Norman: University of Oklahoma Press.

Inbar, Efraim. 1999. *Rabin and Israel's National Security.* Baltimore: John's Hopkins University Press.

Institute for Counter-Terrorism (ICT). 2001. *Countering Suicide Terrorism.* Herzliya, Israel: International Policy Institute for Counter-Terrorism.

Jenkins, Brian N. 1975. "Will Terrorists Go Nuclear?" Rand Report P-5541. Santa Monica, CA: Rand Corp.

Jenkins, Brian N. 1985. *International Terrorism.* Washington, DC: Rand Corp.

Jervis, Robert. 1976. *Perception and Misperception in International Politics.* Princeton, NJ: Princeton University Press.

Kaufmann, Chaim D. 1996. "Possible and Impossible Solutions to Ethnic Civil Wars." *International Security* 20 (Spring): 136–75.

Kaufmann, Chaim D. 1998. "When All Else Fails: Ethnic Population Transfers and Partitions in the Twentieth Century." *International Security* 23 (Fall): 120–56.

Kramer, Martin. 1990. "The Moral Logic of Hizballah." In *Origins of Terrorism,* ed. Walter Reich. New York: Cambridge University Press.

Kramer, Martin. 1996. "Fundamentalist Islam at Large: Drive for Power." *Middle East Quarterly* 3 (June): 37–49.

Kydd, Andrew, and Barbara F.Walter. 2002. "Sabotaging the Peace: The Politics of Extremist Violence." *International Organization* 56 (2): 263–96.

Laqueur, Walter. 1987. *The Age of Terrorism.* Boston: Little, Brown.

Lebow, Richard Ned. 1981. *Between Peace and War: The Nature of International Crisis.* Baltimore, MD: Johns Hopkins University Press.

Lewis, Bernard. 1968. *The Assassins.* New York: Basic Books. Makovsky, David, and Alon Pinkas. 1994. "Rabin: Killing Civilians Won't Kill the Negotiations." *Jerusalem Post,* 13 April.

Merari, Ariel. 1990. "The Readiness to Kill and Die: Suicidal Terrorism in the Middle East." In *Origins of Terrorism,* ed.Walter Reich. New York: Cambridge University Press.

Mish'al, Khalid. 2000. "Interview." *BBC Summary of World Broadcasts,* 17 November.

Mishal, Shaul, andAvraham Sela. 2000. *The Palestinian Hamas.* New York: Columbia University Press.

Niebuhr, Reinhold. 1960. *Moral Man and Immoral Society.* New York: Scribner.

Nusse, Andrea. 1998. *Muslim Palestine: The Ideology of Hamas.* Amsterdam: Harwood Academic.

O'Neill, Richard. 1981. *Suicide Squads.* NewYork: Ballantine Books. Pape, Robert A. 1996. *Bombing to Win: Air Power and Coercion in War.* Ithaca, NY: Cornell University Press.

Pape, Robert A. 1997. "Why Economic Sanctions Do Not Work." *International Security* 22 (Fall): 90–136.

Pape, Robert A. 2002. "The Universe of Suicide Terrorist Attacks World-wide, 1980–2001." University of Chicago. Typescript.

Post, Jerrold M. 1990. "Terrorist Psycho-Logic: Terrorist Behavior as a Product of Psychological Forces." In *Origins of Terrorism*, ed. Walter Reich. New York: Cambridge University Press.

Przeworski, Adam, Michael E. Alvarez, Jose Antonio Cheibub, and Fernando Limongi. 2000. *Democracy and Development: Political Institutions and Well-Being in the World, 1950–1990.* Cambridge, UK: Cambridge University Press.

Rabin, Yitzhaq. 1994. "Speech to Knessett." *BBC Summary of World Broadcasts,* 20 April.

Rabin, Yitzhaq. 1995. "Interview." *BBC Summary of World Broadcasts,* 8 September.

Rapoport, David C. 1971. *Assassination and Terrorism.* Toronto: CBC Merchandising.

Rapoport, David C. 1984. "Fear and Trembling: Terrorism in Three Religious Traditions." *American Political Science Review* 78 (September): 655–77.

Reagan, Ronald. 1990. *An American Life.* New York: Simon and Schuster.

Reich, Walter, ed. 1990. *Origins of Terrorism.* New York: Cambridge University Press.

Sauvagnargues, Philippe. 1994. "Opposition Candidate." *Agence France Presse,* 14 August.

Schalk, Peter. 1997. "Resistance and Martyrdom in the Process of State Formation of Tamililam." In *Martyrdom and Political Resistance,* ed. Joyed Pettigerw. Amsterdam: VU University Press, 61–83.

Schelling, Thomas. 1966. *Arms and Influence.* New Haven, CT: Yale University Press.

Schmid, Alex P., and Albert J. Jongman. 1988. *Political Terrorism.* New Brunswick, NJ: Transaction Books.

Sciolino, Elaine. 2002. "Saudi Warns Bush." *New York Times,* 27 January.

Shallah, Ramadan. 2001. "Interview." *BBC Summary of World Broadcasts,* 3 November.

Shiqaqi, Khalil, et al. 2002. *The Israeli-Palestinian Peace Process.* Portland, OR: Sussex Academic Press.

Sprinzak, Ehud. 2000. "Rational Fanatics." *Foreign Policy,* No. 120 (September/October): 66–73.

"Sri Lanka Opposition Leader Promises Talk with Rebels." 1994. *Japan Economic Newswire,* 11 August.

St. John, Peter. 1991. *Air Piracy, Airport Security, and International Terrrorism.* New York: Quorum Books.

Theodoulou, Michael. 1995. "New Attacks Feared." *The Times* (London), 21 August. FBIS-NES-95-165, 25 August 1995.

Tuchman, Barbara W. 1966. *The Proud Tower.* New York: Macmillan.

World Islamic Front. 1998. "Jihad Against Jews and Crusaders." Statement, 23 February.

8

Beyond the Abu Sayyaf

Steven Rogers

Washington has made the fight against radical Muslim separatists in the Philippines a critical front in its war on terrorism. But its one-size-fits-all approach reflects a dangerous misunderstanding of the problem—and could make things worse.

On October 18, 2003, President George W. Bush stood before the Philippine Congress and declared that the Philippines and the United States are "bound by the strongest ties that two nations can share." The statement was not just the sort of rhetorical flourish that often dominates a U.S. leader's address to a former colony. The long-simmering Muslim separatist rebellion in the southern Philippines has been identified as a critical battle in the war on terror, and the Philippine government has become a key U.S. ally as a result.

In January 2002, 600 U.S. soldiers were sent to support Philippine forces fighting the Abu Sayyaf, a loosely organized gang of Islamist bandits entrenched on the southern Philippine islands of Basilan and Jolo. The operation was a failure: a year after the deployment, U.S. forces had withdrawn with their enemy still in place and the Philippine government suffering from a damaging scandal. Since then, the focus of U.S. assistance has changed: military and development aid to the Philippines has soared to well more than $100 million a year, and President Bush has urged the Philippine Congress to increase its own military appropriations to meet the separatist Muslim threat.

The need for action is real. The chaos and criminality sown by the Abu Sayyaf and the Moro Islamic Liberation Front (MILF) have created an environment ripe for exploitation by international terrorists, and Philippine

Steven Rogers, "Beyond the Abu Sayef," *Foreign Affairs*, Jan.–Feb. 2004, p. 15. Reprinted by permission.

government attempts to address the situation have been ineffective. But Washington's flawed understanding of the problem has hamstrung the mission and lowered its chances of success. Policymakers treat the conflict as a case of a violent Muslim population terrorizing its Christian neighbors under the influence of radical Islamist agitators. They emphasize reports of al Qaeda support and the presence of operatives from the Southeast Asian Jemaah Islamiyah network. They have failed to recognize, however, that terrorists did not create the conflict in the southern Philippines and do not control any of the combatants. The troubles are rooted in specific local issues that predate the war on terror by centuries, and neither soldiers nor money will end Mindanao's war.

MINDANAO'S WAR

Conflict has plagued the southern islands of the Philippines since 1566, when Spanish forces, fresh from centuries of war against Muslims in their homeland, found their traditional enemies in their new colony. Muslim ferocity and Spanish torpor combined to leave Mindanao unconquered, but the reflexive Spanish hostility toward Muslims was passed on to Christian Filipinos, and Muslims responded in kind. American forces finally subdued the Muslim chieftains in the early twentieth century but ruled Mindanao as an entity separate from the rest of the Philippines. The divided populations were joined only with Philippine independence in 1946.

Ethnic tensions plagued this union from the start. Separatist sentiment flared into conflict in 1970, after years of government-sponsored Christian migration into Muslim regions, and Libya stepped in to support the Muslims, serving as midwife to the Moro National Liberation Front (MNLF). As fighting ground to a bloody stalemate, Muslim leaders urged Philippine president Ferdinand Marcos to negotiate with Muslim rebels. Dependent on oil imported from Muslim countries, Marcos complied, and a peace agreement was concluded in 1976.

With the truce signed, Marcos left control of Mindanao to his subordinates, who looked after their own interests. Military forces in the area were virtually abandoned. Soldiers went into business, by themselves or with local political overlords. Former rebels took to crime, often receiving official protection in return for a cut of the profits. Manila's influence over Mindanao dwindled, and the style of governance embraced by the region's feudal lords quickly inspired a new round of rebellion.

In 1978, disgruntled MNLF members under the leadership of a Cairo-educated cleric named Hashim Salamat formed the MILF. Salamat's strong religious identity and non-negotiable goal of an independent Islamic state proved more compelling than the MNLF's Libyan-influenced socialism. The MILF quickly grew to include some 12,000 armed men—concentrated mostly on Mindanao—and claimed the mantle of Muslim resistance. Since then, despite two decades of warfare and negotiation, government forces have been unable to establish lasting control over MILF territory.

In 1990, contact between a young militant named Abdurajak Janjalani and Osama bin Laden's brother-in-law Mohammed al-Khalifa led to the founding of another Muslim separatist group, the Abu Sayyaf, which quickly entrenched itself on the islands of Basilan and Jolo, west of Mindanao. The new group proclaimed a radical Islamist ideology and gained early notoriety with grenade attacks on Christian targets. Before long, however, it had diverted its energy to ransom-driven kidnapping. Soon, members of the criminal underground had emerged in key leadership positions, and the group's Islamic identity was subordinated to the quest for profit. After Janjalani's death in 1998, the Abu Sayyaf deteriorated into a loose federation of bandit chiefs bound mainly by convenience.

Despite the Islamist foundations of both the Abu Sayyaf and the MILF, the extent of their links to global terrorism is debatable. MILF fighters have trained in Pakistan and with the Taliban and have had contact with members of al Qaeda and Jemaah Islamiyah. There is no evidence, however, that the MILF is directed by outside powers, and its limited arsenal corroborates this independence. Its new chief, Al-Haj Murad, who took over after Salamat's death earlier this year, is not considered a religious extremist. The Abu Sayyaf similarly shows no sign of significant outside support, despite having initially received aid and military training from foreign terrorists. (Widely circulated rumors of Iraqi funding spring from a single, unreliable source.) The group's most important outside connections are not terrorists at all; they are police, military, and government officials, who sell firepower and immunity to the brigands for a share of the spoils.

COLLISION COURSE

In March 2000, the Abu Sayyaf took 51 hostages on Basilan. A month later they kidnapped 30 more, of varied nationalities, from a Malaysian resort. The tactic proved lucrative: they exchanged hostages for large ransom payments, including $25 million from the Libyan government. As cash flooded the impoverished islands, men flocked to the group, attracted less by ideology than by the promise of large guns and fast boats. In May 2001, an Abu Sayyaf group seized several Filipinos and two American missionaries in another resort raid, setting the group on a collision course with Washington.

In the first months of this minor crisis, the Bush administration viewed the hostages as victims of crime. There was no talk of terrorism and little enthusiasm for military action, or even for restoring much military aid to the Philippines. After September 11, however, the United States rapidly reversed its position. Manila was suddenly reclassified as a staunch ally in the war on terror, and Washington rediscovered the ties between Mindanao and jihad. The Abu Sayyaf was tagged a terrorist organization, and in January 2002, 600 U.S. soldiers joined 4,000 Filipino troops on Basilan. Philippine laws restrict foreign troops to training roles, but the Americans, though designated as trainers, entered hostile territory with explicit authorization to fire if attacked.

Critics immediately disputed Washington's claim that the Abu Sayyaf was a terrorist organization, rather than a criminal syndicate. They argued that the

MILF posed a far greater danger and that the size of the operation against the Abu Sayyaf was disproportionate to the threat. Many Filipinos suggested that the exercise was intended to secure a U.S. base in Mindanao or prepare for a later move against the MILF and the communist New People's Army.

Although U.S. soldiers gained local approval by building roads and bridges, the military outcome was ambiguous at best. The American hostages turned up elsewhere, discovered by Filipino troops unconnected to the operation; their captors had apparently slipped through a U.S. Navy cordon. One hostage was killed during the rescue. The operation halted the Abu Sayyaf's dramatic expansion, but most of the group's leaders and troops escaped.

In February 2003, American and Filipino officials announced another, larger exercise directed at the Abu Sayyaf presence on Jolo. As forces prepared for the operation, an unnamed Pentagon spokesman declared, "This is an actual combined operation, and it is U.S. forces accompanying and actively participating in Philippine-led offensive operations." The next day, White House spokesman Ari Fleischer added, "The Armed Forces of the Philippines will conduct operations supported by U.S. troops against the Abu Sayyaf group. The Armed Forces of the Philippines has the lead, and U.S. forces will assist them." In the Philippines, this was interpreted as a declaration that U.S. troops would be illegally deployed in a combat role. The subsequent outcry forced the cancellation of the exercise.

Days later, a bomb exploded outside an airport in the primarily Christian city of Davao. The next month, another explosion hit a crowded Davao wharf, and just before Philippine President Gloria Macapagal-Arroyo left for a visit to Washington in May a blast in the Christian town of Koronadal raised the combined toll to 50 dead and 200 wounded. Arroyo has blamed the recent bombings on the MILF, without citing any convincing evidence. The MILF, which had not previously designed attacks to maximize civilian casualties, has denied involvement.

Arroyo returned from Washington with a substantial aid package, but the MILF has not been added to Washington's list of terrorist organizations, despite suggestions from Manila officials that the designation was "inevitable." Negotiations brokered by Malaysia and encouraged by the United States are in progress. The focus of turmoil has since moved to Manila, underscoring the connection between Mindanao's conflict and the fragile state of Philippine democracy. In July, convicted Indonesian terrorist Fathur Rohman al-Ghozi and two Abu Sayyaf members walked out of Manila's national police headquarters. The escape, which clearly had inside help, provoked outrage in American and Australian counterterrorism circles and severely embarrassed Arroyo.

Two weeks later, several hundred soldiers seized a commercial complex in a 19-hour mutiny, accusing senior military officials of selling arms to the rebels and staging the recent bombings to encourage American support. Arroyo called the rebellion an attempted coup, but the participants claimed that they were only trying to publicize legitimate grievances.

The al-Ghozi escape, the mutiny, and subsequent attempts to capitalize on allegations of corruption within Arroyo's family appear to be coordinated moves aimed at undermining the Philippine administration and its generally pro–U.S. policies. Arroyo is running in the 2004 election, and opposition figures still consider her a leading contender. Several other candidates are prominent allies of Joseph Estrada, Arroyo's spectacularly inept predecessor. Estrada built his successful campaign around quasi-populist demagoguery, rallying discontent with the existing political order without offering any practical alternative. His administration had few definable policies beyond the pursuit of self-interest, and it oversaw a precipitous decline in political, economic, and security conditions, particularly on Mindanao. There is no shortage of grounds on which to criticize Arroyo's administration, but if her successor adopts the Estrada model, the consequences—for Mindanao, for the Philippines, and for the struggle against terrorism in Southeast Asia—will be severe.

TREATING CAUSES, NOT SYMPTOMS

The situation in the Philippines is not an international crisis demanding immediate intervention. But if it is ignored or subjected to simplistic short-term solutions, it could easily become one. Discussions of a constructive U.S. role typically focus on promoting security and development, but this approach fails to recognize a simple truth: the traditional prerogatives of power in the southern Philippines are fundamentally incompatible with either. A thin veneer of democratic institutions covers a society that remains essentially feudal, conforming less to democratic ideals than to the style of the datus, the warrior-chiefs of old. Leadership is personal and paternalistic and functions largely above the law; power flows from guns and money.

President Bush has lauded Arroyo's commitment to bringing terrorists to justice. His praise is somewhat justified, but terrorism and banditry cannot really be controlled until the members of the political and military elite who cooperate with terrorists and turn the powers of the state to their own ends are brought to justice as well. The Philippine government has the capacity to do so—it controls the money, the justice system, and the armed forces—but it lacks the will. Manila's elites seem reluctant to start a trend that might eventually result in restrictions on their own power.

Military action alone is not sufficient as a strategy. There is no central terrorist cell or evil genius in Mindanao to provide a discrete target for American action. In the face of overwhelming force guerrillas simply disperse and take refuge; if one leader is removed, several others emerge. Military force is nonetheless a necessary component of any solution, because security is a prerequisite for progress in other spheres of life. Development aid is necessary as well: Mindanao's enduring poverty is an effective incubator for violence. Neither military nor development aid will succeed, though, until the problems of collusion and corruption are decisively addressed.

Washington cannot root out corruption in the Philippines. The Philippines' desperate need for U.S. aid, however, could provide an incentive for reform. U.S. policymakers must make clear, accordingly, that the United States will discontinue aid if Manila does not take sustained, aggressive action against the abuse of power.

Such demands might draw protest from Manila's political elite, but, if presented effectively, they would gain considerable sympathy among most of the population. There is a growing constituency for change in the Philippines. Public discontent is high, focused on a governing class that has traditionally functioned above the law. Issues that for decades had only been discussed in private—such as cooperation between government officials and terrorist leaders—have finally entered public debate. Such discontent is a powerful and unharnessed force. With effective leadership, it could bring great benefits; exploited by self-interested demagogues, it could do great damage. Washington cannot lead a movement to reform the Philippine system of justice, but it can at least align itself with the right side.

ACTING LOCALLY

Applying the simplistic terms of the war on terror to the fight against the Philippines' Islamic extremists obscures the enormous complexity of the situation. But continued fighting on Mindanao could indeed generate the kind of chaos that terrorists are apt to exploit, channeling the anger and lawlessness of a centuries-old ethnic and political conflict to their own ends.

For U.S. policymakers, therefore, Mindanao is both an object lesson and a test case. As open sponsors of terrorism fall to political pressure or military action, the focus of Washington's efforts will shift to terrorist groups operating within countries that, like the Philippines, are at least nominally friendly. Respecting the laws and political processes of foreign governments, even when seriously flawed, can be frustrating. The answer, however, is not to ignore constraints but to find ways of operating effectively within them.

The conflict in the Philippines defies the moral clarity and aggressive rhetoric that the Bush administration has favored since September 11, and recognizing that is the key to progress. In the end, only the Philippine government can bring peace. If negotiations are unaccompanied by real change and Mindanao returns to the status quo, as in past attempts to secure an end to violence, the rebellion will surely resume. At best, the United States can help suppress the rebels militarily while encouraging negotiations and boosting Manila's political will to achieve the meaningful reform necessary for lasting peace. Such a strategy will not assure success, but neither will it make the conflict worse. Moreover, it is the only course available, since the conflict in the southern Philippines is not some nefarious external conspiracy or a clash of civilizations but the internal problem of an allied sovereign state.

9

The Protean Enemy

Jessica Stern

WHAT'S NEXT FROM AL QAEDA?

Having suffered the destruction of its sanctuary in Afghanistan two years ago, al Qaeda's already decentralized organization has become more decentralized still. The group's leaders have largely dispersed to Pakistan, Iran, Iraq, and elsewhere around the world (only a few still remain in Afghanistan's lawless border regions). And with many of the planet's intelligence agencies now focusing on destroying its network, al Qaeda's ability to carry out large-scale attacks has been degraded.

Yet despite these setbacks, al Qaeda and its affiliates remain among the most significant threats to U.S. national security today. In fact, according to George Tenet, the CIA's director, they will continue to be this dangerous for the next two to five years. An alleged al Qaeda spokesperson has warned that the group is planning another strike similar to those of September 11. On May 12, simultaneous bombings of three housing complexes in Riyadh, Saudi Arabia, killed at least 29 people and injured over 200, many of them Westerners. Intelligence officials in the United States, Europe, and Africa report that al Qaeda has stepped up its recruitment drive in response to the war in Iraq. And the target audience for its recruitment has also changed. They are now younger, with an even more "menacing attitude," as France's top investigative judge on terrorism-related cases, Jean-Louis Bruguiere, describes them. More of them are converts to Islam. And more of them are women.

What accounts for al Qaeda's ongoing effectiveness in the face of an unprecedented onslaught? The answer lies in the organization's remarkably

Jessica Stern, "The Protean Enemy," *Foreign Affairs,* July–Aug. 2003, p. 27. Reprinted by permission.

protean nature. Over its life span, al Qaeda has constantly evolved and shown a surprising willingness to adapt its mission. This capacity for change has consistently made the group more appealing to recruits, attracted surprising new allies, and—most worrisome from a Western perspective—made it harder to detect and destroy. Unless Washington and its allies show a similar adaptability, the war on terrorism won't be won anytime soon, and the death toll is likely to mount.

MALLEABLE MISSIONS

Why do religious terrorists kill? In interviews over the last five years, many terrorists and their supporters have suggested to me that people first join such groups to make the world a better place—at least for the particular populations they aim to serve. Over time, however, militants have told me, terrorism can become a career as much as a passion. Leaders harness humiliation and anomie and turn them into weapons. Jihad becomes addictive, militants report, and with some individuals or groups—the "professional" terrorists—grievances can evolve into greed: for money, political power, status, or attention.

In such "professional" terrorist groups, simply perpetuating their cadres becomes a central goal, and what started out as a moral crusade becomes a sophisticated organization. Ensuring the survival of the group demands flexibility in many areas, but especially in terms of mission. Objectives thus evolve in a variety of ways. Some groups find a new cause once their first one is achieved—much as the March of Dimes broadened its mission from finding a cure for polio to fighting birth defects after the Salk vaccine was developed. Other groups broaden their goals in order to attract a wider variety of recruits. Still other organizations transform themselves into profit-driven organized criminals, or form alliances with groups that have ideologies different from their own, forcing both to adapt. Some terrorist groups hold fast to their original missions. But only the spry survive.

Consider, for example, Egyptian Islamic Jihad (EIJ). EIJ's original objective was to fight the oppressive, secular rulers of Egypt and turn the country into an Islamic state. But the group fell on hard times after its leader, Sheikh Omar Abdel Rahman, was imprisoned in the United States and other EIJ leaders were killed or forced into exile. Thus in the early 1990s, Ayman al-Zawahiri decided to shift the group's sights from its "near enemy"—the secular rulers of Egypt—to the "far enemy," namely the United States and other Western countries. Switching goals in this way allowed the group to align itself with another terrorist aiming to attack the West and able to provide a significant influx of cash: Osama bin Laden. In return for bin Laden's financial assistance, Zawahiri provided some 200 loyal, disciplined, and well-trained followers, who became the core of al Qaeda's leadership.

A second group that has changed its mission over time to secure a more reliable source of funding is the Islamic Movement of Uzbekistan (IMU), which, like EIJ, eventually joined forces with the Taliban and al Qaeda. The IMU's original mission was to topple Uzbekistan's corrupt and repressive post-Soviet dictator, Islam Karimov. Once the IMU formed an alliance with the Taliban's leader, Mullah Omar, however, it began promoting the Taliban's anti-American and anti-Western agenda, also condemning music, cigarettes, sex, and alcohol. This new puritanism reduced its appeal among its original, less-ideological supporters in Uzbekistan—one downside to switching missions.

Even Osama bin Laden himself has changed his objectives over time. The Saudi terrorist inherited an organization devoted to fighting Soviet forces in Afghanistan. But he turned it into a flexible group of ruthless warriors ready to fight on behalf of multiple causes. His first call to holy war, issued in 1992, urged believers to kill American soldiers in Saudi Arabia and the Horn of Africa but barely mentioned Palestine. The second, issued in 1996, was a 40-page document listing atrocities and injustices committed against Muslims, mainly by Western powers. With the release of his third manifesto in February 1998, however, bin Laden began urging his followers to start deliberately targeting American civilians, rather than soldiers. (Some al Qaeda members were reportedly distressed by this shift to civilian targets and left the group.) Although this third declaration mentioned the Palestinian struggle, it was still only one among a litany of grievances. Only in bin Laden's fourth call to arms—issued to the al Jazeera network on October 7, 2001, to coincide with the U.S. aerial bombardment of Afghanistan—did he emphasize Israel's occupation of Palestinian lands and the suffering of Iraqi children under un sanctions, concerns broadly shared in the Islamic world. By extending his appeal, bin Laden sought to turn the war on terrorism into a war between all of Islam and the West. The events of September 11, he charged, split the world into two camps—believers and infidels—and the time had come for "every Muslim to defend his religion."

One of the masterminds of the September 11 attacks, Ramzi bin al-Shibh, later described violence as "the tax" that Muslims must pay "for gaining authority on earth." This comment points to yet another way that al Qaeda's ends have mutated over the years. In his putative autobiography, Zawahiri calls the "New World Order" a source of humiliation for Muslims. It is better, he says, for the youth of Islam to carry arms and defend their religion with pride and dignity than to submit to this humiliation. One of al Qaeda's aims in fighting the West, in other words, has become to restore the dignity of humiliated young Muslims. This idea is similar to the anticolonialist theoretician Frantz Fanon's notion that violence is a "cleansing force" that frees oppressed youth from "inferiority complexes," "despair," and "inaction," making them fearless and restoring their self-respect. The real target audience of violent attacks is therefore not necessarily the victims and their sympathizers, but the perpetrators and their sympathizers. Violence becomes a way to bolster support for the organization and the movement it represents. Hence, among the justifications for "special operations" listed in al Qaeda's terrorist manual are "bringing new members to the organization's ranks" and "boosting Islamic morale and lowering that of the enemy." The United States may have become al Qaeda's principal enemy, but raising the morale of Islamist fighters and their sympathizers is now one of its principal goals.

FRIENDS OF CONVENIENCE

Apart from the flexibility of its mission, another explanation for al Qaeda's remarkable staying power is its willingness to forge broad—and sometimes unlikely—alliances. In an effort to expand his network, bin Laden created the International Islamic Front for Jihad Against the Jews and Crusaders (IIF) in February 1998. In addition to bin Laden and EIJ's Zawahiri, members included the head of Egypt's Gama'a al Islamiya, the secretary-general of the Pakistani religious party known as the Jamiat-ul-Ulema-e-Islam (jui), and the head of Bangladesh's Jihad Movement. Later, the IIF was expanded to include the Pakistani jihadi organizations Lashkar-e-Taiba, Harkat-ul-Mujahideen, and Sipah-e-Sahaba Pakistan, the last an anti-Shi'a sectarian party. Senior al Qaeda lieutenant Abu Zubaydah was captured at a Lashkar-e-Taiba safe house in Faisalabad in March 2002, suggesting that some of Lashkar-e-Taiba's members are facilitating and assisting the movement of al Qaeda members in Pakistan. And Indian sources claim that Lashkar-e-Taiba is now trying to play a role similar to that once played by al Qaeda itself, coordinating and in some cases funding pro-bin Laden networks, especially in Southeast Asia and the Persian Gulf.

In addition to its formal alliances through the IIF, bin Laden's organization has also nurtured ties and now works closely with a variety of still other groups around the world, including Ansar al Islam, based mainly in Iraq and Europe; Jemaah Islamiah in Southeast Asia; Abu Sayyaf and the Moro Islamic Liberation Front in the Philippines; and many Pakistani jihadi groups. In some cases, al Qaeda has provided these allies with funding and direction. In others, the groups have shared camps, operatives, and logistics. Some "franchise groups," such as Jemaah Islamiah, have raised money for joint operations with al Qaeda.

Perhaps most surprising (and alarming) is the increasing evidence that al Qaeda, a Sunni organization, is now cooperating with the Shi'a group Hezbollah, considered to be the most sophisticated terrorist group in the world. Hezbollah, which enjoys backing from Syria and Iran, is based in southern Lebanon and in the lawless "triborder" region of South America, where Paraguay, Brazil, and Argentina meet. The group has also maintained a fundraising presence in the United States since the 1980s. According to the CIA's Tenet, however, the group has lately stepped up its U.S. activities and was recently spotted "casing and surveilling American facilities." Although low-level cooperation between al Qaeda and Hezbollah has been evident for some time—their logistical cooperation was revealed in the trial of al Qaeda operatives involved in the 1998 embassy bombing attacks in east Africa—the two groups have formed a much closer relationship since al Qaeda was evicted from its base in Afghanistan. Representatives of the two groups have lately met up in Lebanon, Paraguay, and an unidentified African country. According to a report in Israel's Ha'aretz newspaper, Imad Mughniyah, who directs Hezbollah in the triborder area, has also been appointed by Iran to coordinate the group's activities with Hamas and Palestinian Islamic Jihad.

The triborder region of South America has become the world's new Libya, a place where terrorists with widely disparate ideologies—Marxist Colombian rebels, American white supremacists, Hamas, Hezbollah, and others—meet to swap tradecraft. Authorities now worry that the more sophisticated groups will invite the American radicals to help them. Moneys raised for terrorist organizations in the United States are often funneled through Latin America, which has also become an important stopover point for operatives entering the United States. Reports that Venezuela's President Hugo Chavez is allowing Colombian rebels and militant Islamist groups to operate in his country are meanwhile becoming more credible, as are claims that Venezuela's Margarita Island has become a terrorist haven.

As these developments suggest and Tenet confirms, "mixing and matching of capabilities, swapping of training, and the use of common facilities" have become the hallmark of professional terrorists today. This fact has been borne out by the leader of a Pakistani jihadi group affiliated with al Qaeda, who recently told me that informal contacts between his group and Hezbollah, Hamas, and others have become common. Operatives with particular skills loan themselves out to different groups, with expenses being covered by the charities that formed to fund the fight against the Soviet Union in Afghanistan.

Meanwhile, the Bush administration's claims that al Qaeda cooperated with the "infidel" (read: secular) Saddam Hussein while he was still in office are now also gaining support, and from a surprising source. Hamid Mir, bin Laden's "official biographer" and an analyst for al Jazeera, spent two weeks filming in Iraq during the war. Unlike most reporters, Mir wandered the country freely and was not embedded with U.S. troops. He reports that he has "personal knowledge" that one of Saddam's intelligence operatives, Farooq Hijazi, tried to contact bin Laden in Afghanistan as early as 1998. At that time, bin Laden was publicly still quite critical of the Iraqi leader, but he had become far more circumspect by November 2001, when Mir interviewed him for the third time. Mir also reports that he met a number of Hezbollah operatives while in Iraq and was taken to a recruitment center there.

NEW-STYLE NETWORKS

Al Qaeda seems to have learned that in order to evade detection in the West, it must adopt some of the qualities of a "virtual network": a style of organization used by American right-wing extremists for operating in environments (such as the United States) that have effective law enforcement agencies. American antigovernment groups refer to this style as "leaderless resistance." The idea was popularized by Louis Beam, the self-described ambassador-at-large, staff propagandist, and "computer terrorist to the Chosen" for Aryan Nations, an American neo-Nazi group. Beam writes that hierarchical organization is extremely dangerous for insurgents, especially in "technologically advanced societies where electronic surveillance can often penetrate the structure, revealing its chain of command." In leaderless organizations, however, "individuals and groups operate independently of each other, and never report to a central headquarters or single leader for direction or instruction, as would those who belong to a typical pyramid organization." Leaders do not issue orders or pay operatives; instead, they inspire small cells or individuals to take action on their own initiative.

Lone-wolf terrorists typically act out of a mixture of ideology and personal grievances. For example, Mir Aimal Kansi, the Pakistani national who shot several CIA employees in 1993, described his actions as "between jihad and tribal revenge"—jihad against America for its support of Israel and revenge against the CIA, which he apparently felt had mistreated his father during Afghanistan's war against the Soviets. Meanwhile, John Allen Muhammad, one of the alleged "Washington snipers," reportedly told a friend that he endorsed the September 11 attacks and disapproved of U.S. policy toward Muslim states, but he appears to have been principally motivated by anger at his ex-wife for keeping him from seeing their children, and some of his victims seem to have been personal enemies. As increasingly powerful weapons become more and more available, lone wolves, who face few political constraints, will become more of a threat, whatever their primary motivation.

The Internet has also greatly facilitated the spread of "virtual" subcultures and has substantially increased the capacity of loosely networked terrorist organizations. For example, Beam's essay on the virtues of "leaderless resistance" has long been available on the Web and, according to researcher Michael Reynolds, has been highlighted by radical Muslim sites. Islamist Web sites also offer on-line training courses in the production of explosives and urge visitors to take action on their own. The "encyclopedia of jihad," parts of which are available on-line, provides instructions for creating "clandestine activity cells," with units for intelligence, supply, planning and preparation, and implementation.

The obstacles these Web sites pose for Western law enforcement are obvious. In one article on the "culture of jihad" available on-line, a Saudi Islamist urges bin Laden's sympathizers to take action without waiting for instructions. "I do not need to meet the Sheikh and ask his permission to carry out some operation," he writes, "the same as I do not need permission to pray, or to think about killing the Jews and the Crusaders that gather on our lands." Nor does it make any difference whether bin Laden is alive or dead: "There are a thousand bin Ladens in this nation. We should not abandon our way, which the Sheikh has paved for you, regardless of the existence of the Sheikh or his absence." And according to U.S. government officials, al Qaeda now uses chat rooms to recruit Latino Muslims with U.S. passports, in the belief that they will arouse less suspicion as operatives than would Arab-Americans. Finally, as the late neo-Nazi William Pierce once told me, using the Web to recruit "leaderless resisters" offers still another advantage: it attracts better-educated young people than do more traditional methods, such as radio programs.

Already the effects of these leaderless cells have been felt. In February 2002, Ahmed Omar Saeed Sheikh, the British national who was recently sentenced to death for his involvement in the abduction and murder of Wall Street Journal reporter Daniel Pearl, warned his Pakistani interrogators that they would soon confront the threat of small cells, working independently of the known organizations that Pakistani President Pervez Musharraf had vowed to shut down. Sure enough, soon after Omar Sheikh made this threat, unidentified terrorists killed 5 people in an Islamabad church known to be frequented by U.S. embassy personnel, and another group killed 11 French military personnel in Karachi in May. And in July, still other unidentified terrorists detonated a truck bomb at the entrance of the U.S. consulate in Karachi, killing 12 Pakistanis.

JOINING THE FAMILY

Virtual links are only part of the problem; terrorists, including members of bin Laden's IIF, have also started to forge ties with traditional organized crime groups, especially in India. One particularly troubling example is the relationship established between Omar Sheikh and an ambitious Indian gangster named Aftab Ansari. Asif Reza Khan, the "chief executive" for Ansari's Indian operations, told interrogators that he received military training at a camp in Khost, Afghanistan, belonging to Lashkar-e-Taiba, and that "leaders of different militant outfits in Pakistan were trying to use his network for the purpose of jihad, whereas [Ansari] was trying to use the militants' networks for underworld operations."

Khan told his interrogators that the don provided money and hideouts to his new partners, in one case transferring $100,000 to Omar Sheikh—money that Omar Sheikh, in turn, wired to Muhammad Atta, the lead hijacker in the September 11 attacks. According to Khan, Ansari viewed the $100,000 gift as an "investment" in a valuable relationship.

Still another set of unlikely links has sprung up in American prisons, where Saudi charities now fund organizations that preach radical Islam. According to Warith Deen Umar, who hired most of the Muslim chaplains currently active in New York State prisons, prisoners who are recent Muslim converts are natural recruits for Islamist organizations. Umar, incidentally, told *The Wall Street Journal* that the September 11 hijackers should be honored as martyrs, and he traveled to Saudi Arabia twice as part of an outreach program designed to spread Salafism (a radical Muslim movement) in U.S. prisons.

Another organization now active in U.S. prisons is Jamaat ul-Fuqra, a terrorist group committed to purifying Islam through violence. (Daniel Pearl was abducted and murdered in Pakistan while attempting to interview the group's leader, Sheikh Gilani, to investigate the claim that Richard Reid—who attempted to blow up an international flight with explosives hidden in his shoes—was acting under Gilani's orders.) The group functions much like a cult in the United States; members live in poverty in compounds, some of which are heavily armed. Its members have been convicted of fraud, murder, and several bombings, but so far, most of their crimes have been relatively small scale. Clement Rodney Hampton-El, however, convicted of participating with Omar Abdel Rahman in a 1993 plot to blow up New York City landmarks, was linked to the group, and U.S. law enforcement authorities worry that the Fuqra has since come under the influence of al Qaeda.

Still another surprising source of al Qaeda recruits is Tablighi Jamaat (TJ), a revivalist organization that aims at creating better Muslims through "spiritual jihad": good deeds, contemplation, and proselytizing. According to the historian Barbara Metcalf, TJ has traditionally functioned as a self-help group, much like Alcoholics Anonymous, and most specialists claim that it is no more prone to violence than are the Seventh-Day Adventists, with whom TJ is frequently compared. But several Americans known to have trained in al Qaeda camps were brought to Southwest Asia by TJ and appear to have been recruited into jihadi organizations while traveling under TJ auspices. For example, Jose Padilla (an American now being held as an "enemy combatant" for planning to set off a "dirty" radiological bomb in the United States) was a member of TJ, as were Richard Reid and John Walker Lindh (the so-called American Taliban). According to prosecutors, the "Lackawanna Six" group (an alleged al Qaeda sleeper cell from a Buffalo, New York, suburb) similarly first went to Pakistan to receive TJ religious training before proceeding to the al Farooq training camp in Afghanistan. A Pakistani TJ member told me that jihadi groups openly recruit at the organization's central headquarters in Raiwind, Pakistan, including at the mosque. And TJ members in Boston say that a lot of Muslims end up treating the group, which is now active in American inner cities and prisons, as a gateway to jihadi organizations.

As such evidence suggests, although it may have been founded to create better individuals, TJ has produced offshoots that have evolved into more militant outfits. In October 1995, Pakistani authorities uncovered a military plot to assassinate Prime Minister Benazir Bhutto and establish a theocracy. Most of the officers involved in the attempted coup were members of TJ. The group is said to have been strongly influenced by retired Lieutenant General Javed Nasir, who served as Pakistan's intelligence chief from 1990 to 1993 but was sacked under pressure from the United States for his support of militant Islamists around the world.

Totalitarian Islamist revivalism has become the ideology of the dystopian new world order. In an earlier era, radicals might have described their grievances through other ideological lenses, perhaps anarchism, Marxism, or Nazism. Today they choose extreme Islamism.

Radical transnational Islam, divorced from its countries of origin, appeals to some jobless youths in depressed parts of Europe and the United States. As the French scholar Olivier Roy points out, leaders of radical Islamic groups often come from the middle classes, many of them having trained in technical fields, but their followers tend be working-class dropouts.

Focusing on economic and social alienation may help explain why such a surprising array of groups has proved willing to join forces with al Qaeda. Some white supremacists and extremist Christians applaud al Qaeda's rejectionist goals and may eventually contribute to al Qaeda missions. Already a Swiss neo-Nazi named Albert Huber has called for his followers to join forces with Islamists. Indeed, Huber sat on the board of directors of the Bank al Taqwa, which the U.S. government accuses of being a major donor to al Qaeda. Meanwhile, Matt Hale, leader of the white-supremacist World Church of the Creator, has published a book indicting Jews and Israelis as the real culprits behind the attacks of September 11. These groups, along with Horst Mahler (a founder of the radical leftist German group the Red Army Faction), view the September 11 attacks as the first shot in a war against globalization, a phenomenon that they fear will exterminate national cultures. Leaderless resisters drawn from the ranks of white supremacists or other groups are not currently capable of carrying out massive attacks on their own, but they may be if they join forces with al Qaeda.

MODERN METHODOLOGY

Al Qaeda has lately adopted innovative tactics as well as new alliances. Two new approaches are particularly alarming to intelligence officials: efforts to use surface-to-air missiles to shoot down aircraft and attempts to acquire chemical, nuclear, or biological weapons.

In November 2002, terrorists launched two shoulder-fired SA-7 missiles at an Israeli passenger jet taking off from Mombasa, Kenya, with 271 passengers on board. Investigators say that the missiles came from the same batch as those used in an earlier, also unsuccessful attack on a U.S. military jet in Saudi Arabia. And intelligence officials believe that Hezbollah contacts were used to smuggle the missiles into Kenya from Somalia.

Meanwhile, according to Barton Gellman of *The Washington Post*, documents seized in Pakistan in March 2003 reveal that al Qaeda has acquired the necessary materials for producing botulinum and salmonella toxins and the chemical agent cyanide—and is close to developing a workable plan for producing anthrax, a far more lethal agent. Even more worrisome is the possibility that al Qaeda, perhaps working with Hezbollah or other terrorist groups, will recruit scientists with access to sophisticated nuclear or biological weapons programs, possibly, but not necessarily, ones that are state-run.

To fight such dangerous tactics, Western governments will also need to adapt. In addition to military, intelligence, and law enforcement responses, Washington should start thinking about how U.S. policies are perceived by potential recruits to terrorist organizations. The United States too often ignores the unintended consequences of its actions, disregarding, for example, the negative message sent by Washington's ongoing neglect of Afghanistan and of the chaos in postwar Iraq. If the United States allows Iraq to become another failed state, groups both inside and outside the country that support al Qaeda's goals will benefit.

Terrorists, after all, depend on the broader population for support, and the right U.S. policies could do much to diminish the appeal of rejectionist groups. It does not make sense in such an atmosphere to keep U.S. markets closed to Pakistani textiles or to insist on protecting intellectual property with regard to drugs that needy populations in developing countries cannot hope to afford.

In countries where extremist religious schools promote terrorism, Washington should help develop alternative schools rather than attempt to persuade the local government to shut down radical madrasahs. In Pakistan, many children end up at extremist schools because their parents cannot afford the alternatives; better funding for secular education could therefore make a positive difference.

The appeal of radical Islam to alienated youth living in the West is perhaps an even more difficult problem to address. Uneasiness with liberal values, discomfort with uncertain identities, and resentment of the privileged are perennial problems in modern societies. What is new today is that radical leaders are using the tools of globalization to construct new, transnational identities based on death cults, turning grievances and alienation into powerful weapons. To fight these tactics will require getting the input not just of moderate Muslims, but of radical Islamist revivalists who oppose violence.

To prevent terrorists from acquiring new weapons, meanwhile, Western governments must make it harder for radicals to get their hands on them. Especially important is the need to continue upgrading security at vulnerable nuclear sites, many of which, in Russia and other former Soviet states, are still vulnerable to theft. The global system of disease monitoring—a system sorely tested during the SARs epidemic—should also be upgraded, since biological attacks may be difficult to distinguish from natural outbreaks. Only by matching the radical innovation shown by professional terrorists such as al Qaeda—and by showing a similar willingness to adapt and adopt new methods and new ways of thinking—can the United States and its allies make themselves safe from the ongoing threat of terrorist attack?

10

The Future
of Political Islam

Graham E. Fuller

IT'S NOT OVER 'TIL IT'S OVER

Were the attacks of September 11, 2001, the final gasp of Islamic radicalism or the opening salvo of a more violent confrontation between Muslim extremists and the West? And what does the current crisis imply for the future of the Islamic world itself? Will Muslims recoil from the violence and sweeping anti-Westernism unleashed in their name, or will they allow Osama bin Laden and his cohort to shape the character of future relations between Muslims and the West?

The answers to these questions lie partly in the hands of the Bush administration. The war on terrorism has already dealt a major blow to the personnel, infrastructure, and operations of bin Laden's al Qaeda network. Just as important, it has burst the bubble of euphoria and sense of invincibility among radical Islamists that arose from the successful jihad against the Soviet occupation of Afghanistan. But it is not yet clear whether the war will ultimately alleviate or merely exacerbate the current tensions in the Muslim world.

Depending on one's perspective, the attacks on the World Trade Center and the Pentagon can be seen either as a success, evidence that a few activists can deal a grievous blow to a superpower in the name of their cause, or as a failure, since the attackers brought on the demise of their state sponsor and most likely of their own organization while galvanizing nearly global

Graham Fuller, "The Future of Political Islam," *Foreign Affairs*, March–April 2002, p. 48. Reprinted by permission.

opposition. To help the latter lesson triumph, the United States will have to move beyond the war's first phase, which has punished those directly responsible for the attacks, and address the deeper sources of political violence and terror in the Muslim world today.

THE MANY FACES OF ISLAMISM

President Bush has repeatedly stressed that the war on terrorism is not a war on Islam. But by seeking to separate Islam from politics, the West ignores the reality that the two are intricately intertwined across a broad swath of the globe from northern Africa to Southeast Asia. Transforming the Muslim environment is not merely a matter of rewriting school textbooks or demanding a less anti-Western press. The simple fact is that political Islam, or Islamism—defined broadly as the belief that the Koran and the Hadith (Traditions of the Prophet's Life) have something important to say about the way society and governance should be ordered—remains the most powerful ideological force in that part of the world.

The Islamist phenomenon is hardly uniform, however; multiple forms of it are spreading, evolving, and diversifying. Today one encounters Islamists who may be either radical or moderate, political or apolitical, violent or quietist, traditional or modernist, democratic or authoritarian. The oppressive Taliban of Afghanistan and the murderous Algerian Armed Islamic Group (known by its French acronym, GIA) lie at one fanatic point of a compass that also includes Pakistan's peaceful and apolitical preaching-to-the-people movement, the Tablighi Jamaat; Egypt's mainstream conservative parliamentary party, the Muslim Brotherhood; and Turkey's democratic and modernist Fazilet/Ak Party.

Turkey's apolitical Nur movement embraces all aspects of science as compatible with Islam because secular scientific knowledge reinforces the wonder of God's world. Indonesia's syncretic Nahdatul Ulama eschews any Islamic state at all in its quest to further appreciation of God's role in human life. Islamist feminist movements are studying the Koran and Islamic law (the shari`a) in order to interpret the teachings for themselves and distinguish between what their religion clearly stipulates and those traditions arbitrarily devised and enforced by patriarchal leaders (such as mandatory head-to-toe covering or the ban on female driving in Saudi Arabia). These are but a few among the vast array of movements that work in the media, manage Web sites, conduct massive welfare programs, run schools and hospitals, represent flourishing Muslim nongovernmental organizations, and exert a major impact on Muslim life.

Islamism has become, in fact, the primary vehicle and vocabulary of most political discourse throughout the Muslim world. When Westerners talk about political ideals, they naturally hark back to the Magna Carta, the American

Revolution, and the French Revolution. Muslims go back to the Koran and the Hadith to derive general principles about good governance (including the ruler's obligation to consult the people) and concepts of social and economic justice. Neither Islam nor Islamism says much about concrete state institutions, and frankly nobody knows exactly what a modern Islamic state should look like—since few have ever existed and none provides a good model. But Islamists today use general Islamic ideals as a touchstone for criticizing, attacking, or even trying to overthrow what are perceived as authoritarian, corrupt, incompetent, and illegitimate regimes.

No other ideology has remotely comparable sway in the Muslim world. The region's nationalist parties are weak and discredited, and nationalism itself has often been absorbed into Islamism; the left is marginalized and in disarray; liberal democrats cannot even muster enough supporters to stage a demonstration in any Muslim capital. Like it or not, therefore, various forms of Islamism will be the dominant intellectual current in the region for some time to come—and the process is still in its infancy. In the end, modern liberal governance is more likely to take root through organically evolving liberal Islamist trends at the grassroots level than from imported Western modules of "instant democracy."

A DYNAMIC PHENOMENON

Most Western observers tend to look at the phenomenon of political Islam as if it were a butterfly in a collection box, captured and skewered for eternity, or as a set of texts unbendingly prescribing a single path. This is why some scholars who examine its core writings proclaim Islam to be incompatible with democracy—as if any religion in its origins was about democracy at all.

Such observers have the question wrong. The real issue is not what Islam is, but what Muslims want. People of all sorts of faiths can rapidly develop interpretations of their religion that justify practically any political quest. This process, moreover, is already underway among Muslims. Contemporary Islam is a dynamic phenomenon. It includes not only bin Laden and the Taliban, but also liberals who are clearly embarking on their own Reformation with potentially powerful long-term consequences. Deeply entrenched traditionalists find these latter stirrings a threat, but many more Muslims, including many Islamists, see such efforts to understand eternal values in contemporary terms as essential to a living faith.

Regrettably, until recently Islam had been living (with striking periodic exceptions) in a state of intellectual stagnation for many hundreds of years. Western colonizers further vitiated and marginalized Islamic thought and institutions, and postindependence leadership has done no better, tending to draw on quasi-fascist Western models of authoritarian control. Only now is Islam emerging into a period of renewed creativity, freedom, and independence. Much of this new activity, ironically, is occurring in the freedom of the West, where dozens of Islamic institutes are developing new ideas and employing modern communications to spur debate and disseminate information.

The process of diversification and evolution within modern Islamism is driven by multiple internal forces, but these developments are always ultimately contingent on the tolerance of local regimes, the nature of local politics, and the reigning pattern of global power. Most regimes see almost any form of political Islam as a threat, since it embodies a major challenge to their unpopular, failing, and illegitimate presidents-for-life or isolated monarchs. How the regime responds to the phenomenon often plays a major role in determining how the local Islamist movement develops.

Does the regime permit elections and free political discussion? How repressive is it, and how violent is the political culture in which it operates? How do existing economic and social conditions affect the political process? The answers to these questions go a long way toward describing how Islamists—like all other political actors—will behave in any particular country. That said, these days nearly all Islamists push hard for democracy, believing that they will benefit from it and flourish within it. They also have discovered the importance of human rights—at least in the political field—precisely because they are usually the primary victims of the absence of rights, filling regional jails in disproportionate numbers.

Some skepticism is due, of course, about the ability of Islamists to run effective and moderate governments, especially when the three Islamic state models to date—Iran, Sudan, and the Taliban's Afghanistan—have all failed dramatically in this area. Only Iran has lately shown signs of exciting evolution within an Islamic framework. But it is worth recalling that all of those regimes came to power by social revolution, military coup, or civil war, virtually guaranteeing continuing despotism regardless of which party was in charge.

The true test of any Islamist party comes when it gains office by the ballot box and must then adhere while in power to the democratic norms it touted in opposition. History unfortunately gives few precedents here. Turkey's brief experience under an elected Islamist-led coalition comes closest, but the government was removed by the military after a year of mixed performance, leaving the experiment unfinished. Secular Turks continue to elect Islamist mayors in major cities across the country, however, including Istanbul and Ankara, because they deliver what constituents want.

Americans brought up to venerate the separation of church and state may wonder whether a movement with an explicit religious vision can ever create a democratic, tolerant, and pluralistic polity. But if Christian Democrats can do it, there is no reason in principle why Islamists cannot. This is what the cleric President Mohammed Khatami is trying to achieve in Iran, in fact, although his efforts are being blocked by a hard-line clerical faction. Non-Muslims should understand that democratic values are latent in Islamic thought if one wants to look for them, and that it would be more natural and organic for the Muslim world to derive contemporary liberal practices from its own sources than to import them wholesale from foreign cultures. The key question is whether it will actually do so.

WHO'S BESIEGING WHOM?

The liberal evolution of political Islam faces some formidable obstacles. The first, as noted, comes from the local political scene, where Islamists are routinely suppressed, jailed, tortured, and executed. Such circumstances encourage the emergence of secret, conspiratorial, and often armed groups rather than liberal ones.

The second obstacle comes from international politics, which often pushes Islamist movements and parties in an unfortunate direction. A familiar phenomenon is the Muslim national liberation movement. In more than a dozen countries, large, oppressed Muslim minorities, who are also ethnically different from their rulers, have sought autonomy or independence—witness the Palestinians, Chechens, Chinese Uighurs, Filipino Moros, and Kashmiris, among others. In these cases, Islam serves to powerfully bolster national liberation struggles by adding a "holy" religious element to an emerging ethnic struggle. These causes have attracted a kind of Muslim "foreign legion" of radicalized, volunteer mujahideen, some of whom have joined al Qaeda.

A third obstacle comes from the Islamists' own long list of grievances against the forces and policies perceived to be holding Muslims back in the contemporary world, many of them associated with liberalism's supposed avatar, the United States. The litany includes U.S. support for authoritarianism in the Muslim world in the name of stability or material interests such as ensuring the flow of oil, routine U.S. backing of Israeli policies, and Washington's failure to press for democratic political processes out of fear that they might bring Islamist groups to power.

Islamists, too, deserve criticism for playing frequently opportunistic political games—like so many other fledgling parties. Where they exist legally, they often adopt radical postures on Islamic issues to embarrass the government. The major Islamist pas movement in Malaysia, for example—which now governs two of the country's ten states—has called for full implementation of the shari`a and application of traditional Muslim punishments (including amputations and stoning), in part to show up the poor Islamic credentials of the central government. In Egypt and Kuwait, meanwhile, Islamist groups regularly call for more conservative social measures, partly to score political points, and have often inhibited the intellectual freedom on Islamic issues which these societies desperately require. Such posturing tends to bid up the level of Islamic strictness within the country in question in a closed atmosphere of Islamic political correctness. Still, most Islamists have quite concrete domestic agendas related to local politics and social issues that are far removed from the transnational, apocalyptic visions of a bin Laden.

Ironically, even as Westerners feel threatened by Islam, most in the Muslim world feel themselves besieged by the West, a reality only dimly grasped in the United States. They see the international order as dramatically skewed against them and their interests, in a world where force and the potential for force dominate the agenda. They are overwhelmed by feelings of political impotence. Muslim rulers fear offending their protectors in Washington, Muslim publics have little or no influence over policy within their own states, bad leaders cannot be changed, and public expression of dissent is punished, often brutally. This is the "stability" in the Middle East to which the United States seems wedded.

Under such conditions, it should not be surprising that these frustrated populations perceive the current war against terrorism as functionally a war against Islam. Muslim countries are the chief target, they contend, Muslims everywhere are singled out for censure and police attention, and U.S. power works its will across the region with little regard for deeper Muslim concerns. A vicious circle exists: dissatisfaction leads to anti-regime action, which leads to repression, which in turn leads to terrorism, U.S. military intervention, and finally further dissatisfaction. Samuel Huntington's theory of a "clash of civilizations" is seemingly vindicated before the Muslim world's eyes.

THEIR MUSLIM PROBLEM—AND OURS

Several regimes have decided to play the dangerous game of trying to "out-Islam the Islamists," embracing harsh social and intellectual interpretations of Islam themselves so as to bolster their credentials against Islamist opposition. Thus in Egypt, the government-controlled University of al-Azhar, a prestigious voice in interpreting Islam, issues its own brand of intolerant fundamentalist rulings; Pakistan does something similar. The issue here is not the actual Islamist agenda but whose Islamist writ will dominate. Islam is simply the vehicle and coinage of the struggle between the state and its challengers.

In a comparable fashion, Islam and Islamist movements today provide a key source of identity to peoples intent on strengthening their social cohesion against Western cultural assault. Religious observance is visibly growing across the region, often accompanied by the "Arabization" of customs in clothing, food, mosque architecture, and ritual—even in areas such as Africa and East Asia, where no such customs had previously existed and where claims to cultural authenticity or tradition are weak to say the least. Association with the broader umma, the international Muslim community, is attractive because it creates new bonds of solidarity that can be transformed into increased international clout.

Islam and Islamist concepts, finally, are often recruited into existing geopolitical struggles. In the 1980s, for example, the rivalry between Saudi Arabia and Iran, often cloaked as a simple Sunni versus Shi`a competition, was as much political as it was religious. The Saudis hoped that their puritanical and intolerant Wahhabi vision of Islam would prevail over the Iranian revolutionary vision. For better or worse it did, partly because the Saudis could bankroll movements and schools far outside Saudi borders, and partly because many Sunnis considered Iran's Shi`ism anathema. The radical Islamic groups one sees today in the Philippines, Central Asia, the Caucasus, Afghanistan, and Pakistan, among other places, are partly the fruits of this export of Wahhabism, nourished by local conditions, ideological and material needs, and grievances.

Islam has thus become a vehicle and vocabulary for the expression of many different agendas in the Muslim world. The West is not at war with the religion itself, but it is indeed challenged by the radicalism that some groups have embraced. Muslims may too readily blame the West for their own problems, but their frustrations and current grievances are real. Indeed, the objective indicators of living conditions in the Islamic world—whether political, economic, or social—are generally turning down. Cultures and communities under siege naturally tend to opt for essentialism, seeking comfort and commonality in a back-to-basics view of religion, a narrowing and harshening of cultural and nationalist impulses, and a return to traditional community values. Muslims under pressure today are doing just this, retreating back to the solid certainties of essentialist Islam while their societies are in chaos. When Grozny was flattened by Russian troops, the Chechens declared Islamic law— clinging to an unquestioned traditional moral framework for comfort, familiarity, and reassuring moral discipline.

As a result, even as liberalization is occurring within some Islamist movements, much of the Islamic community is heading in the other direction, growing more austere and less tolerant and modernist. The same harsh conditions produce a quest for heroes, strongmen, and potential saviors. One of the saddest commentaries today, in fact, is the Muslim thirst for heroes who will stand up and defy the dominant U.S.-led order—a quest that has led them to cheer on the Saddam Husseins and bin Ladens of the world.

The Muslim world is therefore in a parlous condition. Some in the West may think that Islam's problem is not their problem, that Muslims just need to face reality and get on with it. But the September 11 attacks showed that in a globalized world, their problems can become our problems. The U.S. tendency to disregard popular Muslim concerns as Washington cooperates with oppressive and insecure regimes fosters an environment in which acts of terrorism become thinkable and, worse, even gratifying in the eyes of the majority. The vast bulk of Muslims, of course, will go no further than to cheer on those who lash out. But such an environment is perhaps the most dangerous of all, because it legitimizes and encourages not the tolerant and liberalizing Islamists and peacemakers, but the negativistic hard-liners and rejectionists.

THE SILENT MUSLIM MAJORITY

Few Muslims around the world want to inflict endless punishment on the United States or go to war with it. Most of them recognize what happened on September 11 as a monstrous crime. But they still hope that the attacks will serve as a "lesson" to the United States to wake up and change its policies toward the Middle East. Most would emphatically reject, however, a key contention of President George W. Bush, that those who sympathize with the attacks are people who "hate freedom." Nearly all Muslims worldwide admire and aspire to the same political freedoms that Americans take for granted. A central complaint of theirs, in fact, is that U.S. policies have helped block the freedoms necessary to develop their personal and national capacities in comparable ways.

Muslim societies may have multiple problems, but hating American political values is not among them. U.S. policymakers would be wise to drop this simplistic, inaccurate, and self-serving description of the problem. They should instead consider what steps the United States can take to spread those political values to areas where they have been noticeable chiefly by their absence.

For Muslims who live in the West, the attacks of September 11 posed a moment of self-definition. However acutely attuned they might have been to the grievances of the broader Muslim world, the vast majority recognized that it was Western values and practices with which they identified most. This reaction suggests there may be a large silent majority in the Islamic world, caught between the powerful forces of harsh and entrenched regimes on the one hand and the inexorable will of an angry superpower on the other. Right now they have few channels of expression between acceptance of a miserable status quo and siding with the world-wreckers' vision of apocalyptic confrontation. How can the United States help mobilize this camp? What can make the members of this silent majority think they are anything but ringside spectators at a patently false clash of civilizations unfolding before their eyes?

Today most moderate Islamists, as well as the few Muslim liberals around, maintain a discouragingly low profile. Although they have condemned the September 11 attacks, they have been reluctant to scrutinize the conditions of their own societies that contribute to these problems. This myopia stems partly from an anxiety about signing on to the sweeping, unpredictable, and open-ended U.S. agenda for its war on terrorism. That said, however, it also stems from a failure of will to preach hard truths when society is under siege.

Given the authoritarian realities of life in the region, what acceptable outlets of expression are available? Islamists and other social leaders should find some way of setting forth a critique of Muslim society that will galvanize a call for change. Even if presidents-for-life cannot be removed, other demands can be made—for better services, more rights, freer economies. It is inexcusable that a Muslim civilization that led the entire world for a thousand years in the arts and sciences today ranks near the bottom of world literacy rates. Although conditions for women vary widely in the Muslim world, overall their levels of education and social engagement are depressingly low—not just a human scandal but also a prime indicator of underdevelopment. When highly traditional or fanatic groups attempt to define Islam in terms of a social order from a distant past, voices should be raised to deny them that monopoly.

The United States, meanwhile, should contribute to this effort by beginning to engage overseas Muslims vigorously, including those Islamic clerics who enjoy great respect and authority as men of uncompromised integrity. Both sides will benefit from a dialogue that initially will reveal deep fissures in thought and approach, but that over time may begin to bridge numerous gaps. Many of these clerics represent undeniably moderate forces within political Islam, but their own understanding of the West, though far from uniformly hostile, is flawed and often initially unsympathetic. They could learn from visits to the United States and dialogue with Americans—if ever they were granted visas.

It is worth noting, however, that this process will be fought hard by elements on both sides. The first group of opponents will be the friendly Muslim tyrants themselves, those regimes that stifle critiques from respected independent clerics and restrict their movements. The second group of opponents will come from the United States and will try to discredit the Muslim travelers by pointing to rash statements about Israel they may have made at one point or another. Given the passions aroused in the Middle East by the Arab-Israeli conflict, very few if any prominent Muslim figures will have the kind of liberal record of interfaith dialogue and tolerance that Americans find natural and appropriate. That should not disqualify them as potential interlocutors, however. Given the importance of the issues involved and the realities of the situation, the initial litmus test for being included in the conversation should be limited to a prohibition on incitement to terrorism and advocacy of war.

TURKISH DELIGHT?

Americans need to be mindful of the extent to which Islam is entwined with politics throughout the Muslim world. This connection may pose problems, but it is a reality that cannot be changed by mere appeals for secularism. The United States should avoid the Manichean formulation adopted by Bush that nations are either "with us or with the terrorists"; that is not what is going on, any more than Islamism is what bin Laden calls "a struggle between Islam and unbelief." The real story is the potential rise of forces in the Muslim world that will change not Islam itself, but rather the human understanding of Islam, laying the groundwork for a Muslim Reformation and the eventual emergence of a politics at once authentically Islamist yet also authentically liberal and democratic. The encouragement of such trends should be an important objective of U.S. policy.

One successful model that merits emulation is Turkey. This is not because Turkey is "secular"; in fact, Turkish "secularism" is actually based on total state control and even repression of religion. Turkey is becoming a model precisely because Turkish democracy is beating back rigid state ideology and slowly and reluctantly permitting the emergence of Islamist movements and parties that reflect tradition, a large segment of public opinion, and the country's developing democratic spirit. Political Islam in Turkey has evolved rapidly out of an initially narrow and nondemocratic understanding of Islam into a relatively responsible force, whether it overlaps entirely with American ideals or not.

Other promising cases to explore include Kuwait, Bahrain, Morocco, Jordan, Yemen, Malaysia, and Indonesia—all of which are at differing stages of political and social liberalization and evolution. All are working to avoid the social explosion that comes with repression of Islamic politics as a vehicle of change. Opening the political process enables people to sort out the effective moderates from the rhetorical radicals and reactionaries. Significantly, citizens of these states have not been prominent among the major terrorist groups of the world, unlike citizens of the U.S. allies Egypt and Saudi Arabia.

Most great religions have elements of both tolerance and intolerance built into them: intolerance because they believe they carry the truth, perhaps the sole truth, and tolerance because they also speak of humanity, the common origins of mankind, concepts of divine justice, and a humane order for all. Violence does not flow from religion alone—even bigoted religion. After all, the greatest horrors and killing machines in history stemmed from the Western, secular ideologies of fascism and communism. Religion is not about to vanish from the face of the earth, even in the most advanced Western nations, and certainly not in the Islamic world. The West will have to deal with this reality and help open up these embittered societies. In the process, the multiple varieties of Islam—the key political realities of today—will either evolve in positive directions with popular support, or else be discredited when they deliver little but venom. Muslim publics will quickly know the difference when offered a choice.

Terrorists must be punished. But will Washington limit itself to a merely punitive agenda to treat only the symptoms of crisis in the Muslim world? A just settlement for the Palestinians and support of regional democratization remain among the key weapons that can fight the growth of terrorism. It will be a disaster for the United States, and another cruel chapter in the history of the Muslim world, if the war on terrorism fails to liberalize these battered societies and, instead, exacerbates those very conditions that contribute to the virulent anti-Americanism of today. If a society and its politics are violent and unhappy, its mode of religious expression is likely to be just the same.

11

America's Imperial Strategy

G. John Ikenberry

THE LURES OF PREEMPTION

In the shadows of the Bush administration's war on terrorism, sweeping new ideas are circulating about U.S. grand strategy and the restructuring of today's unipolar world. They call for American unilateral and preemptive, even preventive, use of force, facilitated if possible by coalitions of the willing—but ultimately unconstrained by the rules and norms of the international community. At the extreme, these notions form a neoimperial vision in which the United States arrogates to itself the global role of setting standards, determining threats, using force, and meting out justice. It is a vision in which sovereignty becomes more absolute for America even as it becomes more conditional for countries that challenge Washington's standards of internal and external behavior. It is a vision made necessary—at least in the eyes of its advocates—by the new and apocalyptic character of contemporary terrorist threats and by America's unprecedented global dominance. These radical strategic ideas and impulses could transform today's world order in a way that the end of the Cold War, strangely enough, did not.

The exigencies of fighting terrorism in Afghanistan and the debate over intervening in Iraq obscure the profundity of this geopolitical challenge. Blueprints have not been produced, and Yalta-style summits have not been convened, but actions are afoot to dramatically alter the political order that the

G. John Ikenberry, "America's Imperial Ambition," *Foreign Affairs*, Sept.–Oct. 2002, p. 44. Reprinted by permission.

United States has built with its partners since the 1940s. The twin new realities of our age—catastrophic terrorism and American unipolar power—do necessitate a rethinking of the organizing principles of international order. America and the other major states do need a new consensus on terrorist threats, weapons of mass destruction (WMD), the use of force, and the global rules of the game. This imperative requires a better appreciation of the ideas coming out of the administration. But in turn, the administration should understand the virtues of the old order that it wishes to displace.

America's nascent neoimperial grand strategy threatens to rend the fabric of the international community and political partnerships precisely at a time when that community and those partnerships are urgently needed. It is an approach fraught with peril and likely to fail. It is not only politically unsustainable but diplomatically harmful. And if history is a guide, it will trigger antagonism and resistance that will leave America in a more hostile and divided world.

PROVEN LEGACIES

The mainstream of American foreign policy has been defined since the 1940s by two grand strategies that have built the modern international order. One is realist in orientation, organized around containment, deterrence, and the maintenance of the global balance of power. Facing a dangerous and expansive Soviet Union after 1945, the United States stepped forward to fill the vacuum left by a waning British Empire and a collapsing European order to provide a counter-weight to Stalin and his Red Army.

The touchstone of this strategy was containment, which sought to deny the Soviet Union the ability to expand its sphere of influence. Order was maintained by managing the bipolar balance between the American and Soviet camps. Stability was achieved through nuclear deterrence. For the first time, nuclear weapons and the doctrine of mutual assured destruction made war between the great powers irrational. But containment and global power-balancing ended with the collapse of the Soviet Union in 1991. Nuclear deterrence is no longer the defining logic of the existing order, although it remains a recessed feature that continues to impart stability in relations among China, Russia, and the West.

This strategy has yielded a bounty of institutions and partnerships for America. The most important have been the NATO and U.S.-Japan alliances, American-led security partnerships that have survived the end of the Cold War by providing a bulwark for stability through commitment and reassurance. The United States maintains a forward presence in Europe and East Asia; its alliance partners gain security protection as well as a measure of regularity in their relationship with the world's leading military power. But Cold War balancing has yielded more than a utilitarian alliance structure; it has generated a political order that has value in itself.

This grand strategy presupposes a loose framework of consultations and agreements to resolve differences: the great powers extend to each other the respect of equals, and they accommodate each other until vital interests come into play. The domestic affairs of these states remain precisely that—domestic. The great powers compete with each other, and although war is not unthinkable, sober statecraft and the balance of power offer the best hope for stability and peace.

George W. Bush ran for president emphasizing some of these themes, describing his approach to foreign policy as "new realism": the focus of American efforts should shift away from Clinton-era preoccupations with nation building, international social work, and the promiscuous use of force, and toward cultivating great-power relations and rebuilding the nation's military. Bush's efforts to integrate Russia into the Western security order have been the most important manifestation of this realist grand strategy at work. The moderation in Washington's confrontational rhetoric toward China also reflects this emphasis. If the major European and Asian states play by the rules, the great-power order will remain stable. (In a way, it is precisely because Europe is not a great power—or at least seems to eschew the logic of great-power politics—that it is now generating so much discord with the United States.)

The other grand strategy, forged during World War II as the United States planned the reconstruction of the world economy, is liberal in orientation. It seeks to build order around institutionalized political relations among integrated market democracies, supported by an opening of economies. This agenda was not simply an inspiration of American businessmen and economists, however. There have always been geopolitical goals as well. Whereas America's realist grand strategy was aimed at countering Soviet power, its liberal grand strategy was aimed at avoiding a return to the 1930s, an era of regional blocs, trade conflict, and strategic rivalry. Open trade, democracy, and multilateral institutional relations went together. Underlying this strategy was the view that a rule-based international order, especially one in which the United States uses its political weight to derive congenial rules, will most fully protect American interests, conserve its power, and extend its influence.

This grand strategy has been pursued through an array of postwar initiatives that look disarmingly like "low politics": the Bretton Woods institutions, the World Trade Organization (WTO), and the Organization for Economic Cooperation and Development are just a few examples. Together, they form a complex layer cake of integrative initiatives that bind the democratic industrialized world together. During the 1990s, the United States continued to pursue this liberal grand strategy. Both the first Bush and the Clinton administrations attempted to articulate a vision of world order that was not dependent on an external threat or an explicit policy of balance of power. Bush the elder talked about the importance of the transatlantic community and articulated ideas about a more fully integrated Asia-Pacific region. In both cases, the strategy offered a positive vision of alliance and partnership built around common values, tradition, mutual self-interest, and the preservation of stability. The Clinton administration likewise attempted to describe the post-Cold War order in terms of the expansion of democracy and open markets. In this vision, democracy provided the foundation for global and regional community, and trade and capital flows were forces for political reform and integration.

The current Bush administration is not eager to brandish this Clinton-looking grand strategy, but it still invokes that strategy's ideas in various ways. Support for Chinese entry into the WTO is based on the liberal anticipation that free markets and integration into the Western economic order will create pressures for Chinese political reform and discourage a belligerent foreign policy. Administration support for last year's multilateral trade-negotiating round in Doha, Qatar, also was premised on the economic and political benefits of freer trade. After September 11, U.S. Trade Representative Robert Zoellick even linked trade expansion authority to the fight against terrorism: trade, growth, integration, and political stability go together. Richard Haass, policy planning director at the State Department, argued recently that "the principal aim of American foreign policy is to integrate other countries and organizations into arrangements that will sustain a world consistent with U.S. interests and values"—again, an echo of the liberal grand strategy. The administration's recent protectionist trade actions in steel and agriculture have triggered such a loud outcry around the world precisely because governments are worried that the United States might be retreating from this postwar liberal strategy.

AMERICA'S HISTORIC BARGAINS

These two grand strategies are rooted in divergent, even antagonistic, intellectual traditions. But over the last 50 years they have worked remarkably well together. The realist grand strategy created a political rationale for establishing major security commitments around the world. The liberal strategy created a positive agenda for American leadership. The United States could exercise its power and achieve its national interests, but it did so in a way that helped deepen the fabric of international community. American power did not destabilize world order; it helped create it. The development of rule-based agreements and political-security partnerships was good both for the United States and for much of the world. By the end of the 1990s, the result was an international political order of unprecedented size and success: a global coalition of democratic states tied together through markets, institutions, and security partnerships.

This international order was built on two historic bargains. One was the U.S. commitment to provide its European and Asian partners with security protection and access to American markets, technology, and supplies within an open world economy. In return, these countries agreed to be reliable partners providing diplomatic, economic, and logistical support for the United

States as it led the wider Western postwar order. The other is the liberal bargain that addressed the uncertainties of American power. East Asian and European states agreed to accept American leadership and operate within an agreed-upon political-economic system. The United States, in response, opened itself up and bound itself to its partners. In effect, the United States built an institutionalized coalition of partners and reinforced the stability of these mutually beneficial relations by making itself more "user-friendly"— that is, by playing by the rules and creating ongoing political processes that facilitated consultation and joint decision-making. The United States made its power safe for the world, and in return the world agreed to live within the U.S. system. These bargains date from the 1940s, but they continue to shore up the post–Cold War order. The result has been the most stable and prosperous international system in world history. But new ideas within the Bush administration—crystallized by September 11 and U.S. dominance—are unsettling this order and the political bargains behind it.

A NEW GRAND STRATEGY

For the first time since the dawn of the Cold War, a new grand strategy is taking shape in Washington. It is advanced most directly as a response to terrorism, but it also constitutes a broader view about how the United States should wield power and organize world order. According to this new paradigm, America is to be less bound to its partners and to global rules and institutions while it steps forward to play a more unilateral and anticipatory role in attacking terrorist threats and confronting rogue states seeking WMD. The United States will use its unrivaled military power to manage the global order.

This new grand strategy has seven elements. It begins with a fundamental commitment to maintaining a unipolar world in which the United States has no peer competitor. No coalition of great powers without the United States will be allowed to achieve hegemony. Bush made this point the centerpiece of American security policy in his West Point commencement address in June: "America has, and intends to keep, military strengths beyond challenges— thereby making the destabilizing arms races of other eras pointless, and limiting rivalries to trade and other pursuits of peace." The United States will not seek security through the more modest realist strategy of operating within a global system of power balancing, nor will it pursue a liberal strategy in which institutions, democracy, and integrated markets reduce the importance of power politics altogether. America will be so much more powerful than other major states that strategic rivalries and security competition among the great powers will disappear, leaving everyone—not just the United States—better off.

This goal made an unsettling early appearance at the end of the first Bush administration in a leaked Pentagon memorandum written by then Assistant Secretary of Defense Paul Wolfowitz. With the collapse of the Soviet Union, he wrote, the United States must act to prevent the rise of peer competitors in

Europe and Asia. But the 1990s made this strategic aim moot. The United States grew faster than the other major states during the decade, it reduced military spending more slowly, and it dominated investment in the technological advancement of its forces. Today, however, the new goal is to make these advantages permanent—a fait accompli that will prompt other states to not even try to catch up. Some thinkers have described the strategy as "breakout," in which the United States moves so quickly to develop technological advantages (in robotics, lasers, satellites, precision munitions, etc.) that no state or coalition could ever challenge it as global leader, protector, and enforcer.

The second element is a dramatic new analysis of global threats and how they must be attacked. The grim new reality is that small groups of terrorists—perhaps aided by outlaw states—may soon acquire highly destructive nuclear, chemical, and biological weapons that can inflict catastrophic destruction. These terrorist groups cannot be appeased or deterred, the administration believes, so they must be eliminated. Secretary of Defense Donald Rumsfeld has articulated this frightening view with elegance: regarding the threats that confront the United States, he said, "There are things we know that we know. There are known unknowns. That is to say, there are things that we know we don't know. But there are also unknown unknowns. There are things we don't know we don't know. . . . Each year, we discover a few more of those unknown unknowns." In other words, there could exist groups of terrorists that no one knows about. They may have nuclear, chemical, or biological weapons that the United States did not know they could get, and they might be willing and able to attack without warning. In the age of terror, there is less room for error. Small networks of angry people can inflict unimaginable harm on the rest of the world. They are not nation-states, and they do not play by the accepted rules of the game.

The third element of the new strategy maintains that the Cold War concept of deterrence is outdated. Deterrence, sovereignty, and the balance of power work together. When deterrence is no longer viable, the larger realist edifice starts to crumble. The threat today is not other great powers that must be managed through second-strike nuclear capacity but the transnational terrorist networks that have no home address. They cannot be deterred because they are either willing to die for their cause or able to escape retaliation. The old defensive strategy of building missiles and other weapons that can survive a first strike and be used in a retaliatory strike to punish the attacker will no longer ensure security. The only option, then, is offense.

The use of force, this camp argues, will therefore need to be preemptive and perhaps even preventive—taking on potential threats before they can present a major problem. But this premise plays havoc with the old international rules of self-defense and United Nations norms about the proper use of force. Rumsfeld has articulated the justification for preemptive action by stating that the "absence of evidence is not evidence of absence of weapons of mass destruction." But such an approach renders international norms of self-defense—enshrined by Article 51 of the UN Charter—almost meaningless.

The administration should remember that when Israeli jets bombed the Iraqi nuclear reactor at Osirak in 1981 in what Israel described as an act of self-defense, the world condemned it as an act of aggression. Even British Prime Minister Margaret Thatcher and the American ambassador to the UN, Jeane Kirkpatrick, criticized the action, and the United States joined in passing a UN resolution condemning it.

The Bush administration's security doctrine takes this country down the same slippery slope. Even without a clear threat, the United States now claims a right to use preemptive or preventive military force. At West Point, Bush put it succinctly when he stated that "the military must be ready to strike at a moment's notice in any dark corner of the world. All nations that decide for aggression and terror will pay a price." The administration defends this new doctrine as a necessary adjustment to a more uncertain and shifting threat environment. This policy of no regrets errs on the side of action—but it can also easily become national security by hunch or inference, leaving the world without clear-cut norms for justifying force.

As a result, the fourth element of this emerging grand strategy involves a recasting of the terms of sovereignty. Because these terrorist groups cannot be deterred, the United States must be prepared to intervene anywhere, anytime to preemptively destroy the threat. Terrorists do not respect borders, so neither can the United States. Moreover, countries that harbor terrorists, either by consent or because they are unable to enforce their laws within their territory, effectively forfeit their rights of sovereignty. Haass recently hinted at this notion in *The New Yorker*:

> What you are seeing in this administration is the emergence of a new principle or body of ideas . . . about what you might call the limits of sovereignty. Sovereignty entails obligations. One is not to massacre your own people. Another is not to support terrorism in any way. If a government fails to meet these obligations, then it forfeits some of the normal advantages of sovereignty, including the right to be left alone inside your own territory. Other governments, including the United States, gain the right to intervene. In the case of terrorism, this can even lead to a right of preventive . . . self-defense. You essentially can act in anticipation if you have grounds to think it's a question of when, and not if, you're going to be attacked.

Here the war on terrorism and the problem of the proliferation of WMD get entangled. The worry is that a few despotic states—Iraq in particular, but also Iran and North Korea—will develop capabilities to produce weapons of mass destruction and put these weapons in the hands of terrorists. The regimes themselves may be deterred from using such capabilities, but they might pass along these weapons to terrorist networks that are not deterred. Thus another emerging principle within the Bush administration: the possession of WMD by unaccountable, unfriendly, despotic governments is itself a threat that must be countered. In the old era, despotic regimes were to be lamented but ultimately tolerated. With the rise of terrorism and weapons of mass destruction, they are now unacceptable threats. Thus states that are not technically in violation of any existing international laws could nevertheless be targets of American force—if Washington determines that they have a prospective capacity to do harm.

The recasting of sovereignty is paradoxical. On the one hand, the new grand strategy reaffirms the importance of the territorial nation-state. After all, if all governments were accountable and capable of enforcing the rule of law within their sovereign territory, terrorists would find it very difficult to operate. The emerging Bush doctrine enshrines this idea: governments will be held responsible for what goes on inside their borders. On the other hand, sovereignty has been made newly conditional: governments that fail to act like respectable, law-abiding states will lose their sovereignty.

In one sense, such conditional sovereignty is not new. Great powers have willfully transgressed the norms of state sovereignty as far back as such norms have existed, particularly within their traditional spheres of influence, whenever the national interest dictated. The United States itself has done this within the western hemisphere since the nineteenth century. What is new and provocative in this notion today, however, is the Bush administration's inclination to apply it on a global basis, leaving to itself the authority to determine when sovereign rights have been forfeited, and doing so on an anticipatory basis.

The fifth element of this new grand strategy is a general depreciation of international rules, treaties, and security partnerships. This point relates to the new threats themselves: if the stakes are rising and the margins of error are shrinking in the war on terrorism, multilateral norms and agreements that sanction and limit the use of force are just annoying distractions. The critical task is to eliminate the threat. But the emerging unilateral strategy is also informed by a deeper suspicion about the value of international agreements themselves. Part of this view arises from a deeply felt and authentically American belief that the United States should not get entangled in the corrupting and constraining world of multilateral rules and institutions. For some Americans, the belief that American sovereignty is politically sacred leads to a preference for isolationism. But the more influential view—particularly after September 11—is not that the United States should withdraw from the world but that it should operate in the world on its own terms. The Bush administration's repudiation of a remarkable array of treaties and institutions—from the Kyoto Protocol on global warming to the International Criminal Court to the Biological Weapons Convention—reflects this new bias. Likewise, the United States signed a formal agreement with Russia on the reduction of deployed nuclear warheads only after Moscow's insistence; the Bush administration wanted only a "gentlemen's agreement." In other words, the United States has decided it is big enough, powerful enough, and remote enough to go it alone.

Sixth, the new grand strategy argues that the United States will need to play a direct and unconstrained role in responding to threats. This conviction is partially based on a judgment that no other country or coalition—even the European Union—has the force-projection capabilities to respond to terrorist and rogue states around the world. A decade of U.S. defense spending and modernization has left allies of the United States far behind. In combat operations, alliance partners are increasingly finding it difficult to mesh with U.S. forces. This view is also based on the judgment that joint operations and the use of force through coalitions tend to hinder effective operations. To some observers, this lesson became clear in the allied bombing campaign over Kosovo. The sentiment was also expressed during the U.S. and allied military actions in Afghanistan. Rumsfeld explained this point earlier this year, when he said, "The mission must determine the coalition; the coalition must not determine the mission. If it does, the mission will be dumbed down to the lowest common denominator, and we can't afford that."

No one in the Bush administration argues that NATO or the U.S.-Japan alliance should be dismantled. Rather, these alliances are now seen as less useful to the United States as it confronts today's threats. Some officials argue that it is not that the United States chooses to depreciate alliance partnerships, but that the Europeans are unwilling to keep up. Whether that is true, the upgrading of the American military, along with its sheer size relative to the forces of the rest of the world, leaves the United States in a class by itself. In these circumstances, it is increasingly difficult to maintain the illusion of true alliance partnership. America's allies become merely strategic assets that are useful depending on the circumstance. The United States still finds attractive the logistical reach that its global alliance system provides, but the pacts with countries in Asia and Europe become more contingent and less premised on a vision of a common security community.

Finally, the new grand strategy attaches little value to international stability. There is an unsentimental view in the unilateralist camp that the traditions of the past must be shed. Whether it is withdrawal from the Anti-Ballistic Missile Treaty or the resistance to signing other formal arms-control treaties, policymakers are convinced that the United States needs to move beyond outmoded Cold War thinking. Administration officials have noted with some satisfaction that America's withdrawal from the ABM Treaty did not lead to a global arms race but actually paved the way for a historic arms-reduction agreement between the United States and Russia. This move is seen as a validation that moving beyond the old paradigm of great-power relations will not bring the international house down. The world can withstand radically new security approaches, and it will accommodate American unilateralism as well. But stability is not an end in itself. The administration's new hawkish policy toward North Korea, for example, might be destabilizing to the region, but such instability might be the necessary price for dislodging a dangerous and evil regime in Pyongyang.

In this brave new world, neoimperial thinkers contend that the older realist and liberal grand strategies are not very helpful. American security will not be ensured, as realist grand strategy assumes, by the preservation of deterrence and stable relations among the major powers. In a world of asymmetrical threats, the global balance of power is not the linchpin of war and peace. Likewise, liberal strategies of building order around open trade and democratic institutions might have some long-term impact on terrorism, but they do not address the immediacy of the threats. Apocalyptic violence is at our doorstep, so efforts at strengthening the rules and institutions of the international community are of little practical value. If we accept the worst-case imagining of "we don't know what we don't know," everything else is secondary: international rules, traditions of partnership, and standards of legitimacy. It is a war. And as Clausewitz famously remarked, "War is such a dangerous business that the mistakes which come from kindness are the very worst."

IMPERIAL DANGERS

Pitfalls accompany this neoimperial grand strategy, however. Unchecked U.S. power, shorn of legitimacy and disentangled from the postwar norms and institutions of the international order, will usher in a more hostile international system, making it far harder to achieve American interests. The secret of the United States' long brilliant run as the world's leading state was its ability and willingness to exercise power within alliance and multinational frameworks, which made its power and agenda more acceptable to allies and other key states around the world. This achievement has now been put at risk by the administration's new thinking.

The most immediate problem is that the neoimperialist approach is unsustainable. Going it alone might well succeed in removing Saddam Hussein from power, but it is far less certain that a strategy of counterproliferation, based on American willingness to use unilateral force to confront dangerous dictators, can work over the long term. An American policy that leaves the United States alone to decide which states are threats and how best to deny them weapons of mass destruction will lead to a diminishment of multilateral mechanisms—most important of which is the nonproliferation regime.

The Bush administration has elevated the threat of WMD to the top of its security agenda without investing its power or prestige in fostering, monitoring, and enforcing nonproliferation commitments. The tragedy of September 11 has given the Bush administration the authority and willingness to confront the Iraqs of the world. But that will not be enough when even more complicated cases come along—when it is not the use of force that is needed but concerted multilateral action to provide sanctions and inspections. Nor is it certain that a preemptive or preventive military intervention will go well; it might trigger a domestic political backlash to American-led and military-focused interventionism. America's well-meaning imperial strategy could undermine the principled multilateral agreements, institutional infrastructure, and cooperative spirit needed for the long-term success of nonproliferation goals.

The specific doctrine of preemptive action poses a related problem: once the United States feels it can take such a course, nothing will stop other countries from doing the same. Does the United States want this doctrine in the hands of Pakistan, or even China or Russia? After all, it would not require the intervening state to first provide evidence for its actions. The United States argues that to wait until all the evidence is in, or until authoritative international bodies support action, is to wait too long. Yet that approach is the only basis that the United States can use if it needs to appeal for restraint in the actions of others. Moreover, and quite paradoxically, overwhelming American conventional military might, combined with a policy of preemptive strikes, could lead hostile states to accelerate programs to acquire their only possible deterrent to the United States: WMD. This is another version of the security dilemma, but one made worse by a neoimperial grand strategy.

Another problem follows. The use of force to eliminate WMD capabilities or overturn dangerous regimes is never simple, whether it is pursued unilaterally or by a concert of major states. After the military intervention is over, the target country has to be put back together. Peacekeeping and state building are inevitably required, as are long-term strategies that bring the UN, the World Bank, and the major powers together to orchestrate aid and other forms of assistance. This is not heroic work, but it is utterly necessary. Peacekeeping troops may be required for many years, even after a new regime is built. Regional conflicts inflamed by outside military intervention must also be calmed. This is the "long tail" of burdens and commitments that comes with every major military action.

When these costs and obligations are added to America's imperial military role, it becomes even more doubtful that the neoimperial strategy can be sustained at home over the long haul—the classic problem of imperial overstretch. The United States could keep its military predominance for decades if it is supported by a growing and increasingly productive economy. But the indirect burdens of cleaning up the political mess in terrorist-prone failed states levy a hidden cost. Peacekeeping and state building will require coalitions of states and multilateral agencies that can be brought into the process only if the initial decisions about military intervention are hammered out in consultation with other major states. America's older realist and liberal grand strategies suddenly become relevant again.

A third problem with an imperial grand strategy is that it cannot generate the cooperation needed to solve practical problems at the heart of the U.S. foreign policy agenda. In the fight on terrorism, the United States needs cooperation from European and Asian countries in intelligence, law enforcement, and logistics. Outside the security sphere, realizing U.S. objectives depends even more on a continuous stream of amicable working relations with major states around the world. It needs partners for trade liberalization, global financial stabilization, environmental protection, deterring transnational organized crime, managing the rise of China, and a host of other thorny challenges. But it is impossible to expect would-be partners to acquiesce to

America's self-appointed global security protectorate and then pursue business as usual in all other domains.

The key policy tool for states confronting a unipolar and unilateral America is to withhold cooperation in day-to-day relations with the United States. One obvious means is trade policy; the European response to the recent American decision to impose tariffs on imported steel is explicable in these terms. This particular struggle concerns specific trade issues, but it is also a struggle over how Washington exercises power. The United States may be a unipolar military power, but economic and political power is more evenly distributed across the globe. The major states may not have much leverage in directly restraining American military policy, but they can make the United States pay a price in other areas.

Finally, the neoimperial grand strategy poses a wider problem for the maintenance of American unipolar power. It steps into the oldest trap of powerful imperial states: self-encirclement. When the most powerful state in the world throws its weight around, unconstrained by rules or norms of legitimacy, it risks a backlash. Other countries will bridle at an international order in which the United States plays only by its own rules. The proponents of the new grand strategy have assumed that the United States can single-handedly deploy military power abroad and not suffer untoward consequences; relations will be coarser with friends and allies, they believe, but such are the costs of leadership. But history shows that powerful states tend to trigger self-encirclement by their own overestimation of their power. Charles V, Louis XIV, Napoleon, and the leaders of post-Bismarck Germany sought to expand their imperial domains and impose a coercive order on others. Their imperial orders were all brought down when other countries decided they were not prepared to live in a world dominated by an overweening coercive state. America's imperial goals and modus operandi are much more limited and benign than were those of age-old emperors. But a hard-line imperial grand strategy runs the risk that history will repeat itself.

BRING IN THE OLD

Wars change world politics, and so too will America's war on terrorism. How great states fight wars, how they define the stakes, how they make the peace in its aftermath—all give lasting shape to the international system that emerges after the guns fall silent. In mobilizing their societies for battle, wartime leaders have tended to describe the military struggle as more than simply the defeat of an enemy. Woodrow Wilson sent U.S. troops to Europe not only to stop the kaiser's army but to destroy militarism and usher in a worldwide democratic revolution. Franklin Roosevelt saw the war with Germany and Japan as a struggle to secure the "four great freedoms." The Atlantic Charter was a statement of war aims that called not just for the defeat of fascism but for a new dedication to social welfare and human rights within an open and stable world system.

To advance these visions, Wilson and Roosevelt proposed new international rules and mechanisms of cooperation. Their message was clear: If you bear the burdens of war, we, your leaders, will use this dreadful conflict to usher in a more peaceful and decent order among states. Fighting the war had as much to do with building global relations as it did with vanquishing an enemy.

Bush has not fully articulated a vision of postwar international order, aside from defining the struggle as one between freedom and evil. The world has seen Washington take determined steps to fight terrorism, but it does not yet have a sense of Bush's larger, positive agenda for a strengthened and more decent international order.

This failure explains why the sympathy and goodwill generated around the world for the United States after September 11 quickly disappeared. Newspapers that once proclaimed, "We are all Americans," now express distrust toward America. The prevailing view is that the United States seems prepared to use its power to go after terrorists and evil regimes, but not to use it to help build a more stable and peaceful world order. The United States appears to be degrading the rules and institutions of international community, not enhancing them. To the rest of the world, neoimperial thinking has more to do with exercising power than with exercising leadership.

In contrast, America's older strategic orientations—balance-of-power realism and liberal multilateralism—suggest a mature world power that seeks stability and pursues its interests in ways that do not fundamentally threaten the positions of other states. They are strategies of co-option and reassurance. The new imperial grand strategy presents the United States very differently: a revisionist state seeking to parlay its momentary power advantages into a world order in which it runs the show. Unlike the hegemonic states of the past, the United States does not seek territory or outright political domination in Europe or Asia; "America has no empire to extend or utopia to establish," Bush noted in his West Point address. But the sheer power advantages that the United States possesses and the doctrines of preemption and counterterrorism that it is articulating do unsettle governments and people around the world. The costs could be high. The last thing the United States wants is for foreign diplomats and government leaders to ask, How can we work around, undermine, contain, and retaliate against U.S. power?

Rather than invent a new grand strategy, the United States should reinvigorate its older strategies, those based on the view that America's security partnerships are not simply instrumental tools but critical components of an American-led world political order that should be preserved. U.S. power is both leveraged and made more legitimate and user-friendly by these partnerships. The neoimperial thinkers are haunted by the specter of catastrophic terrorism and seek a radical reordering of America's role in the world. America's commanding unipolar power and the advent of frightening new terrorist threats feed this imperial temptation. But it is a grand strategic vision that, taken to the extreme, will leave the world more dangerous and divided—and the United States less secure.

12

History and the Hyperpower

Eliot A. Cohen

EMPIRE'S NEW CLOTHES

Most historians cringe at talk of the "lessons of history." Trained as specialists and wary of sweeping comparisons, they flinch from attempts to make past events speak directly to current policy. They remind us of what makes circumstances unique, highlighting differences where others see similarities.

Politicians and policymakers, on the other hand, have few compunctions about drawing on historical analogies to frame and explain policy choices. Scholars may wince at their shallow thinking and imprecision, but such practitioners always have the last word. And even if we try to understand our world purely in its own terms, implicit, historically grounded beliefs—in trends and turning points, analogies and metaphors, parallels and lessons—inevitably shape our views. Better, then, to ask explicitly how history should inform our understanding of the present.

The historical analogy making the rounds of late is the notion that the United States today is an empire that can and should be compared with imperial powers of the past. This idea gained immediacy when U.S. soldiers trod in the footsteps of Alexander the Great in Afghanistan and U.S. tanks rumbled through the ancient imperial heartland of Mesopotamia: ruling and remaking distant, recalcitrant peoples looks very much like an imperial project.

Eliot Cohen, "History and the Hyperpower," *Foreign Affairs*, July–Aug. 2004, p. 49.
Reprinted by permission.

Casual talk of a Pax Americana—harking back to the Pax Britannica, itself an echo of the Pax Romana—implies that the United States is following a pattern of imperial dominance that holds precedents and lessons. The metaphor of empire merits neither angry rejection nor gleeful embrace. It instead deserves careful scrutiny, because imperial history contains analogies and parallels that bear critically on the current U.S. predicament.

CURRENCIES OF POWER

An empire is a multinational or multiethnic state that extends its influence through formal and informal control of other polities. The Indian writer Nirad Chaudhuri put it well: "There is no empire without a conglomeration of linguistically, racially, and culturally different nationalities and the hegemony of one of them over the rest. The heterogeneity and the domination are of the very essence of imperial relations. An empire is hierarchical. There may be in it, and has been, full or partial freedom for individuals or groups to rise from one level to another; but this has not modified the stepped and stratified structure of the organization."

Most people throughout history have lived under imperial rule. The current international system, with nearly two hundred independent states and not a single confessed empire, is a historical anomaly. Most empires, however, have had only regional scope and limited ambitions. In the nineteenth century, the French, Russian, Turkish, and Austro-Hungarian Empires jostled one another at the margins and waged war in conjunction with other allies, but none towered over the rest. Of past empires, only ancient Rome and the British Empire in the nineteenth century had enough power and influence to dominate the international system. Each exerted not only military strength, but also cultural influence; each made international economic order possible; each was envied, resented, and ultimately displacednot by a single foe but by a combination of enemies abroad and weaknesses within.

How does the United States compare with Britain and Rome? Start with the reserve currency of empire: military strength. Rome's legions hacked their way to world power, suffering a series of military disasters in the process: Gauls, Greeks, Carthaginians, Persians, and numerous barbarian bands inflicted on Roman forces defeats of a kind that U.S. troops have not suffered since the early days of the Korean War. The legions shed their blood in internecine warfare, clashes among rival dictators, and massive revolts by humiliated clients and mutinous subjects—ills without contemporary American parallel. Rome recruited many of its soldiers from conquered lands. These soldiers owed allegiance chiefly to their own leaders and fellow troops, not to a government, constitution, or homeland. Thus, although Rome dominated its world, it did so with none of the assurance or domestic solidity of the United States.

The British army, meanwhile, relied on pluck, not numbers. Its force was negligible compared with the great conscript armies of continental Europe; Bismarck once scoffed that if the British were to land their army on the Baltic coast, he would send the Berlin police force to arrest it. From 1815 to 1914, the British Empire essentially withdrew from the game of continental warfare, a fact that British statesmen recognized as a restraint on their behavior. As for the Royal Navy, it ruled the seas but teetered constantly on the verge of technological obsolescence and (as it believed) overall inferiority. The French introduced ironclad warships before the British did, and even when the British made a breakthrough—as with the Dreadnought class big-gun battleships—it was with the knowledge that their technological rivals, Germany and the United States, would soon follow suit.

U.S. military power is of a different order entirely. The United States now accounts for between 40 and 50 percent of global defense spending, more than double the total spending of its European allies (whose budgets are so riddled with inefficiencies that, aside from territorial defense, peacekeeping, and some niche capabilities, the European pillar of NATO is militarily irrelevant). In virtually every sphere of warfare, the United States dominates, an unprecedented phenomenon in military history. On and above the earth and on and below the sea, U.S. military technology far surpasses that of any potential opponent. No other power has the ability to move large and sophisticated forces around the globe; to coordinate and direct its own forces and those of its allies; to keep troops equipped, fed, and healthy; and to support those troops with precision firepower and unsurpassed amounts of information and intelligence.

Viewed from within, of course, the picture looks very different. U.S. soldiers know all too well their own deficiencies and vulnerabilities: they grouse about aging trucks, jammed rifles, and intermittent data links. Viewed from the outside, however, the world has seen nothing like the U.S. military. British infantrymen in 1900 shot more accurately than their continental European counterparts but did not differ all that much from them in terms of equipment and unit skills (and the Tommies found themselves inferior to Boer citizen-soldiers equipped with German-made rifles). Today, an average U.S. battalion has better kit—from body armor to night vision devices—than any comparable unit in the world; with a few exceptions (mostly allies of the United States), it trains more effectively in the field; and it has officers and sergeants groomed by a military schooling system more thorough than any in history.

This qualitative advantage looms even larger at the higher levels of the armed forces. No other military has the B-2 bombers or the satellite constellation, the aircraft carriers or the long-range unmanned aircraft of the U.S. Navy and Air Force. No other country is remotely close to having the resources afforded by a $400 billion defense budget or the accumulated military-industrial capital of years of spending on construction and infrastructure. No other research establishment can match that of the United States, which receives more money than the entire defense budget of its largest European ally.

Put thus, U.S. military power seems to invite hubris. But again, viewed from within the picture appears different. Generals and admirals fret over forces stretched too thin, anticipate threats from unconventional and irregular opponents who will avoid U.S. strengths and seek out weaknesses, and worry that their political masters will succumb to the intoxication of great power or their fellow citizens will fail to understand the commitment of money and blood that any war requires. Such leaders understand better than their civilian superiors the fragility of great military strength. But that does not undermine the basic fact of U.S. predominance. Augustus lost his legions in the Teutoburger Wald, Disraeli his regiments at Isandhlwana in both cases, succumbing to primitive opponents inferior in weaponry and, according to the imperial powers, culture as well. Not even in Vietnam, where the odds of such a debacle's occurring were highest, did U.S. forces suffer a similar defeat. Today, the legions of the United States have no match, and the gap between them and other militaries is only growing.

No empire, of course, can sustain itself by raw military power alone. It requires, at the very minimum, sufficient resources to generate power. Here, too, the contrasts between the United States and its imperial predecessors are striking. Rome was a city, Britain a set of moderately sized islands on the periphery of Eurasia. The United States spans a vast, rich continent. In the middle of the nineteenth century, the United Kingdom's population numbered only slightly more than half that of France and considerably less than those of the rising powers—Germany, the United States, and Russia. Its once-impressive economic lead over the rest of Europe had dwindled everywhere but in the area of finance. By the end of the century, it had fallen behind Germany in the production of steel and electrical power. The United States, in contrast, is the third most populous country on the planet and, unlike most developed countries, has a birth rate at or near replacement rate. It accounts for just under a third of the world's economic production. It does not live off plunder or accumulated finance or the farming of large estates. Its economy remains the largest, most productive, and most dynamic on the planet.

The might of Rome and Britain depended on ideas as much as on power or resources: imperial power resided in science, literature, and education. Gauls learned Latin, and Indians learned English. Yet the United States can claim greater influence in the realm of ideas as well. In the ancient world, Greek was the language of philosophy; in the nineteenth and early twentieth centuries, German was the language of science. Today, English is the lingua franca of the planet for everything from air traffic control to entertainment. U.S. universities dominate in higher education, while low- and middle-brow American culture floods a planet that simultaneously loathes and embraces Spielberg, Starbucks, and MTV. American music, food, idiom, work styles, and manners are inescapable.

DEFINING DOMINANCE

And yet, can the United States be an empire? Raymond Aron famously called the United States "the imperial republic," but even that title sits uncomfortably with Americans. On the whole, the United States has proven itself reluctant to exercise prolonged formal control over states or peoples who do not have the option of becoming its citizens. A country whose sacred texts begin "We the people" and talk of "inalienable rights," which celebrates self-government and legal equality, can never comfortably enjoy imperial rule as traditionally understood. And indeed, even the United States' most overtly imperial endeavor—rule over Cuba and the Philippines following the Spanish-American War—generated internal opposition and ended in a remarkably swift, self-imposed retreat.

A longer historical perspective, moreover, suggests that democracy and empire are ultimately incompatible. The tragedy of Athens in Thucydides' Peloponnesian War lies in democracy's difficulty in withstanding the pressures of imperial necessity, compulsions that corrupt and even destroy the freedoms at the root of democracy. The British empire could liberalize domestically and exert dominion externally only so long as Britons believed their subjects to be inferior, childlike, or incapable of self-government, a prejudice undermined by the spread of democratic principles. Whether or not one agrees with the current U.S. attempt to create a democratic Iraq, no one dares suggest (at least not publicly) that Iraqis are, by virtue of history, culture, faith, or race, incapable of ruling themselves.

When the United Kingdom granted independence to the Irish Republic after World War I, it acknowledged the fundamental principle of self-determination—a concession, some observers have noted, that spelled the end of the British empire and perhaps of all European empires. In the twentieth century, three waves of disintegration—the first induced by nationalism and World War I, the second by World War II, the third by the collapse of the Soviet Union—brought an end to the empires that had dominated the three previous centuries: the Austro-Hungarian, Turkish, British, French, Dutch, Portuguese, and Russian.

To be sure, influence and even a few possessions linger, and the imperial era left a strong legacy in everything from institutions and attitudes to street names and school systems. And some forms of imperial rule persist. What is the European and U.S. presence in Yugoslavia, for example, if not a kind of neocolonialism? Dour white men may no longer raise flags and color overseas possessions in red on their maps, but that hardly changes the reality of hierarchy and subordination in international politics. American claims of benign intentions to spread democracy are surely no less and no more sincere than the missions civilisatrices of imperial powers in the past.

But the basic fact remains: empires have dissolved, and they will not return. To talk about the United States as an empire is, from this point of view, to engage in useless and potentially dangerous anachronism, a temptation to hubris, overstretch, and disregard of the claims of the international community.

In the end, however, the applicability of a particular term (debates about empire tend to degenerate into semantic squabbles) does not matter. The fact of the overwhelming power of the United States does. No potential adversary comes close to it, and, for the moment, there is no question of a countervailing coalition to block, let alone replace, it. Its roots lie in a growing and extraordinarily productive population, a stable political system, and a military that is unsurpassable in the foreseeable future. And the United States will not, as some hope and others fear, bind itself to an international institutional and legal order that will domesticate and restrain it. If nothing else, domestic politics would prohibit it. No U.S. leader in the next decade or two will call for a dramatic reduction in defense spending or deny that this country must be the strongest in the world, ready to exert its power globally and act unilaterally if necessary.

The "Age of Empire" may indeed have ended, then, but an age of American hegemony has begun. And regardless of what one calls it or how long it will last, U.S. statesmen today cannot ignore the lessons and analogies of imperial history.

ANXIETIES OF INFLUENCE

The logic of the Cold War was one of ideological struggle and bipolar contest. The logic of contemporary international politics is that of predominance and its discontents. The first lesson of imperial history is that the absence of rivals does not diminish the challenges for statesmen. Indeed, to crawl inside the heads of British statesmen in the nineteenth century (or, more imaginatively, of Roman leaders during the republic and early empire) is to find leaders weighted down by anxieties.

One overwhelming problem results from the sheer scope of imperial politics. In virtually any government, a handful of people make the critical decisions on foreign and security policy. The larger the empire, the less likely that this small group will know what it must about the nature and extent of imperial problems. Leaders face an unattractive set of options: mastering the challenges of one segment of their political universe while scanting others; dealing with all problems superficially; or devolving large areas of policy to proconsuls and viceroys.

The imperial power faces another fundamental disadvantage in its contests with smaller states or political movements: its leaders cannot focus in the way their opponents can. Smaller actors who recognize this can manipulate an imperial center's politics. Both the Indian National Congress and the Irish Republican Army contained astute students of British politics who knew how to wrestle with a metropolitan government that only intermittently concentrated its attention on the problems of India or Ireland. The stumbles and follies of U.S. foreign policy result in part from a similar problem: its demands simply exceed the capacity of the handful of men and women who manage them. The U.S. decision-making elite, moreover, has none of the social uniformity and cohesion of the Roman Senate (with its ladder of political-military-religious advancement, intermarriage, and adoption) or the British upper class (with its network of universities, clubs, country houses, and regiments). The openness of the American elite may make it more dynamic, but it also makes it harder to lead.

The universal enmity that hegemonic power breeds presents another, and perhaps graver, challenge to imperial statesmen. Empires have no peers and precious few friends. Indeed, to the imperial mind, "friendship" means a relationship in which clients render services and patrons provide protection. The result, as Great Britain found out at least twice during its heyday (first during the American Revolution, when the European powers turned against a global empire forged during the Seven Years' War, then in the Boer War, when European sympathy went exclusively to the unruly British subjects), is diplomatic and military isolation. An empire's opponent always looks like the underdog, the imperial power always the bully. The victories of insurgents become inspiring tales of audacity and sacrifice, the triumphs of legions the inevitable consequence of superior technology, training, and numbers. The empire's claims to act for the good of the international system will always be dismissed (often rightly) as the mere exercise of self-interest. (In moments of reflection, the more honest imperialists confess as much: Rome introduced the Britons to Latin, togas, arcades, baths, and banquets, of which Tacitus remarked, "The unsuspecting Britons spoke of such novelties as civilization, when in fact they were only a feature of their enslavement.")

The inevitability of anti-imperial sentiment may help explain the tide of anti-Americanism that has swept much of the world since September 11, 2001. Some of that antipathy surely emerged in reaction to the personality of an assertive U.S. president whose manner and core beliefs aggravate the elites of Europe and the Middle East. Some surely results from understandable apprehension about U.S. courses of action, in the Middle East especially. But some also stems from the swirl of hostility to the colossus, to all it embodies, and, indeed, to the very fact of its existence. The consequences of that hostility may be managed and mitigated in the years ahead, but some level of antipathy will remain, perhaps grow, and conceivably become dangerous. To be an empire, or something like an empire, is to be envied, resented, suspected, mistrusted, and, often enough, hated.

THE ART OF UNDERSTATEMENT

From imperial problems arise maxims of imperial policy. Few outside of university classics departments read the major Greek and Roman historians today, but their works still have much to offer. The ancient world considered Rome's success both a marvel and a puzzle: the Romans seemed to lack a deep culture, wise statesmen, and invariably successful armies, yet they managed to conquer their world and keep it. The ancients wondered how they did it, and so too did political philosophers of the Renaissance and the Enlightenment, such as Machiavelli and Montesquieu.

Polybius and many who followed him sought an explanation in the role of the Senate, a body that, although internally divided, provided a degree of steadiness to otherwise turbulent policy. Underlying the turmoil of Roman politics, these authors claimed, was a consistent imperial style that persisted despite the rise and fall of consuls and dictators. That style had some simple rules. "Above all, their constant maxim was to divide," Montesquieu observed, and it is such a simple guide to conduct in foreign affairs that its importance is easily overlooked. It was no accident that Rome never faced a coalition of the many powers and peoples that opposed it. Rome's rise was neither foreordained nor without perils: it faced more numerous enemies, more wily commanders, and more ferocious warriors than it had at its command. It picked its fights, however, and took care not to take on the great powers of the world all at once or to allow unified powers to arise against it—a piece of wisdom that, two millennia later, imperial Germany failed to learn. In 2003, the United States stumbled into similar wisdom when, after decades of benign indifference to the formation of a European Union under Franco-German direction, it realized the merits of siding with the weaker factions inside the EU. (It turned out, however, to be inept in its conduct of a policy that Roman statesmen would have found trivial.)

Reflecting on the practices of the Romans as described by Livy, Machiavelli noted, "One of the great prudences men use is to abstain from menacing or injuring anyone with words." Roman statesmen did not generally bluster or fume. They did not threaten or menace. Instead, they made requests and promises and followed through on both. When the simply clad Roman senator Gaius Popilius Laenas delivered Rome's demand that Antiochus IV withdraw from Egypt, he did not threaten the Syrian king. Rather, he walked over to the problematic monarch and with his staff drew a circle around him in the sand, insisting on an answer to the Senate before Antiochus stepped out of it. The Seleucid king turned pale and acceded, and this act of submission destroyed his reputation in his own luxurious court.

Great Britain, too, made an art of imperial understatement. Throughout the nineteenth century, its leaders assiduously sought to prevent a grand coalition from rising against it, even if that meant accommodating U.S. or Japanese claims. U.S. statesmen today might similarly benefit from maintaining a discreet silence and avoiding offense until absolutely necessary. In retrospect, for example, the brusque manner of the Bush administration's rejection of the Kyoto Protocol, the International Criminal Court, and other measures dear to European hearts created a climate of opinion that made the prewar crisis over Iraq much worse than it need have been. And even if the administration had decided to punish its wayward allies for not supporting the war, it should never have publicly announced its decision to ban their companies from postwar reconstruction contracts, but merely excluded them without saying a word.

U.S. power is so obvious a fact, particularly to non-Americans, that there is no need to remind anyone of it. If the United States intends to exercise its power effectively, even against the wishes of its allies, it should do so with a bland smile, not boastful words. Weaker states will inevitably view the strongest power as arrogant, inconsiderate, and demanding. There is no need to make it any worse than it must be: Roman discretion offers as important a historical example as Roman assertion.

MAKING VIRTUE OF NECESSITY

The military burden of past empires fell not only on the power at the center. The British had their Indian Army, the Romans auxiliaries who proved indispensable to the success of armies built around the legion, itself a masterpiece of ancient military organization. Even the United States has, and will have, far too few soldiers for the tasks at hand. In some ways, Washington has succeeded at handling its own auxiliaries: NATO is, in practical terms, a military alliance that allows the United States to bring forces other than its own to bear on the unstable periphery of Europe. But in other ways, the United States has yet to master the art of developing foreign military institutions, especially when it must do so swiftly. And history suggests that the hope expressed by some U.S. leaders—of handing off peacekeeping and humanitarian intervention to smaller powers—is misplaced: the auxiliaries did not fight without the legionaries there to back them up, and the British interlaced the Indian Army with British units and officers.

For Britain, like Rome, imperial governance required proconsuls. The viceroy of India wielded enormous authority, which he often exercised at variance with the views of the government back home. Belief in the superior judgment of "the man on the spot" was the unofficial credo of the British Empire, and although centralizing tendencies existed, they had to yield to the necessities of distance. London had few promising alternatives before the advent of near-instantaneous communication, and travel times in the empire were measured in weeks, not hours. Around the necessity of delegation grew up cultures of initiative, authority, and responsibility, without which empire could not have survived.

The United States does not rule parts of the world in the way the European empires did, but it faces similar challenges. Theater combatant commanders (formerly known as commanders-in-chief, or cincs) have served as its proconsuls. Their standing in their regions has usually dwarfed that of ambassadors and assistant secretaries of state. They have had the regional outlook, the sophisticated staffs, and the resources to make things happen. It is small wonder that much of U.S. policy abroad has been effectively militarized, at the expense of a State Department whose collective strength has rarely matched the quality of individual diplomats.

As happened in the case of Rome (although to a far lesser degree), these U.S. proconsuls have become politicized. Once out of uniform (and, in some cases, even before) they endorse or denounce politicians; once retired, one recently ran for president, an activity usually reserved for successful commanders in great conflicts. No retired American general, of course, will cross the Rubicon in arms, and their various missteps in recent years will likely cause most of them to return to the dignified silence that characterized many of their predecessors. The phenomenon is revealing, however, because of what it says about the weakness of the civilian side of the U.S. policymaking apparatus—which has created the vacuum into which generals are drawn.

The United States needs to develop its own versions of viceroys, legates, residents, and procurators. The troubles of Iraq following the overthrow of Saddam Hussein showed that, however skilled its armies, the United States has neither the cadre of administrators nor the organizations necessary to establish order and begin establishing domestic institutions that will prevent a relapse into violence and disorder. Indeed, in this respect especially, the imperial analogy breaks down. In the old days, the great powers—for reasons of pride, greed, and sheer competitiveness—desired colonies. In the twenty-first century, in contrast, the projection of power into another country results not from the lure of profit or ambition but from the fear of chaos. Formal colonial rule has lost all legitimacy. And yet, what can substitute for it? International administration of the kind found in Kosovo and Bosnia has a mixed record at best; although the United Nations can usefully provide legitimacy for such rule, and although individuals and organizations have served valiantly and effectively (the name Sergio Vieira de Mello comes to mind), the UN's failures outweigh its successes. And even those successes have required the backing of military powers acting out of traditional self-interest. To legitimize colonial rule by some other name, and to create institutions that can conduct it, has become one of the great challenges of contemporary statecraft—necessary not only to ease the misery of anarchy, but also to avert the dangers posed by anarchy in the age of weapons of mass destruction and suicide bombers.

THE CHOICE

History "gives no comfort to the many able, subtle, dedicated minds that crave finality and certitude," Jacques Barzun once noted. But it does offer training for the tough-minded who can tolerate uncertainty and operate within it.

In the end, it makes very little difference whether one thinks of the United States as an empire or as something else—a hyperpower *sui generis,* a new order of political entity. Many of the practical problems it faces resemble those faced by past empires, and that alone requires reflection. The results of such reflection, however, are sobering, because soon comes a time when empire no longer looks quite as attractive as it does at the peak of its success and influence. Thucydides captured this by juxtaposing two speeches by the Athenian statesman Pericles. In the great funeral oration delivered over the first casualties of the war with Sparta, he celebrates Athens as "the school of Hellas," "a pattern to others" rather than "imitators ourselves." In words that may remind some of John F. Kennedy at the outset of his presidency, he calls a generation to greatness. Yet after setbacks in war and the ravages of the plague, he warns his countrymen that "to recede is no longer possible, if indeed any of you in the alarm of the moment has become enamored of the honesty of such an unambitious part. For what you hold is, to speak somewhat plainly, a tyranny; to take it perhaps was wrong, to let go is unsafe."

Herein lies one of the curses of empire: to let go never looks safe, and indeed rarely is. The United Kingdom withdrew from its leading role in world affairs without too much damage to itself (although at the price of massive bloodshed in places such as India and Yemen), but that had much to do with the readiness of the United States to take its place—to fill the vacuum left by British power and take up the British role in many parts of the world. Nor did the British have much choice in their withdrawal from empire, other than by, as Machiavelli put it, "anticipating necessity," pulling back just before forces too strong for them to master would have compelled them.

The United States today also has less choice about its role in world affairs than its worried leaders and their critics, or its anxious friends and numerous enemies, think. The logic of empire is a logic of extension, and the strategic conundrum of empire is that of overcommitment and overstretch. Despite the wishes of French and Chinese politicians, no countervailing state or federation will restore a balance-of-power system akin to that of Europe in the eighteenth and nineteenth centuries, at least not in the near future. Despite the wishes of idealists, no international institution has proven capable of effective action in the absence of the power generated and exercised by states. And a third possibility—anarchy unleashed after a disgusted United States recalls its legions in a spurt of democratic disgust at and indifference to the rest of the planet—is too horrifying to contemplate. The real alternatives, then, are U.S. hegemony exercised prudently or foolishly, consistently or fecklessly, safely or dangerously—and for this, U.S. leaders must look back to school themselves in the wisdom that will make such statesmanship possible.

13

A Duty to Prevent

Lee Feinstein and Anne-Marie Slaughter

The unprecedented threat posed by terrorists and rogue states armed with weapons of mass destruction cannot be handled by an outdated and poorly enforced nonproliferation regime. The international community has a duty to prevent security disasters as well as humanitarian ones—even at the price of violating sovereignty.

DISARMING ROGUES

The Bush administration has proclaimed a doctrine of unilateral preemption as a core part of its National Security Strategy. The limits of this approach are demonstrated daily in Iraq, where the United States is bearing the burden for security, reconstruction, and reform essentially on its own. Yet the world cannot afford to look the other way when faced with the prospect, as in Iraq, of a brutal ruler acquiring nuclear weapons or other weapons of mass destruction (WMD). Addressing this danger requires a different strategy, one that maximizes the chances of early and effective collective action. In this regard, and in comparison to the changes that are taking place in the area of intervention for the purposes of humanitarian protection, the biggest problem with the Bush preemption strategy may be that it does not go far enough.

In the name of protecting state sovereignty, international law traditionally prohibited states from intervening in one another's affairs, with military force or otherwise. But members of the human rights and humanitarian protection communities came to realize that, in light of the humanitarian catastrophes of the 1990s, from famine to genocide to ethnic cleansing, those principles will

Lee Feinstein and Anne-Marie Slaughter, "A Duty to Prevent," *Foreign Affairs*, Jan.–Feb. 2004, p. 136. Reprinted by permission.

not do. The world could no longer sit and wait, reacting only when a crisis caused massive human suffering or spilled across borders, posing more conventional threats to international peace and security. As a result, in late 2001, an international commission of legal practitioners and scholars, responding to a challenge from the UN secretary-general, proposed a new doctrine, which they called "The Responsibility to Protect." This far-reaching principle holds that today un member states have a responsibility to protect the lives, liberty, and basic human rights of their citizens, and that if they fail or are unable to carry it out, the international community has a responsibility to step in.

We propose a corollary principle in the field of global security: a collective "duty to prevent" nations run by rulers without internal checks on their power from acquiring or using WMD. For many years, a small but determined group of regimes has pursued proliferation in spite of—and, to a certain extent, without breaking—the international rules barring such activity. Some of these nations cooperate with one another, trading missile technology for uranium-enrichment know-how, for example. Their cooperation, dangerous in itself, also creates incentives for others to develop a nuclear capacity in response. These regimes can also provide a ready source of weapons and technology to individuals and terrorists. The threat is gravest when the states pursuing WMD are closed societies headed by rulers who menace their own citizens as much as they do their neighbors and potential adversaries.

Such threats demand a global response. Like the responsibility to protect, the duty to prevent begins from the premise that the rules now governing the use of force, devised in 1945 and embedded in the UN Charter, are inadequate. Both new principles respond to a growing recognition, born of logic and experience, that in the twenty-first century maintaining global peace and security requires states to be proactive rather than reactive. And both recognize that un members have responsibilities as well as rights.

The duty to prevent has three critical features. First, it seeks to control not only the proliferation of WMD but also people who possess them. Second, it emphasizes prevention, calling on the international community to act early in order to be effective and develop a menu of potential measures aimed at particular governments—especially measures that can be taken well short of any use of force. Third, the duty to prevent should be exercised collectively, through a global or regional organization.

OLD RULES, NEW THREATS

We live in a world of old rules and new threats. This period did not begin on September 11, 2001. Before then, politicians and public figures were already lacing their millennium speeches with calls for a new global financial architecture, new definitions of national self-interest and humanitarian intervention, and new ways of organizing international institutions. They recognized that the existing rules and institutions created to address the economic, political, and security problems of the last century were inadequate for solving a new generation of threats to world order: failed states; regional economic crises; sovereign bankruptcies; the spread of HIV/AIDS and other new viruses; global warming; the rise of global criminal networks; and trafficking in arms, money, women, workers, and drugs.

Although the worst threats to the international order in the 1990s arose from internal conflicts—civil wars, ethnic bloodletting, and resurgent nationalism—the cardinal doctrines of the post-1945 order apply to wars between nations, not within them. The UN Charter binds states only to refrain from the use or threat of force in "their international relations" and explicitly protects their "domestic jurisdiction" from outside interference. And a broad doctrine prohibiting intervention in a state's internal affairs is well established in customary law.

Granted, under the charter, the UN Security Council may take action when it determines the existence of a threat to international peace and security. And nothing prevents it from identifying a government with no internal checks on its power that possesses or seeks to acquire WMD as a threat to the peace and taking measures against it. But articulating and acknowledging a specific duty to prevent such governments from even acquiring WMD will shift the burden of proof from suspicious nations to suspected nations and create the presumption of a need for early and, therefore, more effective action.

Consider, for instance, how recognizing a duty to prevent could have changed the debate over the war in Iraq. Under existing law, the Bush administration could justify intervention only by arguing that Iraq held WMD in violation of Security Council resolutions. Even though Saddam Hussein's Iraq was subject to special Security Council restrictions precisely because of its earlier illegal nuclear program and use of chemical weapons, the United States could not argue that Saddam posed a threat warranting intervention simply because of his absolute power, his past behavior, and his expressed intentions. Now suppose that last March, the United States and the United Kingdom had accepted a proposal by France, Germany, and Russia to blanket Iraq with inspectors instead of attacking it. Presumably those inspectors would have found what U.S. forces seem to be finding today—evidence of Iraq's intention and capacity to build WMD, but no existing stocks. Would the appropriate response then have been to send the inspectors home and leave Saddam's regime intact? The better answer would have been to recognize from the beginning the combined threat posed by the nature of his regime and his determination to acquire and use WMD. Invoking the duty to prevent, the Security Council could have identified Iraq as a subject of special concern and, as it was blanketing the country with inspectors, sought to prosecute Saddam for crimes against humanity committed back in the 1980s.

The inability to prevent WMD proliferation by dangerous regimes is a concern that has confounded at least the last three U.S. administrations. President George H.W. Bush defined the issue in terms of "outlaw" states, to distinguish regimes that followed international rules from those that defied them. President Bill Clinton used the term "rogue states" until 2000, when his administration began referring to "states of concern" to signal that the goal of U.S. policy was eventually to reintegrate states, if not their dictatorial rulers, into the international system. The present administration's use of the term "axis of evil" suggests a sterner version of the first Bush administration's approach. It leaves little room for diplomacy, forcing the United States to either advocate regime change or do nothing.

All these approaches, moreover, miss a key point. It is not states that are the danger, but their rulers—a relatively small group of identifiable individuals who seek absolute power at home or sponsor terrorism abroad. These rulers and their regimes can be identified by evaluating their behavior according to criteria already documented in the UN system: the rule of law and human rights; rights of association and organization; freedom of expression and belief; and personal autonomy and economic rights. The international system remains uncomfortable distinguishing one country from another, but such distinctions are already embedded in the UN system and they should be emphasized as the basis for effective international action to deal with the dangers we now face.

WHERE SOVEREIGNTY STOPS

In the wake of Somalia, Haiti, Rwanda, Bosnia, and Kosovo, a halting process of revising old rules to meet today's threats has begun. In the fall of 2002, Secretary-General Kofi Annan repeated a challenge he first made to UN members in 1999, urging the Security Council to discuss "the best way to respond to threats of genocide or other comparable massive violations of human rights." Although the Security Council has yet to heed Annan's call, the Canadian government did, appointing former Australian Foreign Minister Gareth Evans and Annan's Special Adviser Mohamed Sahnoun to head a distinguished global commission of diplomats, politicians, scholars, and nongovernmental activists. In December 2001, the commission issued a report, titled "The Responsibility to Protect," that took on nothing less than the redefinition of sovereignty itself. The Evans–Sahnoun Commission argued that the controversy over using force for humanitarian purposes stemmed from a "critical gap" between the unavoidable reality of mass human suffering and the existing rules and mechanisms for managing world order. To fill this gap, the commission identified an emerging international obligation—the "responsibility to protect"—which requires states to intervene in the affairs of other states to avert or stop humanitarian crises.

This concept challenges the traditional understanding of sovereignty by suggesting that it implies responsibilities as well as rights. According to the commission, sovereignty means that "the state authorities are responsible for the functions of protecting the safety and lives of citizens and promotion of their welfare;" that "the national political authorities are responsible to the citizens internally and to the international community through the UN;" and that "the agents of state are responsible for their actions; that is to say they are accountable for their acts of commission and omission."

The commission's boldest contribution, however, was to argue that the responsibility to protect binds both the individual states and the international community as a whole. The commission insists that an individual state has the primary responsibility to protect the individuals within it. But where the state fails to carry it out, a secondary responsibility to protect falls on the international community acting through the UN, even if enforcing it requires infringing on state sovereignty. Thus, "where a population is suffering serious harm, as a result of internal war, insurgency, repression or state failure, and the state in question is unwilling or unable to halt or avert it, the principle of non-intervention yields to the international responsibility to protect."

BEHIND CLOSED DOORS

By the time the Evans–Sahnoun Commission issued its report, in December 2001, much of the world was focused on the most dramatic of the world's new threats: an emerging breed of catastrophic terrorism. The prospect that al Qaeda or a comparable group might gain access to WMD drove the Bush administration in the fall of 2002 to announce a doctrine of preemption in its National Security Strategy. In the ensuing controversy, humanitarian concerns took a back seat to the imperatives of national security, narrowly defined. But today the links between the two sets of issues, especially the need to tackle them with proactive strategies, are becoming more evident..

The commission's effort to redefine basic concepts of sovereignty and international community in the context of humanitarian law are highly relevant to international security, in particular to efforts to counter governments that both possess WMD and systematically abuse their own citizens. After all, the danger posed by WMD in the hands of governments with no internal checks on their power is the prospect of mass, indiscriminate murder. Whether individuals are targeted for execution over time or vaporized in a single instant, the result is the same: a massive and senseless loss of life. We argue, therefore, that a new international obligation arises to address the unique dangers of proliferation that have grown in parallel with the humanitarian catastrophes of the 1990s.

The duty to prevent is the responsibility of states to work in concert to prevent governments that lack internal checks on their power from acquiring WMD or the means to deliver them. In cases where such regimes already possess such weapons, the first responsibility is to halt these programs and prevent the regimes from transferring WMD capabilities or actual weapons. The duty to prevent would also apply to states that sponsor terrorism and are seeking to obtain WMD.

This responsibility would apply to cases where the underlying set of agreements restricting WMD programs—the Nonproliferation Treaty (NPT), the

Biological Weapons Convention, and the Chemical Weapons Convention—has not prevented a regime without internal checks from pursuing dangerous weapons, or when such a state withdraws from its obligations or cheats on them, or when a gap in existing rules needs to be filled to prevent such a regime from acquiring WMD or the means to deliver them.

Why emphasize the absence of internal checks on a government's power? We are not trying to distinguish "good" governments from "bad" governments, much less democracies from nondemocracies. Nor are we arguing that governments that have internal checks on their behavior always obey international law; they are bound by the same international norms restricting the development and use of weapons of WMD as are other states, and their compliance must be monitored too. But the behavior of open societies is subject to scrutiny, criticism, and countermeasures by opponents, at home and abroad. Also, existing nonproliferation agreements can circumscribe these states' behavior or, if political circumstances change dramatically, as they did, say, in South Africa in 1989 and in Argentina and Brazil in the 1990s, they can provide a path for states to give up their nuclear ambitions or, in the case of Pretoria, even their weapons.

On the other hand, the international community may only discover the danger posed by a closed society with no opposition when it is too late. In such cases, standard diplomatic tools are simply not up to the job. The greatest potential danger to the international community is posed by rulers whose power over their own people and territory is so absolute that no matter how brutal, aggressive, or irrational they become, no force within their own society can stop them. Their rule is absolute precisely because they have terrified, brainwashed, and isolated their populations and have either destroyed internal opposition or subdued it by "closing" their societies, restricting information as much as possible. Such leaders may simply seek to consolidate their power and to be left alone. But if they choose to menace other countries or support terrorist groups, it is far more difficult to find out what they are doing and take effective measures to stop them.

Just as the responsibility to protect cannot apply to all regimes that abuse their citizens' human rights, the duty to prevent cannot apply to all closed societies with WMD programs. To be practical, the duty has to be limited and applied to cases when it can produce beneficial results. It applies to Kim Jong Il's North Korea, but not to Hu Jintao's (or even Mao's) China. Existing nonproliferation tools, updated to close loopholes, would continue to apply to most countries, and the effectiveness of these rules would be reinforced by the perception of greater determination to deal firmly with the most serious cases.

THE USUAL SUSPECTS

The main international nonproliferation agreements stigmatize weapons or certain categories of weapons rather than regimes or leaders. Aiming at the weapons themselves rather than the states or regimes that develop or acquire them has been judged to be a more objective basis for international action. The problem with this approach is that its opening proposition is to treat North Korea as if it were Norway. This flaw has exposed the nonproliferation regime to abuse by determined and defiant regimes, especially those headed by dictatorial rulers. It is also the weakness that makes the NPT and, more broadly, the nonproliferation system vulnerable to charges that the only ones restrained by nonproliferation agreements are those nations that do not need restraining.

In truth, the NPT—the cornerstone of international efforts to prevent the spread of WMD—has helped stanch nuclear proliferation in the overwhelming majority of cases. It has also provided a pathway for states seeking to terminate their nuclear programs. But the NPT has not prevented a small group of determined states, including Iran, Iraq, and North Korea, from traveling down the nuclear path. These states, sometimes operating within the scope of the treaty, managed to develop advanced nuclear programs and, in the case of North Korea, the material for actually producing nuclear weapons.

How did this happen? In the name of fairness and due process, the NPT does not make it possible to meaningfully distinguish parties to the treaty that are in good standing from parties with clear nuclear designs. Parties may take action against a state that breaches the treaty only when clear evidence of the breach emerges—but by then their options may be limited and it may already be too late. Mohammed ElBaradei, director-general of the International Atomic Energy Agency, summarized the treaty's approach when he said recently of planned inspections into a clandestine uranium enrichment program in Tehran, "Let me point out here that what we do in Iran is what we do everywhere else. We treat Iran exactly as we treat all other member states." Of course, the agreement Iran struck with France, Germany, and the United Kingdom last October to halt its uranium-enrichment activities is a welcome development. But it comes too late. At this stage, international pressure might succeed in freezing Iran's existing program, but it is unlikely to reverse it.

Just as effective gun control in the United States requires both outlawing the most dangerous weapons and ammunition and applying more stringent controls on citizens with criminal records and other risk factors, an effective international nonproliferation campaign must target both WMD and international actors with suspect intentions. It must be based, in other words, on the recognition that leaders without internal checks on their power, or who are sponsors of terror, and who seek to acquire WMD are a unique threat. An international duty to prevent such regimes from acquiring WMD capabilities would allow preventive actions against them, such as bars on their participation in civilian nuclear programs, which have provided cover for illegal weapons programs in Iraq and Iran.

The recent agreement with Iran, though overdue, indicates a growing recognition that the one-size-fits-all approach articulated by ElBaradei is limited and that the legal rules on nonproliferation are evolving in the direction of a duty to prevent. The provisional agreement treats Iran very differently from "all other . . . states." It recognizes that regimes such as Iran's, because they sponsor terrorism, repress democracy, and have clear nuclear designs, are not entitled to the same rights as other NPT members. It also demonstrates the range of preventive options available to deal with proliferation dangers.

EARLY ACTION

Like intervention for humanitarian purposes, international action to counter WMD proliferation can take the form of diplomatic pressure or incentives, economic measures, or coercive action, often in combination. It can also incorporate new strategies, such as indicting individual leaders before the International Criminal Court or a special court for crimes against humanity, grave war crimes, or genocide when such charges apply, as they certainly would have with Saddam Hussein and possibly with Kim Jong Il. Still another alternative could be support for nonviolent resistance movements that are dedicated to democratizing their governments.

To be effective, incentives must be tailored to a state's particular needs. Where a state seeks WMD for their perceived deterrent value, security assurances by a nation or group of nations, formally organized or not, may make adequate alternatives. Where a state trades in sensitive technologies in exchange for hard currency, economic incentives—including assistance from international financial institutions, direct bilateral aid, and trade incentives—may be more appropriate.

Coercive action may take the form of economic penalties, including measures targeted at the state's rulers, their close associates, and their families. Curbs on financial flows or on sensitive trade that provides financial support for a state's weapons programs, including a crackdown on black-market trade, can be a very effective brake. (Counterfeiting and the illegal drug trade are believed to support North Korea's WMD programs.) Coercive action can also include embargoes, informal or otherwise, to block the transfer of weapons or relevant technologies and material. The Bush administration's Proliferation Security Initiative, an 11-nation effort to stop the shipment of WMD, their delivery systems, and related materials at sea, by air, or on land, is a step in the right direction. The initiative is intended to prevent the transfer of nuclear weapons, weapons materials, and missiles, as well as trade in contraband that supports these weapons programs. France and Germany are participating, despite their opposition to the Iraq war, but not China and Russia, whose cooperation is critical to making it an effective system.

A jugular issue is how to monitor compliance with any pledges to freeze or reverse nuclear programs. The Iraq experience suggests that un inspections stopped being effective when Baghdad succeeded in dividing the Security Council and international support for them broke down. When UN Security Council Resolution 1441 revived the inspections, with the unanimous backing of the Security Council, Baghdad grudgingly cooperated with inspectors. Intrusive inspections endorsed by a united Security Council, backed up by the threat of force, may have worked better than they have been given credit for. Although it is easy to dismiss the effectiveness of inspections in closed societies, we need to review systematically the experience of international inspections for lessons learned. It may be that intense international pressure can make a system of rigorous inspections effective enough.

The Bush administration's announcement of a preemption doctrine set off alarm bells in the United States and abroad, chiefly because of the precedent it would set in terms of a unilateral determination that another state poses a sufficient threat to justify a preemptive strike. In truth, the use of force to preempt an imminent threat has always been part of international law, and it has been an option that the United States has held in quiet reserve and occasionally used. In cases in which terrorists appear poised to strike, preemption is clearly the preferred course of action.

Unfortunately, the preemptive use of force is often difficult to justify because clear evidence that a threat is imminent is rare. The U.S. strike on a pharmaceutical plant in Sudan in 1998 was intended as a preemptive strike against a facility suspected of producing chemical weapons, but evidence that activities there were illicit remains thin. Furthermore, preemption is usually impractical because suspected facilities are often difficult to spot or hit. States have taken precautions in recent years in response to the Israeli bombing of Iraq's Osiraq reactor in 1981 and to the NATO and U.S. bombing campaigns in the Balkans and the Middle East. Many facilities are buried in bunkers deep underground and dispersed over wide areas. They are especially difficult to locate in closed societies. This is not to suggest that the use of force should be discounted as ineffective but to highlight that the most effective action is preventive, because undoing a nuclear program is orders of magnitude more difficult than preventing one in the first place.

Nevertheless, as in the Iraq case, keeping force on the table is often a critical ingredient in making diplomacy work. It may be especially necessary for effective inspections and monitoring of WMD programs in closed societies. Force may be considered as part of an interdiction effort, may be targeted at specific dangerous facilities, or may be part of broader military action as a last resort.

The utility of force in dealing with the most serious proliferation dangers is not a controversial proposition. In a little-noticed statement last June, the EU announced a "strategy against proliferation," identifying "coercive measures, including as a last resort the use of force in accordance with the UN Charter" as one of its "key elements." Later that month, the G-8 group of leading industrialized countries, which includes Russia, approached the subject more gingerly but nonetheless agreed that WMD and the spread of international terrorism were "the preeminent threat to international security," and that force ("other measures in accordance with international law") may be needed to deal with them. And, as noted earlier, Kofi Annan himself called on the Security Council to develop criteria for the early authorization of coercive measures.

IN IT TOGETHER

The contentious issue is who decides when and how to use force. No one nation can or should shoulder alone the obligation to prevent a repressive regime from acquiring WMD. Although the Security Council, still reeling from the Iraq crisis last March, now seems more interested in papering over its differences than in tackling these questions, it remains the preferred enforcer of collective measures. The unmatched legitimacy that the UN lends to Security Council actions makes it easier for member states to carry them out and harder for targeted governments to evade them by playing political games. On the other hand, rifts within the council allow states to pursue WMD to advance their programs, leaving individual nations to take matters into their own hands, which further erodes the stature and credibility of the United Nations.

Given the Security Council's propensity for paralysis, alternative means of enforcement must be considered. The second most legitimate enforcer is the regional organization that is most likely to be affected by the emerging threat. After that, the next best option would be another regional organization, such as NATO, with a less direct connection to the targeted state but with a sufficiently broad membership to permit serious deliberation over the exercise of a collective duty. It is only after these options are tried in good faith that unilateral action or coalitions of the willing should be considered.

In any event, the resort to force is subject to certain "precautionary principles." All nonmilitary alternatives that could achieve the same ends must be tried before force may be used, unless they can reasonably be said to be futile. Force must be exerted on the smallest scale, for the shortest time, and at the lowest intensity necessary to achieve its objective; the objective itself must be reasonably attainable when measured against the likelihood of making matters worse. Finally, force should be governed by fundamental principles of the laws of war: it must be a measure of last resort, used in proportion to the harm or the threat of the harm it targets, and with due care to spare civilians.

A SAFER WORLD

Humanitarian protection is emerging as a guiding principle for the international community. In the same vein, we propose a duty to prevent, as a principle that would guide not only the Security Council in its decision-making but also national governments in shaping their foreign policy priorities. Accepting this principle would require the United States to accept that specific criteria be met before preventive action of various types would be authorized. At the same time, the principle addresses many of the problems raised by the approach being advanced by other nations to deal with WMD.

The international legal rules governing nonproliferation, as well as those determining sovereign rights over a given population and territory, are evolving. Nations are interpreting old rules in new ways and trying out new practices in response to new threats. It is impossible to predict when and how a new international consensus will emerge, but now is the time to elaborate new principles that could structure a broad legal regime.

Ours is not a radical proposal. It simply extrapolates from recent developments in the law of intervention for humanitarian purposes—an area in which over the course of the 1990s old rules proved counter-productive at best, murderous at worst. The responsibility to protect is based on a collective obligation to avoid the needless slaughter or severe mistreatment of human beings anywhere—an obligation that stems from both moral principle and national interest. The corollary duty to prevent governments without internal checks from developing WMD capacity addresses the same threat from another source: the prospect of mass murder through the use of WMD, which have a destructive potential far beyond the control of any attacker.

In a world in which such governments can get access to the most devastating weapons and make them available to terrorists, we must take action. We are operating under a set of rules governing the use of force that were framed for a very different world, one of sovereign states, conventional armies, and noninterference in a government's treatment of its own citizens. These rules can continue to serve us well only if they are revised and updated to meet a new set of threats. Accepting a collective duty to prevent is the first step toward sustained self-protection in a new and dangerous era.

14

The Hard Questions

David Carr

The futility of "homeland defense"—Don't even try to close the holes in a country, and a society, designed to be porous.

G et over thinking that America can be made safe. Defending a country as big and commercially robust as the United States raises profound, and probably insurmountable, issues of scale. There has been much talk of "Israelifying" the United States, but America has about forty-seven times as many people as Israel, and roughly 441 times the amount of territory to be defended. New Jersey alone is 753 square miles bigger than Israel, and home to nearly 2.5 million more people. Beyond problems of size, it's all too reasonable to assume that America won't be safe. Righting various asymmetries merely designs—as opposed to prevents—the next attack. When one target is shored up, nimble transnational cells that can turn on a dime simply find new bull's-eyes. Up against those practical realities, homeland security is the national version of the gas mask in the desk drawer—something that lets people feel safer without actually making them so.

If America is riddled with holes and targets, it's because a big society designed to be open is hard to change—impossible, probably. In 2000 more than 350 million non-U.S. citizens entered the country. In 1999 Americans made 5.2 billion phone calls to locations outside the United States. Federal Express handles nearly five million packages every business day, UPS accounts for 13.6 million, and until it became a portal for terror, the Postal Service processed 680 million pieces of mail a day. More than two billion tons of cargo

David Carr, "The Hard Questions: The Futility of Homeland Defense," *Atlantic Monthly*, Jan. 2002, p. 53. Reprinted by permission.

ran in and out of U.S. ports in 1999, and about 7.5 million North Americans got on and off cruise ships last year.

Group targets are plentiful. There are eighty-six college and professional stadiums that seat more than 60,000 people, and ten motor speedways with capacities greater than 100,000; the Indianapolis Motor Speedway seats more than 250,000. Few other countries offer the opportunity to take aim at a quarter million people at once. Also plentiful are tall buildings—until just yesterday the dominant symbol of civic pride. Fifty of the hundred tallest buildings in the world are on U.S. soil. Minneapolis, a mid-size city that doesn't leap to mind as a target, has three of them. And one of its suburbs has the largest shopping mall in the country, the Mall of America, with at least 600,000 visitors a week.

As for trained personnel to defend our borders and targets, the Immigration and Naturalization Service, which oversees the inspection of half a billion people a year, has only 2,000 agents to investigate violations of immigration law. The Postal Service has only 1,900 inspectors to investigate the misuse of mail. According to one estimate, it would take 14,000 air marshals to cover every domestic flight—more than the total number of special agents in the FBI. The former drug czar General Barry McCaffrey has pointed out that at least four different agencies oversee 303 official points of entry into the United States. After staffing increases over the past three years there are 334 U.S. Border Patrol agents guarding the 4,000 miles of Canadian border. The nation has 95,000 miles of shoreline to protect. "No one is in charge," McCaffrey says.

In all the discussion of building a homeland-security apparatus, very little attention has been paid to the fundamental question of whether 100 percent more effort will make people even one percent safer. The current version of America can no more button up its borders than mid-empire Britain could. Not just cultural imperatives are at stake. America makes its living by exporting technology and pop culture while importing hard goods and unskilled labor. The very small percentage of unwanted people and substances that arrive with all the people and things we do want is part of the cost of being America, Inc.

This is not the first time a President has declared a war within U.S. borders. In 1969 President Richard Nixon promised a "new urgency and concerted national policy" to combat the scourge of drugs—an initiative that has lurched along for more than three decades, growing to the point where the government spent $18.8 billion in 2000 trying to solve America's drug problem.

The drug war is progressing only marginally better than the one in Vietnam did. Adolescent use of most drugs has tailed off in the past year or two, but the hard-core population of 10 to 15 million American users can always find narcotics—and at a price that continues to drop. From 1981 to 1998 the price of both cocaine and heroin dropped substantially, while the purity of both drugs rose. From 1978 to 1998 the number of people dying from overdoses doubled, according to the Office of National Drug Control

Policy. The Drug Enforcement Agency estimates that 331 tons of cocaine were consumed in the United States in 2000.

Counterterrorism is the ultimate zero-tolerance affair. Yet the same federal assets deployed in the war on drugs—the Coast Guard, U.S. Customs, the INS, the Border Patrol, the CIA, the FBI, and the DEA—are the first and last lines of defense in this new war. The fight against terror involves a triad that drug warriors can recite in their sleep: global source management, border interdiction, and domestic harm reduction.

In both wars human ingenuity is a relentless foe. Create a new blockade and some opportunist will survey the landscape for an alternative path. "What the war on drugs tells us," says Eric E. Sterling, of The Criminal Justice Policy Foundation, "is that people motivated by the most elementary of capitalist motives are constantly testing and finding ways to get in. Terrorists are as motivated as the most avaricious drug importer, if not more—and they are not going to be deterred by whatever barriers are put up."

Less than ten miles southwest of where the World Trade Center towers stood, the part of the Port of New York and New Jersey that occupies sections of Newark and Elizabeth is back to work. On the day I went there in October, straddle carriers—leggy, improbable contraptions that lift and cradle containers—buzzed around in the shadow of the *Monet,* a large cargo ship. The *Monet* is a floating lesson in friction-free commerce. It is operated by CMA CGM, a French company, but owned by the U.S. subsidiary of a German firm; it is registered in Monrovia, and it sails under the Liberian flag. Like everything else in view, it's massive, capable of holding 2,480 twenty-foot-long container units—the kind familiar from flatbed trucks and freight trains. It left Pusan, Korea, on September 19, stopping in three Chinese cities before sailing across the Pacific and through the Panama Canal and coming to rest in New Jersey on October 22.

The Port of New York and New Jersey is no less international. It's the busiest port on the East Coast. In 2000 the port moved approximately 70 million tons of general and bulk cargo, the equivalent of three million containers, from hundreds of cities around the globe, and half a million freshly built cars. The large containers it processes are stuffed, sealed, and tagged in far-flung locations, and their contents move, mostly unchecked, into the hands of consumers. A conga line of trains and trucks snakes out of the port, bound for a metropolitan market of some 18 million people.

Smuggling goods in containers probably started the day after shipping goods in them did. In a sting last January, U.S. Customs and the DEA seized 126 pounds of heroin concealed in twelve bales of cotton towels on a container ship at the port. That same month two men were charged with importing 3.25 million steroid pills that were seized during a customs examination of a container shipped from Moldavia. And in May of 1999 the DEA and Customs seized 100 kilograms of cocaine hidden under 40,000 pounds of bananas in two refrigerated containers. Sometimes the cargo isn't cargo at all. In October, Italian authorities found a suspected terrorist—an Egyptian-born

Canadian dressed in a business suit—ensconced in a shipping container. His travel amenities included a makeshift toilet, a bed, a laptop computer, two cell phones, a Canadian passport, security passes for airports in three countries, a certificate identifying him as an airline mechanic, and airport maps. The container was headed for Toronto from Port Said, Egypt.

Before September 11 only about two percent of all the containers that move through ports were actually inspected. At Port Newark–Elizabeth there is a single giant on-site x-ray machine to see inside the containers; since September 11 two portable machines have been brought in to supplement it. The Customs Service enforcement team has been temporarily increased by 30 percent, but even that means that a mere 100 inspectors are responsible for more than 5,000 containers every day. The service has been on Alert Level One, which theoretically means that more containers are being inspected. But not even that vigilance—let alone the overtime—can continue indefinitely.

By reputation and appearance, the port is extremely well run, and it had tightened up security even before September 11. In the mid-1990s port officials began requiring every incoming truck driver to obtain an ID badge. One fall morning a man who appeared to be a Sikh, in a brilliant-orange turban and a lengthy beard, drew double takes from the other truckers—as he would anyplace else—when he stopped by the administration building to get his credential. When I was there, foreign crews were restricted from leaving their ships. The Coast Guard required ninety-six hours' notice before a ship arrived, and boarded every vessel before it was allowed into port. Two tugs accompanied each ship on its way in; if the ship were to head toward, say, a bridge support or some other target, the tugs would muscle the ship away.

But commerce, by definition, requires access. The port offers obvious targets because it is a place of business, not a fortified military installation. Tanks of edible oils sit behind a single cyclone fence; tankers of orange-juice concentrate from Brazil stand unguarded in parking lots. Two squad cars, one belonging to the port and the other on loan from the Department of Corrections, were parked at one of the port's major intersections, but anyone can drive around much of the facility without having to pass a single checkpoint. A train moves in or out of the port four times a day, crossing under the New Jersey Turnpike and through a tangle of bridges and elevated freeways that carries 630,000 cars every day. Just across the turnpike, Newark Airport handles roughly 1,000 flights a day.

Testifying one month after the September attacks, Rear Admiral Richard Larrabee, the port commerce director, told a Senate Commerce, Science, and Transportation subcommittee, "As a port director, I cannot give you or my superiors a fair assessment today of the adequacy of current security procedures in place, because I am not provided with information on the risk analysis conducted to institute these measures."

If a container holding heroin slips into the United States, the street price may go down, gangs may be enriched, and drug use may rise. If that same container held chemical or biological agents, or a nuclear weapon, the social costs would be incalculable. Doing nothing to deter such events would be foolish, but doing everything possible would be more foolish still. "There are two things to be considered with regard to any scheme," Jean Jacques Rousseau once observed. "In the first place, 'Is it good in itself?' In the second, 'Can it be easily put into practice?'" In the case of homeland security the answers are yes, and absolutely not.

Some measures, both quotidian and provident, will be taken. Practical approaches to making air travel safe again will emerge incrementally. Newly integrated databases will prevent a recurrence of the dark comedy of errors that allowed many of the hijackers into the country in the first place. Postal workers, it is to be hoped, will be tested for the presence of biological agents with the same alacrity that senators are. But the culture itself will not be re-engineered. America will continue to be a place of tremendous economic dynamism and openness.

At the port the country's muscular determination to remain in business is manifest on every loading dock. But if one looks hard enough, the cost of openness is there to see. In a quiet spot amid the industrial bustle—behind Metro Metals, on the north side of the port facility—is a nasty clump of twisted metal. Some of the girders from the World Trade Center, another brawny symbol of U.S. economic strength that also happens to be owned by the Port Authority, have come to rest here. The stink of that day—the burnt smell of implacable mayhem—hangs near, reminding us that great symbols make irresistible targets.

15

Terrorism and Humanity

What Are We Fighting Against and What Are We Fighting For

Dipak K. Gupta

In a recent forum on terrorism in New York, titled "Fighting Terrorism for Humanity," Nobel Peace Prize winner Elie Wiesel startled the participants by posing the question: "Can terrorism be fought with humanity?"

At first blush, the intellectual gauntlet thrown down by the sagacious gentleman of peace seems almost too dreamy, fit only for an impractical peacenik. It runs contrary to the often repeated promises of "rooting out," "smoking out" or "hunting down" the terrorists. Quick and decisive retaliatory actions seem to be the only solution for the scourge of our modern times.

Yet, when we don't allow our rage to overwhelm reason, we realize the wisdom of Wiesel's challenge. Terrorism, despite its daily use, has remained largely an undefined term reflecting the deep ambivalence in the international community. This ambivalence is amply reflected in the fact that at least three recipients of the Nobel Peace prize have been accused of being "terrorists."

As we mourn our mounting losses since the dreadful days of Sept. 11, 2001, we must realize that what we are fighting is not so much an individual, such as Osama bin Laden or even a group, like al-Qaeda or the Taliban; what we are fighting in the global arena is an idea.

Ideas, not simply a litany of grievances alone, have moved people throughout history; the Minute Men, the volunteers in the Spanish Civil War, the

Dipak Gupta, "Terrorism and Humanity: What are we fighting against and what are we fighting for?" Originally appeared as op–ed, *San Diego Union Tribune*. Reprinted by permission of the author.

Communist sympathizers in support of Che Guevara and even the Freedom Riders, have all been moved by the strength of ideas. Some ideas have advanced what we generally uphold as humanity, others have caused pain and misery.

In the early 20th century, the ideals of nationalism produced terrorism. In the 1940s, it was about ending colonial rule. In the 1960s and '70s, the revolutionary ideals of communism as well as Arab nationalism spawned global terrorism.

Today we face the menace of an idea that holds out promises of Islamic paradise on Earth to many, who have had little to rejoice and are besieged by an overwhelming feeling of losing out. The once proud Islamic nation that stretched from one end of the known world to the other is now reduced to a number of countries, most of which are wracked by poverty, injustice and an overarching feeling of desperation.

Although aspects of economic and even political deprivation are only peripherally linked to terrorism, they supply the essential foundation on which leaders can build their edifice of hate. When this hate threatens our lives and the roots of our civilization, we fight back, but not just against the leaders or their organizations, but the ideas they espouse.

In our battle, we battle not the entire Islamic world, but the idea that a particular brand of Islam should rule the world. The most insidious aspect of the spread of ideologies of the extreme is that in every case, the extremist groups were initially promoted by people in power for political or strategic reasons.

Successive U.S. administrations helped the Taliban and the current leaders of the al-Qaeda movement to fight the Soviet invaders of Afghanistan; Indira Gandhi saw Sikh extremists as instruments of her political ambition; her son Rajiv Gandhi initially supported the separatist Tamil Tigers of Sri Lanka; Hamas was seen by some as the counterweight to the growing popularity of the PLO in Israel.

In each case, the monster turned against Dr. Frankenstein: Indira Gandhi was assassinated by the Sikh extremists; Rajiv Gandhi by the Tamil Tigers; Hamas has been the single most potent source of death and destruction in Israel; and the Islamic extremists are the biggest adversaries of the United States.

The worldwide rise of Islamic extremism can be directly linked to patronage of the Saudi government. Saudi authorities thought that they would be able to buy off the extremists, who would leave them alone and instead, would spread their venom to other parts of the world. Alas, the primary targets of the Islamic extremists also include the desert kingdom.

Similarly, other Islamic nations, most notably Pakistan, Egypt, Yemen, Somalia, Sudan and Indonesia have either actively supported the Islamic extremists or have tried to ignore their nefarious activities. Their support has only undermined their own political stability.

How should this war of ideas be fought? We can fight against a tyrannical regime with our military might, but how do we win over those who hate us more than they love their own lives? The policy that confirms the worst about us to our adversaries only adds fuel to their fire of hatred. Every military action that kills innocent bystanders, regardless of our true intention, gives birth to many more suicide bombers.

Western civilization is rooted in the concept of rule of law. We cannot win over those who violate the law by breaking the law ourselves. Any act that violates the basic principles on which our civilization is based ultimately debases us. Any move that weakens the global consensus isolates us, particularly when the problem should be addressed globally.

This does not mean that we should coddle those who attack us. We should take every action to defeat them, militarily, politically, and most importantly, ideologically. Since the problem is of global importance, we must be steadfast in our opposition to the leaders of those countries whom we support in their effort at mixing religion and politics.

We must impress upon those who are chafing under intolerable poverty that economic development cannot take place in countries where women and minorities are not granted equal status. We must make it clear to the political elite of these countries of the danger of sending the children of the poor to the schools that do not prepare them for the modern world while sending their own to schools in Western nations.

We must tighten international banking laws to deny these organizations, their source of funding. Also, any armed rebellion is ultimately rooted in the perceived injustice; no mass movement can be stopped without addressing its legitimate grievances.

Fighting terrorism is a long-term proposition, and we must be prepared for the long haul. Wiesel is right, terrorism can only be fought with humanity; it is important to know what we are fighting against. But it is even more important to know what we are fighting for.

InfoMarks: Make Your Mark

What Is an InfoMark?

It's a single-click return ticket to any page, any result, any search from InfoTrac College Edition.

An InfoMark is a stable URL, linked to InfoTrac College Edition articles that you have selected. InfoMarks can be used like any other URL, but they're better because they're stable—they don't change. Using an InfoMark is like performing the search again whenever you follow the link—whether the result is a single article or a list of articles.

How Do InfoMarks Work?

If you can "copy and paste," you can use InfoMarks.

When you see the InfoMark icon on a result page, its URL can be copied and pasted into your electronic document—Web page, word processing document, or email. Once InfoMarks are incorporated into a document, the results are persistent (the URLs will not change) and are dynamic.

Even though the saved search is used at different times by different users, an InfoMark always functions like a brand new search. Each time a saved search is executed, it accesses the latest updated information. That means subsequent InfoMark searches might yield additional or more up-to-date information than the original search with less time and effort.

Capabilities

InfoMarks are the perfect technology tool for creating:

- Virtual online readers
- Current awareness topic sites—links to periodical or newspaper sources
- Online/distance learning courses
- Bibliographies, reference lists
- Electronic journals and periodical directories
- Student assignments
- Hot topics

Advantages

- Select from over 15 million articles from more than 5,000 journals and periodicals
- Update article and search lists easily
- Articles are always full text and include bibliographic information
- All articles can be viewed online, printed, or emailed
- Professors and students save time
- Anyone with access to InfoTrac College Edition can use it
- No other online library database offers this functionality
- FREE!

How to Use InfoMarks

There are three ways to utilize InfoMarks—in HTML documents, Word documents, and email

HTML Document

1. Open a new document in your HTML editor (Netscape Composer or FrontPage Express).
2. Open a new browser window and conduct your search in InfoTrac College Edition.
3. Highlight the URL of the results page or article that you would like to InfoMark.
4. Right click the URL and click Copy. Now, switch back to your HTML document.
5. In your document, type in text that describes the InfoMarked item.
6. Highlight the text and click on Insert, then on Link in the upper bar menu.
7. Click in the link box, then press the "Ctrl" and "V" keys simultaneously and click OK. This will paste the URL in the box.
8. Save your document.

Word Document

1. Open a new Word document.
2. Open a new browser window and conduct your search in InfoTrac College Edition.
3. Check items you want to add to your Marked List.
4. Click on Mark List on the right menu bar.
5. Highlight the URL, right click on it, and click Copy. Now, switch back to your Word document.
6. In your document, type in text that describes the InfoMarked item.
7. Highlight the text. Go to the upper bar menu and click on Insert, then on Hyperlink.

8. Click in the hyperlink box, then press the "Ctrl" and "V" keys simultaneously and click OK. This will paste the URL in the box.
9. Save your document.

Email

1. Open a new email window.
2. Open a new browser window and conduct your search in InfoTrac College Edition.
3. Highlight the URL of the results page or article that you would like to InfoMark.
4. Right click the URL and click Copy. Now, switch back to your email window.
5. In the email window, press the "Ctrl" and "V" keys simultaneously. This will paste the URL into your email.
6. Send the email to the recipient. By clicking on the URL, he or she will be able to view the InfoMark.

Contributor Biographies

ABOUT THE EDITOR

Dipak K. Gupta is Distinguished Professor in Political Science at San Diego State University. He is also the Chair of the multidisciplinary program, International Security and Conflict Resolution. Gupta writes in two academic fields: political violence and terrorism, and public policy analysis. In these two areas, his most recent books include *Path to Collective Madness: A Study in Social Order and Political Pathology* (2001) and *Analyzing Public Policy* (2001). He has consulted with the United Nations Terrorism Prevention Department, California Civil Rights Commission, among others. He was contacted by the 9/11 Commission for his writing on terrorism. Gupta is a regular contributor to the opinion section of *San Diego Union-Tribune*.

ABOUT THE AUTHORS

David Carr is a reporter for the *New York Times*. He has written for the *Atlantic* and *New York Magazine* and was formerly the editor of the *Washington City Paper*.

Eliot A. Cohen is the Robert E. Osgood Professor of Strategic Studies at the Paul H. Nitze School of Advanced International Studies (SAIS) of the Johns Hopkins University and founding director of the Philip Merrill Center for Strategic Studies there. He received his Ph.D. in political science at Harvard in 1982. He subsequently taught there and at the Naval War College (Department of Strategy). He has served on the policy planning staff of the Office of the Secretary of Defense. He has written books and articles on a variety of military and national security-related subjects, including, most recently *Supreme Command: Soldiers, Statesmen, and Leadership in Wartime* (Free Press, 2002). He has served as an intelligence officer in the United States Army Reserve, and as a member of the Defense Policy Advisory Board of the Office of the Secretary of Defense.

Lee Feinstein is deputy director of studies and senior fellow at the Council on Foreign Relations. Feinstein served at the Departments of Defense and

State from 1994–2001. He was senior advisor in the Office of the Secretary of Defense on peacekeeping and peace enforcement policy in the Office of the Secretary of Defense from 1994–1995. He served as member of the Policy Planning Staff under Secretary of State Warren Christopher and as Principal Deputy Director of Policy Planning under Secretary of State Madeleine K. Albright. Feinstein was director of the CFR-Freedom House 2002 independent task force on Enhancing US Relations with the UN.

Graham E. Fuller served as an American Foreign Service Officer overseas for twenty years, primarily in the Muslim world. He later became Vice Chairman of the National Intelligence Council at CIA responsible for all long-range strategic forecasting. He then spent 12 years at RAND Corporation as a Senior Political Scientist working on geopolitical issues, the Muslim world and Islam. He has published many articles and books; his latest book is *The Future of Political Islam,* Palgrave 2003.

G. John Ikenberrry is Albert G. Milbank Professor of Politics and International Affairs in the Department of Politics and Woodrow Wilson School at Princeton University. He is the author of *After Victory: Institutions, Strategic Restraint and Order Building after Major Wars* (Princeton, 2001), which won the Schroeder-Jervis Prize for Best Book in International History and Politics by the American Political Science Association. He is also coauthor of *State Power and World Markets* (Norton, 2003), editor of *America Unrivaled: The Future of the Balance of Power* (Cornell, 2003), and coeditor of *International Relatons Theory and the Asia Pacific* (Columbia, 2002).

Alan B. Krueger is the Bendheim Professor of Economics and Public Affairs at Princeton University and Director of Industrial Relations. He has published widely on the economics of education, labor demand, income distribution, social insurance, labor market regulation, and environmental economics. In 1994–1995 he served as Chief Economist at the U.S. Department of Labor. He was named a Sloan Fellow in Economics in 1992, an NBER Olin Fellow in 1989–1990, and awarded the Kershaw Prize by the Association for Public Policy and Management in 1997. In 2002 he was elected a fellow of the American Academy of Arts & Sciences. He received a B.S. degree (with honors) from Cornell University's School of Industrial & Labor Relations, an A.M. in Economics from Harvard University in 1985, and a Ph.D. in Economics from Harvard University in 1987.

David D. Laitin is the Watkins Professor of Political Science at Stanford University. He has conducted field research on culture and nationalism in Somalia, Nigeria, Spain and Estonia. His latest book is *Identity in Formation: The Russian-speaking Populations in the Near Abroad.* He is currently working on the sources of civil war onsets. His paper "Ethnicity, Insurgency and Civil War" (in collaboration with James Fearon) was published in the February 2003 issue of the *American Political Science Review.*

Bernard Lewis received his Ph.D. in the History of Islam from the University of London. He did part of his graduate work in the University of Paris, and spent some months touring the Middle East. He received his first teaching appointment in 1938, as an assistant lecturer in Islamic History at the School of Oriental and African Studies, and remained a University teacher at the University of London and later at Princeton until his formal retirement in 1986. He has researched and is a highly reputed academic in medieval Islamic history, the Ottoman Empire, the contemporary Middle East, and relations between Europe and Islam. His most recent book is *A Middle East Mosaic: Fragments of Life, Letters, and History* (2000).

Robert A. Pape is Associate Professor of Political Science at the University of Chicago. He specializes in international security affairs and is the director of the Chicago Project on Suicide Terrorism.

David C. Rapoport is the editor of *Terrorism and Political Violence*. He received his Ph.D. in Political Theory from the University of California, Berkeley, in 1962. He is Professor Emeritus in Political Science at UCLA and the Founder of the Center for Religious Studies at UCLA. He was an H. F. Guggenheim Fellow from 1989–1991, and he developed the first American course on terrorism in 1970. He is the author and editor of six books, including *Assassination and Terrorism, The Morality of Terrorism, Inside Terrorist Organizations,* and *The Democratic Experience and Political Violence* (with Leonard Weinberg). He also has published over 50 academic articles.

Steven Rogers has lived in the Philippines for over twenty-five years, working as a journalist, political analyst, and risk consultant. He served as a Peace Corps volunteer on Mindanao from 1979 to 1998; since then he has traveled extensively in the Muslim areas of the Philippines and closely monitored events there. His article analyzing the structural and cultural obstacles to economic development and effective democracy in the Philippines, "Philippine Politics and the Rule of Law," appeared in the 4th quarter 2004 issue of the *Journal of Democracy.*

Anne-Marie Slaughter is Dean of the Woodrow Wilson School of Public and International Affairs and the Bert G. Kerstetter '66 University Professor of Politics and International Affairs at Princeton University. Prior to becoming Dean, she was the J. Sinclair Armstrong Professor of International, Foreign and Comparative Law and the Director of Graduate and International Legal Studies at Harvard Law School. She is also the former President of the American Society of International Law. Dean Slaughter is a Fellow of the American Academy of Arts and Sciences and serves on the board of the Council on Foreign Relations. Her book, *A New World Order,* was recently published by Princeton University Press.

Ehud Sprinzak was academic director of the Raoul Wallenberg Scholarship Program and professor of political science at Hebrew University, focusing on terrorism and religious radicalism. He was the 1995 recipient of the Gedalia Gal Fellowship from the Association for the Commemoration of Israel's Intelligence Community and was selected as the 1992 Baruch Yekutieli fellow of the Jerusalem Institute for the Study of Israel. In 1992 Sprinzak was awarded the Landau Prize for best political science book for *The Ascendance of Israel's Radical Right*. Sprinzak held a Ph.D. from Yale University. He passed away in 2002.

Jessica Stern is Lecturer in Public Policy at Harvard University's Kennedy School of Government, where she teaches courses on terrorism and on religion and conflict. She has published extensively on terrorism and national-security affairs, including *Terror in the Name of God: Why Religious Militants Kill*. She served on President Clinton's National Security Council Staff in 1994–1995 and worked as an analyst at Lawrence Livermore National Laboratory. She has a bachelor's degree from Barnard College in chemistry, a master's degree from MIT in technology policy (chemical engineering), and a doctorate from Harvard University in public policy.

Strobe Talbott is President of the Brookings Institution. He served as Deputy Secretary of State from 1994–2001, and Ambassador-at-large and Special Advisor to the Secretary of State for the former Soviet Union (1993–1994). Prior to his service in government, he worked at *Time* magazine for twenty-one years, as a reporter, Washington bureau chief, foreign affairs columnist and editor-at-large. He is the author of nine books, most recently *Engaging India,* a memoir of U.S. diplomacy toward South Asia after the 1998 Indian and Pakistani nuclear tests. He has a B.A. from Yale and an M.Litt. from Oxford.